The Growth Cube

Unlocking the Growth Potential of Your Company

Gary Ross

The Growth Cube

For more information or to order additional copies of this book, please visit or e-mail:

www.TheGrowthCube.com

garyross@InspireYourselfToday.net

FIRST EDITION

Printed in the United States of America

Ebook ISBN-978-1-945091-41-4
Softcover ISBN-978-1-945091-39-1
Hardcover ISBN-978-1-945091-40-7

DEDICATIONS

To three of the greatest leaders I know:
My wife Vicky, my son Tyler, and my daughter Rylee.

It's really you who inspire me; not the other way around.

To my first CEO mentor, Bob Yopko.

*It was under your direction that I first learned
how great leaders build great companies.*

To my customers, and all the associates I have ever led.

You built me.

To God.

Thank you for the opportunity to touch leader's hearts with my book.

CONTENTS

We rejoice in our sufferings
knowing that suffering produces endurance,
endurance produces character,
character produces hope,
and hope does not disappoint us.

Romans 5:3-5

INTRODUCTION

I don't know you, but I know you want more.

You want more from your professional life regardless of how successful you have been. You want more from your personal life regardless how much you have accomplished.

The answer is The Growth Cube^{TM}, a 6-dimensional formula that is the key to unlocking the growth of your company, and your potential as a leader.

What is The Growth Cube?

If you hold up a solid cube in front of you, could you see all sides of the cube at the same time? You can rotate it, look at it from many different angles, yet you will never see all 6 sides at once. This is the same challenge that many company leaders and CEOs encounter while trying to grow their business. Many only focus on 2 or 3 dimensions of their business at one time – some because that's all the time they can afford. But are those the best 2 or 3 opportunities in front of them? Are those areas of focus going to make the biggest increase in company value?

I invented The Growth Cube process to enable you to see all 6 dimensions of your business at the same time. By effectively analyzing and prioritizing across all these dimensions, you can grow your business more successfully than you are today, and it is truly all about growth. According to a 2017 Boston Consulting Group article, "It's easier to trim and optimize and cut costs than to figure out something new. What firms need from their CEOs is growth."

The Growth Cube is not the result of me leading a "storybook" career. I have made mistakes at every level of my career. From the first time I took on the role of managing other people, to running a global services organization for a Fortune 500 company, to being the CEO of two family-owned software companies (one of them to private equity exit), and most recently leading a new technology startup to market. Early on, I realized the blessings of not just my successes, but also of learning from my mistakes. Looking back, I applied The Growth Cube principles before it "officially" became The Growth Cube. Ultimately, these principles helped me achieve my potential and make a lasting impact on the lives of many people.

Did you know that a 10% increase in customer retention yields a 30% increase in the value of your company? This is fundamental. How do we make this happen? I have purposely made this book a practical, working guide with models and tools you can apply immediately to your present company and situation. Like *"The 12 Challenges to Increasing Value"* you will read about later. The ideas, tips, and techniques I share with you are all original content that has been vetted and proven in real companies.

Your people want you to be an awesome leader. They would love to follow your passion, but something you are doing could be holding them back. As you read through The Growth Cube and think about how it fits your situation, I will test you to let go of the preconceived perspectives and assumptions that could be limiting your growth. You may be tempted to cut corners, and you will likely have doubts about my system working for you. I urge you to remain open and courageous. There is no other way down the path of reaching your potential.

I am so excited that you picked up my book and that you want to apply my lessons to your career. I will be with you on your journey from start to finish. By applying The Growth Cube process in your company, you will be energized and inspired— and so will your team and your customers! Get ready to unlock the growth potential of your business!

Positively Yours,

Gary

The Growth Cube

CHAPTER 1 – PEOPLE AND CULTURE.
Creating Raving Associates.

"THE CONTRACT"
A WORD FROM
THOSE YOU LEAD

And in the end, we follow them – not because we are paid. Not because we see some advantage. Not because of the things they have accomplished. Not even because of the dreams they dream.

But simply because of who they are.

The man. The woman. The leader. The boss. Standing up there when the wave hits the rock. Passing out faith and confidence like life jackets. Knowing the currents, holding the doubts. Imagining the delights and terrors of every landfall. Captain. Pirate. Parent. The bearer of countless hopes and expectations.

We give them our trust. We give them our effort.

What we ask in return is that they stay true.

William Ayot

Would you be willing to sign this contract with your people? You would, right? Look at the energy and passion you have available to you. They sit right in front of you every day. Your associates. If you could unleash this kind of relationship and support, you would be unstoppable!

I am here to get you there.

THE GROWTH CUBE™
Unlocking the Growth Potential of Your Company

Early on, as President at one of my companies, I was standing in front of the entire staff. I was feeling them, and they were feeling me, so I just stopped and went off script. I turned off the presentation for a moment and stood out in front of them. All of them wired on this sudden change – wondering what I was going to say. I was not even sure what I was going to say – I just wanted them to know how I felt about them, and us, and our potential together. I wanted to get close to them. I looked at this room full of people – many of whom had been at this company a lot longer than me – and just talked from my heart about what I wanted for the company. My feelings about it. I told them how much I cared about them. I was genuine, and they could feel that. I did not plan this "little conversation," but it felt like the right thing to do. As a result, the ratings on this meeting were some of the highest scores ever! The feedback was awesome. In fact, years later, there were people that still referenced this moment. This is a note the owner shared with me from one associate who talked about this moment:

"At a team meeting years ago, Gary spoke about his feeling for the people in the room and the great potential of the company. Knowing that our leader had the same passion for the company as I do – by seeing the emotion in his eyes and hearing it in his voice – gave me reassurance that we had a bright future."

It is this kind of moment that once again proves to me that if you talk from your heart and have passion, your associates will respond to you as a leader. By putting your heart out there and taking a risk, your associates will have your back and fight for you!

How do we get to this point with our people? How do we build this kind of culture that will give us an edge in the market, with our competitors, and as an added bonus, will also dramatically increase the value of our company? There is a reason that "People" are at the top of The Growth Cube and the first chapter in this book. Creating Raving Associates is one of the top 6 strategies you have as a leader, and getting this first step right will open the doors for all the other goals you want to accomplish with your business.

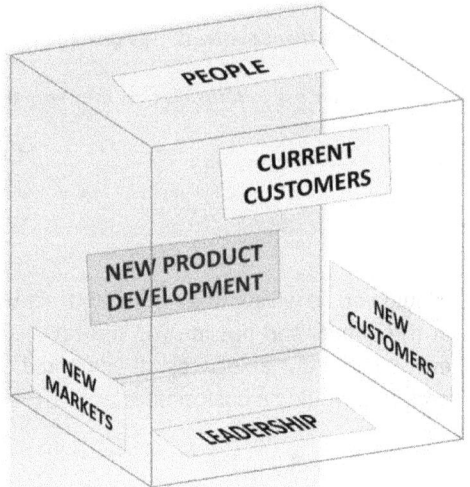

Before I dive into the details of how to make that happen, I want to talk with you about culture, and how you build culture – and specifically a growth culture – in your company. First, I am going to ask you to accept this very basic principle:

YOU AND YOUR COMPANY SUCCEED BECAUSE OF YOUR PEOPLE AND WHAT THEY ARE ABLE TO ACCOMPLISH FOR YOUR CUSTOMERS!

If you do not agree with me, I plan to win you over. If you do agree with me, I can give you a model to accomplish this. This model will help you build a growth culture in your company that will deliver results and inspire your team! They want you to do the things I am going to share with you! Trust me on this. I have lived through this as a CEO many times. Every step. All the sweat. All the roadblocks and hurdles and time. I can tell you it is all worthwhile!

It all starts with you – the leader – and your attitude and commitment to building a team of Raving Associates!

Why do I keep saying "Associates" and not "Employees?" Because we are a team. From the first day I walk into a new company, I never call them "employees." I call them "Associates." I know it's only a word, but it sends a message right away that you are a together in this fight. I am not asking you to run off and do this – but I want to set the tone for my message in this chapter. Look at your attitude and the messages you are sending as a leader. Consider how you view your associates in relation to the team and the goal you are pursuing. If your goal is to reach the top of the mountain, you cannot run to the top of the mountain. When you look back, and your people are still at the base of the mountain, it becomes clear that you are a leader with no followers. You will not win the fight. Your people are willing to lay it all on the line for you if you believe in them, guide them, and support them! You have to get your people to climb the mountain with you and believe in your vision enough to not only watch *you* climb, but to also climb the mountain themselves!

Let me give you an example of a couple inspirational leaders. On June 11, 1963, President John F. Kennedy addressed the nation on the most pressing domestic issue of the day: the struggle to affirm civil rights for all Americans. His administration had sent National Guard troops to accompany the first black students admitted to the University of Mississippi and University of Alabama. In the speech, Kennedy announced that he would be sending civil rights legislation to Congress. Two months later, another leader led about 250,000 Americans of all races on a march in Washington, D.C. in front of the Lincoln Memorial. That leader was Dr. Martin

Luther King, Jr. and the event was marked indelibly into the psyche of the nation by the famous "I Have a Dream" speech.

Did each of these leaders, Kennedy and King, have followers? Regardless of your political or social view, you must admit that they did. In fact, they followed them with passion! Their followers believed in building what their leaders believed. They faced opposition – just like you do today – but they fought for their people and for their mission together. Do you think these leaders had a skill and talent for inspiring people? What if you had followers like this in your company? They would climb the mountain with you, and you would win like never before!

> *"The heart of the question is whether we are going to treat our fellow Americans as we want to be treated."*
> —*John F. Kennedy. 1963.*

Your abilities as a leader of an organization to hire and keep great people, to inspire, to build a culture that gets things done, will ultimately determine your legacy as a leader and your company's success in the market! It all starts here, at the beginning, with how you lead your team and what you deem as a priority. I bet if I came into your company today and did an audit, the chances would be high that I would tell you that you have to focus more of your time on your associates and your team, clarifying with them what you are trying to accomplish, and evaluating your performance in achieving those goals.

My daughter Rylee is a future CEO. She is smart, a hard worker, and brings an awesome combination of analytical and leadership skills – she is going to be successful. I asked Rylee back when she was 11 years old, "What is a leader?"

She responded, "Someone who takes control but does it in a nice way." That was an excellent definition. As a leader, you must walk that fine line between taking control and giving your people room to do their thing. Your ability to move in and out across these spectrums, at the right time and with the right touch, is a talent. How can you, as the leader, be the spark plug and keep momentum toward the goal? How can you keep your associates fired up enough to pursue the goals of the company while at the same time making their personal dreams come true?

There was an international study conducted for *Fortune* magazine that looked at the differences in the workplace cultures of the world's most admired companies verses an average company. What they found is that with average companies, the overriding cultural values are making budget, supporting the decisions of management, and minimizing risks. However, in the most admired companies, the *Fortune* study revealed that the dominant values are innovation, teamwork, customer focus, vision, global reach, and fair treatment of employees.

I know what you are thinking – absolutely! I can see that makes sense, Gary! We are doing all those things.

Are you really? If I came in and audited your company across all the dimensions I just mentioned, what do you think I would find? Would there be untapped opportunity? Is it really working for you today? Are you really getting what you want right now? Are you happy with your growth trajectory and pace? We can change that; we can build a new inflection point of growth for your company.

I hope you are starting to grasp that leadership, culture, and strategy are all related and integrated into each other. We know they are all important, but how do we, as leaders, balance and emphasize defining strategy, building culture, growing the company, and motivating our associates? How do we get them all to work in concert together and not confuse our associates or waste their time in the process?

STRATEGY – STRUCTURE – CULTURE.
Establishing Method to Your Madness.

Let me ask you: Do you have a strategy defined for your business? If I asked you to tell me right now what it is, do you think I would understand within 25 seconds?

What I have learned through leading companies, and actually working through these kind of challenges, is that to be successful at implementing culture initiatives, the strategy has to support it. Even when it does support it, we can mess up the implementation of the idea. How many times have we seen a leader rush back from a conference or a planning meeting with a new blockbuster team-building idea or new book that will "fix the culture" just to find that it is not aligned with the company strategy and therefore does not stick. It becomes the "idea of the month." The key to changing the culture is to first focus on the company strategy and what we are trying to achieve as a company. When the strategy, structure, and culture are out of alignment, there will be a noticeable

tension in the organization. How well would you rate the alignment of these areas in your company today?

I recently conducted a 4-hour workshop for NAWBO (National Association of Women Business Owners) where I presented my ideas for building culture. I featured *The Energy Bus* – including its "10 Rules for the Ride of Your Life," written by Jon Gordon, about the challenges we face in business and in life. One of the leaders in attendance later asked me to come into their company and help her change the culture of her company into a more energized culture. We were both excited about the potential, and as a VP in her company, we were able to build a cross-functional company-wide effort to our initiative, and it started very well. We bought a book for everyone on the team and started to drive new priorities in the company. We did it – we started to generate energy and momentum in a company that was stifled for years! However, it did not stick. It did not last, and it was frustrating because we were on the right track. In the end, it died out like a flame at the end of a wick. Do you know why? Because the CEO was not supportive of the initiative. This kind of culture did not fit within his strategy, and the programs we were implementing did not seem important from his chair. So what did he do? He killed it behind the scenes. His informal and subliminal message to the people on our team was: Why are you wasting your time on this? It's not important.

We were trying to change the culture, and the CEO did not see a reason to change it, and his strategy, which was not even defined, did not support it. We all wasted our time because we found out through a lot of effort (and he said he supported us when we started!), that he did not see the benefit of this team. The team had awesome ideas, and they were being innovative like never before. From this point on, I made a decision to only work with CEOs in my coaching practice. It starts with the person at the top, and it will not succeed without their full commitment.

In 2016, Jay W. Lorsch, Harvard Business School's accomplished Professor, and Emily McTague, his research assistant, conducted interviews with corporate leaders – current and former CEOs who have successfully led major transformations. They found that culture isn't something you "fix." Rather, in the experience of these accomplished leaders, cultural change is what you get after you've put new processes or structures in place to tackle tough business challenges like reworking an outdated strategy or business model. The culture evolves as you do that important work. What Lorsch and McTague found in their research was that culture isn't a final destination. It morphs right along with the company's competitive environment and objectives; if we as leaders use tools such as decision rights (who is authorized to make what decisions), performance measurement, and reward systems to address our particular business challenges, organizational culture will evolve and reinforce our new direction.

"Culture is not the Culprit."
—*Jay Lorsch and Emily McTague*

So you should start with your strategy, and then work your way to the structure and the culture, correct?

I will give you a big tip on how to get this moving forward. If you want to start defining your strategy, start by studying and understanding your customer. Do you know what your customer is trying to accomplish? Ask these questions at your next team meeting: What problem are we are helping our customers solve? Where is our customer's business headed, and how can we help them get positioned to be successful? When you work on this together as a team and start to draft your agreed upon course, you are on your way to defining your strategy and where you want to go as a company. Once you nail this down, stay with it. Building a diverse team is important, and leveraging the specific skills of each player is also important. You are not going to take a great sales leader and throw them into finance. Keep them focused where they have the best chance to succeed. Do the same with your company – stay in the lane you have chosen to pursue. Too many companies diversify so much that they lose focus on what they are good at and what customers loved about them in the first place.

Structuring the organization is complex and sensitive and often involves not only the change in structure but also changing out people who do not buy into or fit the new leadership strategy. In general, I like a flat, lean organization structure, especially in small businesses. Do not put in layers. Keep the CEO owner involved and on the front line with customers. Also place great people who have the skills and energy to get your business to the next level in leadership roles. I have had to make leadership changes and organization restructuring while keeping morale high. I know the challenges you face here. I have also successfully combined top internal talent with outside recruiting to form new leadership teams, both in the U.S. and internationally. This can be sensitive and costly. A coach or partner can help you get through this successfully. All in all, I really enjoy a flat organization structure and an organization that has agility and speed, especially for small businesses trying to compete with larger competitors. Speed should be a competitive differentiator for the smaller company.

I'll give you an example of a successful change I made as a CEO. At one of my companies, we decided that one of our service divisions needed to develop its own strategy and growth path, and not just be a cost of being in the product business. We wanted this division to focus on its own growth and its own financial success. So we set a new strategy. Of course, the structure and the culture needed to be updated in order to support this new strategy as well, so we changed it. Here is a picture of the old culture when we started vs. the new culture that we built:

OLD CULTURE	NEW CULTURE
• Each leader owns all resources. Control is key. • My peer is my competitor. • People are not accountable. "It's not my fault;" "it's not my job." • We know more than our Customers. We will tell the Customer what solutions they need. • Customers were leaving us for competitors who had new products. We had no new products. • Hold time at the Customer support center was unacceptable. • This segment of our business was dying and morale was very low in that division. • Many Customers were unhappy.	• Recognition as a team that Only the Paranoid Survive was real. There were technology inflection points happening in our market. • We must use our strengths – including flexibility and speed and Customer service – to win in the market. • Get involved with the Customer as a company, and understand their environment and their goals. We must get feedback from the Customers through various means: Advisory Board, user groups, early adopters, etc. • We should respect and listen to sales people and other front-line associates who are working directly with customers. • Focus on product innovation and product quality and Customer service – and make sure these operations are performing at a high level. • Develop KPIs and dashboards that tell us how we are executing.

Our goal in this example was not to change the culture. The strategy we chose determined the culture we established. We do not change culture for the sake of changing culture. We do it because we believe it will enable us to get to our goals and achieve our growth strategy.

So did it work? The short answer is, "Yes!" We motivated the team and grew the business, but there were bumps along the way. There was organizational tension as we made this monumental shift in strategy, structure, and culture. Through dedication, we delivered the results, and ultimately put our company onto a new growth vector. If you want more proof that these ideas and models work and clearly demonstrate success, what better way than to look through the eyes of our customer? On the next page is an excerpt from a letter from one of our customers that shows you what our journey looked like through their eyes. Do not think the customers cannot see you changing – they can! (Note – I have changed the name of the company to "ABC Technology" to protect confidentiality.)

CUSTOMER FEEDBACK
AFTER YEARS WORKING WITH GARY AND TEAM

We had a long history of working with ABC Technology. When I came into my position, the company had a positive reputation with a proud history of providing good service and products. However, it also was widely regarded as one that was not on the cutting edge of new technology and had become stagnant.

Gary impressed me early on as someone who was a visionary, and he had a vision for what ABC Technology could become. I am a big believer in technology and finding new solutions to make processes more efficient. I found in Gary a kindred spirit, someone who constantly thinks outside the box and is never satisfied with the status quo, but rather is always looking for new services or products to offer.

Gary created a customer advisory board at ABC Technology, which was an ingenious way to solicit feedback from customers from many different geographies throughout the company's footprint. I was honored when Gary asked me to serve on that board. By listening to the customers – the ones who were actually using the company's products – Gary not only gave customers a sense of empowerment but also took many ideas we gave him and turned them into improvements and enhancements of the products offered.

Through serving on the Customer Advisory Board, I got to know Gary even better and had the opportunity to see how he worked firsthand. Several things impressed me. First, Gary is very inquisitive. He wants to understand the business and market that he is working in. He wants to know his customers, and asks questions until he understands. Second, Gary is a very driven individual. It was very apparent to me that Gary pushes those he works with to succeed, to do more, and to perform at the highest level. Yet, he leads in such a way that he has earned a very high level of respect among his associates. Third, Gary doesn't like to take "no" for an answer. Whether it be software developers, sales staff, or potential customers, Gary always tries to find a way to turn a no into a yes. Finally, Gary gets results.

Under Gary's leadership, ABC Technology developed a new reputation as a cutting-edge technology leader and our particular operation became a showcase for others in our industry looking for the best technology.

Wow! That is inspiring every time I read it. It supports what I am sharing with you. To hear the words from the customer makes you stop in your tracks. The customer is about execution. They do not care about your ideas – they care about how you help them.

You might be thinking that this seems like a lot of work, that you do not have time to undertake this right now, but if you focus on the right areas, it is possible! Many times, organizations need to look outside to gain new ideas – they may be looking inward far too much. I know how you feel – I have faced this at several of my companies. I have faced flat and declining growth situations left by my predecessors, and through a team effort and the principles I am sharing with you in this book, we have been able to successfully turn around sales, profitability, and improve the balance sheet. The formula remains the same. It starts with clearly identifying our new strategy, building the structure and team that can achieve it, and then personally leading that change. These steps, Strategy-Structure-Culture, are the logical way to change your company and make it more valuable to your customers.

I will share one more story about my experience with Strategy-Structure-Culture. Every New Year's Day while everyone was watching football games, I would personally walk around the office and leave a bookmark on everyone's desk with a message from me. Some years I would buy books along with it, but the bookmarks became a symbol of where we were going – a commitment to a strategy for the coming year and how important the associates were going to be in making it happen. See the sample on the next page.

Note the last sentence where we brought out a theme for that year, *"**Bring Your Best Today.**"* This became a theme for our company wide kickoff meeting – held every January – where we would build on this bookmark message and use the momentum from the kickoff meeting and carry it through the rest of the year!

After several years, some associates would hang multiple years of bookmarks on their cubicle walls – next to their family pictures! I was honored by this. It became something special between me and that associate – something with my feelings and how positive I felt about the company and the coming year. This reassured them.

TO OUR AWESOME ASSOCIATES

Three years ago, we focused on 'Only the paranoid survive' – a focus on awareness. Awareness of what was changing in our customers office and with our competitors – and to take on the challenge of creating raving fans and keeping our customers with us – and on new product development and developing products that our customers wanted. We rose to that occasion. We are once again a market leader, we have refreshed our products and our enthusiasm, and we have developed our strategic plans around our goal of growth. To reach this point today, we have taken a remarkable journey – not only from the viewpoint of developing a totally revitalized culture, a new strategic planning skill set, but this year we have added an exciting new goal: developing marketing strategies unique to every market we compete in.

*Now it is all up to you, our associates. There is only one way to succeed. If we each rise to the occasion. If each of our departments rises to the occasion. We can only do that if we do it now. Not tomorrow, not when the pressure turns up. You must **'Bring Your Best Today'**.*

We will help you more specifically establish your strategy in Chapter 3, but I want you to remember this for now: *You cannot change the culture without defining your strategy. If you changed strategy without following through to change the culture, you changed nothing.*

THE INVERTED PYRAMID

The Inverted Pyramid was originally developed by Nordstrom, and it was a key factor in building Nordstrom's legendary reputation for great customer service. Nordstrom, a clothing and consumer goods retailer, has pioneered many ideas on consumer experience, and in fact, this company has built policies into its handbook stating exactly how customers should be treated. The customer focus at Nordstrom captured my attention as a young technology services executive. I was particularly intrigued as to how Nordstrom became known more for its service than for the merchandise it sells. So naturally, I started utilizing it. I implemented it in real companies. I shaped it and worked it based on what was succeeding, and unfortunately, sometimes based on what was not working. I have tested it and refined it at public and private companies; and large and small family companies.

All-in-all, I spent 17 years leading, implementing, and refining the Inverted Pyramid model, and I can tell you that it works! That does not make it easy, but what is your alternative? Continue the path you're on today? Is that really acceptable to you? You picked up this book for a reason, so let's push you forward!

The Inverted Pyramid is a model. It's a philosophy that communicates how you will run the company and what is important. It's a message to all associates, including your top leaders, as to what you value. The goal of the Inverted Pyramid is not just raving associates but also raving fans (customers). That's why successfully implementing the Inverted Pyramid is not only vital to unlocking the first dimension of The Growth Cube, the ability to create raving associates, but it is vital to the second dimension of The Growth Cube, creating raving fans out of your customers.

The Inverted Pyramid
A Growth Culture Increases Company Value!

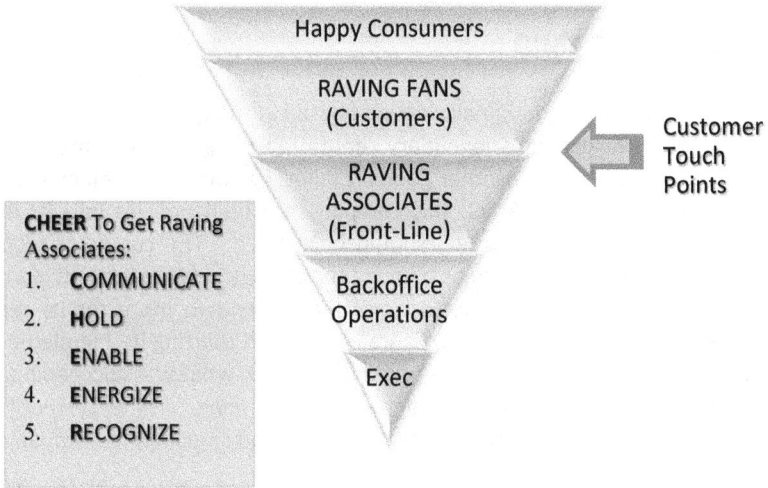

Happy Consumers

RAVING FANS
(Customers)

← Customer Touch Points

RAVING ASSOCIATES
(Front-Line)

CHEER To Get Raving Associates:
1. **COMMUNICATE**
2. **HOLD**
3. **ENABLE**
4. **ENERGIZE**
5. **RECOGNIZE**

Backoffice Operations

Exec

If we are going to build a high-growth company, we need a high-growth culture, and we are not going to come up with high growth in a vacuum that does not include the customer. The premise of my version of The Inverted Pyramid is that it not only turns the organization chart upside down, but it clearly adds the customer – and their customers. The critical fault line of The Inverted Pyramid is the frontline employees who are trying to go above and beyond for customers – what I call the Customer Touchpoints. As a leader, you have to live on that fault line, which is where you make it or break it as a company. Do not sit in your office and separate yourself. Live out there where the customer is touching your company. This is one of my big tips for leaders – my personal secret sauce.

THE CHEER PROCESS – How to Create Raving Associates

If we have successfully defined the roadmap ahead, and we know where we want to go, how do we get everyone in the company fired up and moving in that same direction? How do we achieve our goal of creating raving associates? Get them to CHEER for your company! Can you envision that?

From my experience implementing programs as president and CEO in real companies over the past 17 years, I believe it takes 5 steps to create raving associates that **CHEER** for your company:

Communicate
Hold
Enable
Energize
Recognize

Focus on each one, and take the time to do each of them well, and you will build your team into raving associates!

To Get RAVING ASSOCIATES:
1. **COMMUNICATE**
2. **HOLD**
3. **ENABLE**
4. **ENERGIZE**
5. **RECOGNIZE**

1. COMMUNICATE
The spirit of the Inverted Pyramid management philosophy is that the front-line associates who interact with your customers are vital. Your time invested in building communications to that group, with that group, and those supporting that group, and your company performance at the customer touchpoints, will always offer you great returns. You must know how you are performing for the customer and be able to communicate that performance and other market characteristics to your team. Your communication should be consistent and open, 2-way, and accountable. In this context, 2-way communication makes it a point to continuously gather feedback from your associates in a variety of ways you will read throughout this book. Annually, I recommend an associate survey to get input on leadership by department, but also to gather new ideas for improving products and services. This is invaluable input, and the results and actions should be communicated so the associates know you listened and took them seriously, and you are holding your team accountable to follow-through on agreed actions.

The Quarterly "Town Hall" Team Meeting – A Big Opportunity
You should make it a focus to communicate horizontally and vertically in your company. Do not just communicate down your department silos. Communicate in all directions and to all people. One example of a company-wide communication is the quarterly, all-company team meeting. Your company is a team, and every once in a while, that team should meet together as one. I have tried many formats and techniques, so I will give you some of my best ideas for how to conduct a successful all-company team meeting.

The quarterly all-company team meetings should be 2-3 hours and include one break. Supply good food!

You want the agenda to be mix of various people presenting, some breakout sessions, some customer stuff, and some open Q&A / interaction across all departments. Keep it interesting and energized. Although it is somewhat of a quarterly state of the business, these meetings should be informational, active, and fun. I have many times brought customers into these meetings, always do break out brainstorming, and feature leadership at all levels of the company, not just my direct reports. For example, this could include updates from the various teams across the company.

The reason I like the "Town Hall" meeting format, along with a few key charts and more interaction and breakouts, is that it inspires teambuilding and a locker-room togetherness that confirms we are in this fight together. You should work hard to create an intimate, open, and 2-way dialogue. You should focus on ideas that are generated from associates to evaluate, act on, and communicate the results of our efforts. End the meeting with something fun and spirited; be your best company cheerleader!

*"Inspire teambuilding and a locker-room togetherness
that we are in this fight together!"*

As always, these quarterly meetings are more about the message and the mood that is set than simply presenting the current charts. You do have to update people on the business and hold everyone accountable to achieving the results we set as a team, but we are ultimately looking for involvement and 2-way interaction. As such, presentations should be short, easy to read, and impactful. Video is good. To the extent possible, make sure remote associates have the same experience as your local people in the room. Technology is constantly developing to enable this, but you should work hard and practice this prior to the meeting to make sure there are no major technical difficulties. As an example, how will you plan to include remote associates in the breakouts during the meeting? Many times, we had the remote associates be one breakout team, and we would have someone in attendance be their team leader and spokesperson. Breakouts are a huge opportunity for you as a leader, and it can be a challenge to include the remote associates. But it can be done with technology and proper planning prior to these quarterly meetings.

22

What do you do in the breakout sessions? Focus them around key topics that you want input on. It could be input on a benefit program that you are considering, or on a new recognition program, or a new product you are developing. We use the breakout session at our communication meeting to get involvement, teamwork, and input. Act on this input! After the meeting, communicate a summary of the input received, how you plan to use it, and how the input will help the company succeed. Follow-up!

How often should you do company-wide team meetings? Obviously time is valuable, but so is teambuilding. My recommendation is every quarter. It is just the right length of time between meetings to where some associates will either be new to the company, or existing associates will start to wonder what is going on. These meetings should be mandatory and include every person in the company.

"You are a leader – so lead!"

As the CEO or president, you should personally lead the company-wide meeting. Your associates want to hear directly from you. We would be disappointed if the President of the United States had someone else do their State of the Union. If a head coach walked into the locker room during halftime and didn't say anything, the team could easily lose motivation. Take control and lead!

The company-wide team meeting is also a great opportunity for your leaders to lead and show camaraderie with each other. Leaders should stand up and talk about their direction, their results, and what they are doing to improve. Associates will hold you accountable, and they know what is going on, so just address issues and talk about everything together! Trust your associates.

One example of leadership and trust I can share with you is one of my top 10 all-time team meeting moments. One of our leaders stood up and was updating everyone on the activity in her division. She did not even look at her charts, and really did not care. That's exactly what I want. She got up there and just started laying out her feelings for the associates. She started telling them why we were having issues, what we were doing to fix them, and where they could contribute in order to be part of the solution. She talked from her heart. She was not just talking to her own team, but she spoke with conviction to everyone in the company. She clearly cared about the company. The room was still; the associates were glued in. After her enthusiastic and emotional talk with everyone (I don't even think she

even got through all her charts), the whole room erupted in applause. I mean erupted! That was the most genuine applause from a group of associates for one of their leaders that I have ever seen. The morale of the story: it's not about the charts. It's about you. Be authentic, be honest, and get out there and lead. Your associates will love it, and you will be one step closer to achieving your goal of working with raving associates!

As you might expect, your message is extremely important as you prepare for these team meetings. To be successful, you and your leaders should think deeply about what your message is, what you need input on, and how this meeting can help move the company forward toward its goals. You must figure out a way to communicate complex topics in a positive and understandable manner.

Of course you have your own agenda, but I can tell you what your people want to hear. It's only 3 things:

1. Where are we going, and does it sound exciting?
2. How are we doing on that journey, and are we making progress?
3. Do I like my leaders, and do they care about me?

That's it! Meet those 3 requirements at every quarterly team meeting and you will be on your way to creating raving associates!

The Person Running the Business Needs to be Visible
As you will read throughout this book, I am big on teams and getting associates involved in the business and determining our success. However, I also feel it is important that the leader of the business (the CEO in a small business), is out in front, visible, and available. Not just in these company-wide meetings, but throughout the rest of your day and week. From open-door policies (I have one hour on Friday where any associate can walk into my office and talk about any-thing), to my Friday morning walk-arounds, to attendance at events where associates are having fun, to other types of meetings. The associates want to see you and hear from you directly.

Friday Morning Walk Around
In my very first role as President, I relocated to Europe with my family and led a $50M European operation working with very capable country managers, channel partners, and a headquarters staff operation. I ran into one of my direct reports a few years ago, and do you know the first thing he pointed out and remembered about my tenure there? My "Friday Morning Walk Around." He loved that every

Friday he saw me walking through the departments. I created this activity to get out and see people face-to-face, to see what was "going on." What did I learn about this, and what can I tell you to make it work for you?

1. Say hi to everyone. If you have a big company, handle this one department per week. When I was at one of my companies and did this the first time, I had a 30-year associate tell me, "Mr. Ross, this is the first time I have shaken the hand of our company CEO." Is that amazing? It's also very sad.

2. Use your humor. Keep it light. Don't start "firing questions," and you do not have to talk business with everyone. Ask them what they are doing. Listen – a lot. Learn what each person does. You will uncover nuggets just by listening.

By sharing examples like this with you, I hope I am giving you actionable moves that you utilize to create energized changes in your company. There is no doubt that communication has an impact on creating raving associates, which is our goal here. We have consistently driven up post-meeting associate survey ratings by doing the things I am sharing with you here. I believe in sharing information with our associates and teaching them about the business. I have learned that there is a direct correlation in "my company shares information on how we are doing" to associate satisfaction and retention, so I focus on it!

To Get RAVING ASSOCIATES:
1. COMMUNICATE
2. **HOLD**
3. ENABLE
4. ENERGIZE
5. RECOGNIZE

2. HOLD

Do you know what it feels like to hold someone close? A dear friend, a son or daughter? To be involved in their challenges and their fears? Your associates also have challenges and fears, and beyond the fact that these people could at least use your positivity, not offering support may be affecting their performance. You should be engaged with them and support them. I know there are some personal areas that you do not want to touch as a CEO, but that is not my point. Your associates are not just a number, or a "headcount." They are real people. They are someone's son or daughter. You can motivate them just by caring. This is why "Hold" is our second success factor to create raving associates in your company. I am not sure I can teach this to you. It has to be genuine, and you have to be yourself. Still, I know without a doubt that it's important to creating raving associates.

During one particular annual sales kickoff meeting, I did not present any charts. Instead, I grabbed a chair and sat down with the sales team in a circle, and we just talked for an hour. We talked about many things. About things that were holding them back. About their frustrations. About opportunities. I just let them vent and offered my responses. I had no agenda. It received such high feedback that we started doing it every year after that, and the sales team looked forward to it. We called this session "Gary Unplugged."

Another example of holding your people close is our observance at my companies for 9-11. We would remember and respect the 9-11 tragedy by walking silently from the company lobby and out to the closest flagpole. It was totally optional, but we would draw a sizable group. When we got to the base of the flag, I would say a few words, do a moment of silence, and then open up the floor. A lot of people talked, many about their own family losses or military experiences. I just kind of let it go where it needed to go. There was no plan. Associates talked about these moments for years. These kinds of things take time and attention away from the business, but if our goal is to create raving associates, this is an amazing example of how to help achieve that. Think about how this represents holding people close and builds relationships that last.

Outside of personal reasons for being close to your fellow teammates, there are also strong business reasons for holding your associates in close regard, listening to them, and involving them more deeply in what you are trying to accomplish as a leader:

1. You need ideas – and good ones – to succeed and win in the marketplace.

2. You not only need the ideas, but you have to figure out a way to success-fully execute the implementation those ideas.

3. Holding someone close means listening to struggles and challenges and helping to provide ideas and solutions to solve them.

"As a leader, you should make every associate in the company feel valued."

A few months after I left one of my companies, I received a card in the mail from someone on the front-line in the accounting department. It is a letter I have saved to this day. The letter read, "Gary, thank you for caring so much about the reports

I send out every month from accounting. You were the only one in the company that really read them, and that was so important to me. Thank you."

Yes, I did read them. I knew what she did, and I often asked her many questions about the reports. I got involved. I held her projects and what she was working on closely, and valued her hard work. As a result, she felt it. Involvement is about everyone in the company, from the CEO to the front-line associates. I am very proud of this note because it emphasizes how little steps by a leader can make such a big impact on your associates and their personal and professional performance. There is no doubt that your ability to hold your associates close directly impacts your ability to create a raving associate!

To Get RAVING ASSOCIATES:
1. COMMUNICATE
2. HOLD
3. **ENABLE**
4. ENERGIZE
5. RECOGNIZE

3. ENABLE

So, by now you know that the focus of the Inverted Pyramid is about the ability of your front-line raving associates to be able to take care of our customers, to bring them closer, and make those customers raving fans. However, why is it that 90% of front-line associates, when asked in confidence, will tell you they do not have what they need to delight customers? This is what enabling is all about: making investments in your people so that they can be more effective. If you invest in your people and their ability to perform for your customers, you will achieve many goals as a company.

So how do we do this? How do we enable our associates? Start with the 3 T's:

Training
Tools
Time.

Make Your Training Program a Certification Program
If you really want an effective training process for your associates, build it as a certification program. It should include product, customer, and technical training, and also cross training and learning from their peers. The same onboarding and technical training that you probably utilize today for new hires can be provided to current associates; for example, refresh them on new technologies and new products being released. Videos are excellent in this case. We developed a comprehensive certification program for one of my companies that included multiple levels of training. It offered customer and product training modules, and it provided awards for training accomplishments. It was called a 3-Level Certification

Program. Every associate was required to complete at least level 1, customer facing associates required to complete level 2, and sales associates required to complete level 3. The customer module helped us become thought leaders by learning about the customers' environments and challenges, and the trends and solutions they were deploying in our part of their business. The benefit here is that you now have a formal strategy and framework to become the thought leader your customer wants you to be!

Tools

Invest in the tools and systems that help your associates do their jobs efficiently and effectively; this especially applies to front-line associates. For example, a front-line support, services, or salesperson that has a Customer Relationship Management (CRM) that gives them a 360-degree view of the customer, how we are performing at each customer Touchpoint, and other activity, including contract coverage, support issues, and available upgrade plans. From every department and every position, you should be able to see the customer issues and resolution plans, actions, and results. Through a great system, we have a more complete picture that allows us to serve each customer better.

Time

Most associates want you to let them know the goals and then get out of their way! They do not want to be dragged through a bunch of meetings and reviews that waste time. They want you to have confidence in them and let them have their own time with the option of coaching when they ask for it. Some associates want time to work on developing totally new ideas and concepts.

In the end, it's not just about enabling but retaining that associate as well. These things can help there too.

Hiring New Associates

If you were the general manager of a football team that had all of their quarterbacks injured, and you solved the issue by bringing in one of the top quarterbacks in the league, do you think your team would appreciate that? Would it help you win? I think the answer is a clear, "Yes!" Hiring people into your company can be viewed the same way. Hiring is an enabler. Yes, we want to help current associates get stronger, but sometimes to enable us to succeed, we need to go outside to get new skills. Maybe we are pursuing a new product or a new market where we need more expertise. You should not look at this as a negative. You are adding talent and new skills to the team. Enabling is about building a team with both inside and outside talent.

Now you have decided to go recruit. We all know it is competitive, especially for technology talent. How then do we compete? What is our edge in hiring and interviewing? I see two things:

1. Your environment.
Where do members of the millennial generation most want to work right now? Google. Based on a recent survey by an organization called the National Society of High School Scholars (NSHSS), the reason Google is number 1 is that Google's strategy is to make the office environment so stimulating and fun that employees look forward to coming into the office!

As you may know, Google does not believe in working from home. Neither does Yahoo, which has been recently run by former Google Exec. Marissa Mayer. Google believes there is something to be gained by working as a team in the office together, so they make the environment fun. As leaders, what we can learn is that we need to create unique ideas to make our environment special as well. What is your strategy to do this? The goal is to develop a stellar reputation for treating employees well.

2. Your interviewing and the Critical Success Factor process
If you are interviewing people ineffectively, you could be bringing in the wrong people and just wasting time and money. Worse yet, you may not be bringing them in at all. If you are interviewing and then losing candidates to a competitor, is it because your hiring practices are clunky? Do you know what Google CEO Eric Schmidt believes is the most important skill that any business person can learn? Interviewing. Can you believe this?! Out of all the business skills? That says something about its importance to your company.

So what are you and your team doing to become better at interviewing?

You may have heard a saying, "hire slow, fire fast." I have a different philosophy: *"Hire fast, fire slow."* Why? It's easy to fire someone when they become difficult or ineffective, but why are they this way? Challenge yourself as a leader to think through other roles possible or other potential bosses for that person. I have seen associates totally turn around simply by moving them under a different boss. You are going to cause them personal hardship by firing them – try hard to "re-motivate" them. If you are firing someone you hired within the last year, it is very likely a result of poor interviewing techniques.

I believe in a fast but thorough interview process. Yes, you can be fast and thorough! To achieve this, implement a CSF (Critical Success Factor) hiring process. By using a formalized CSF process, you can move fast and still be effective. I hire fast, but I will admit it is grueling. It is more steps than I see other companies take, and it involves team interviews and grueling questions. If you make it through the process, and we believe you are the right candidate, there are big wins for our company. I believe we are faster than anyone else I have seen. Our speed enables us to make offers before other companies even get to the second round. I am not kidding. I have experienced this! We move. This is a competitive advantage!

I have developed and tested the CSF process in my companies, and it works! We define 5 CSFs for each position, and we grade those on a scorecard as we interview for those positions. Column 1 might be my score on all of those 5 factors, and column 2 might be your score, and so on. By using this format, we hire objectively based on the skills we need.

The owner of one of my companies only used 2 CSFs in his hiring. He used to tell me, "Gary, we only hire people who are smart and have a great attitude." I always felt good about that because he hired me!

The CSFs that you agree are important in advance is the key to hiring. Of course, I look for other specific traits and skills that I believe are vital for the executive team:

1. Vision
I love to see someone come in with a vision of where they want to take their department. It is awesome if they have a track record of doing this, but it is not a deal-breaker if they do not have the experience yet. I know for others it might be, but if you can spot young talent like a sports recruiter might do for a pro team, you can pick up gems of associates who do have vision and will run through the wall to prove themselves. Taking a chance on them motivates them further!

2. Initiative and Positive Energy.
I look for energy and initiative from the people who join our company. I often ask candidates and associates: 'Are you are an energy provider or an energy drainer?' Did you ever meet someone who totally drained the energy out of the room, and out of your conversation? How about someone who adds energy to the room, or brings energy to solving problems? They find a way to make it happen! For candidates specifically, initiative and energy can be something like following-up the

interview with ideas and a summary of how they would attack the role (without me having to ask for it)?

3. Leadership qualities.
Do they have coaching skills that will enable them to coach their team to higher levels of success? Do they have the commitment to their people to create raving associates in their department? There are going to be ups and downs and challenges. Are they a fighter? Are they committed to goals, and do they have a never-give-up attitude? They are going to need it to handle the pressure at the top.

4. Thought Leadership
Whatever your discipline or market experience, you need to have a passion for the customer and your team. This involves pushing yourself into a thought leadership position with your customer. You need to lead the way within your company. Get out there at industry events and network, and contribute and advance the industry. Be visible both socially and physically at networking events. Be the best PR person possible for your company!

Onboarding
Congratulations! You got them to join your team! Now what? All the training and systems and tools we talked about earlier need to be leveraged into an onboarding program for every new associate. This requires focus and attention. As we discussed earlier, start by getting them certified. New hires need more than that, though. They need to meet people across the company, and they should learn the company policies, procedures, culture, and expectations. At one of my companies, we developed a disciplined onboarding program that occurred over a 3-week period (not including the full certification program). You can do this too. Remember, if you can get your new hires up the learning curve and enable them to become effective quicker than your competitors, you will have a competitive advantage, which lends to the potential of increased sales and profitability in a shorter amount of time. And of course, you will be well on your way towards creating a new raving associate!

The Leadership Development Process.
Look at the great coaches in sports. Urban Myer and Nick Saban are strong examples within the world of college football. What sets them apart from other team leaders is that they don't only recruit well; they also work hard to develop their players. They make them better through focused training and development efforts. As a CEO, you should work just as hard at developing your leaders!

I spent 14 years at a large public company where I was promoted 4 times. I moved from director, to VP, and eventually to two roles as president. In my final role there, I managed 600 associates and $150M in revenue responsibility. Throughout that period, I was inside The Program. I saw how they did it, and I learned. I was nothing short of impressed, and through this experience, I now I understand why the market viewed them as a leadership training ground.

I have now taken those ideas and learnings and have adapted them to smaller businesses (under $20M in revenues). I have modified it for small companies and refined it based on what I saw works!

Here are the key tenants of my current leadership development process:

1. Build an annual review to profile and discuss every single manager in your company/division. The profile should include top skills, years with the company, pay, and performance results. It also should include their picture, which is a way to remember that we are talking about people here!

2. If someone is failing, it's the leaders' job to turn it around, coach them, and get them on track. Firing someone is a last resort. If we're not addressing people who are having performance issues, that is the leaders' fault!

3. If someone is doing well and we are not proactively positioning them with more challenges, we are making a mistake. Identify the top 10% of performers in your company. Talk more specifically about them and how you can continue to give them more responsibility in the coming year.

4. For every leader, at least one (preferably more) successors should be identified. How many years away are they from being ready to step in if they had to? This is succession planning.

Let me shift gears here slightly and emphasize something you are going to hear throughout this book. I want you to remember this: your company must learn and become experts at the customers' businesses and how your products and services help them compete more effectively.

How do you do this? Let's take a look at some quotes directly from customers! I have captured below direct correspondences from customers about what they want us to be great at!

WHAT DO CUSTOMERS WANT FROM US?

- "A customer-facing leadership person who fully understands both the product line and our industry/business."
- "People in the company who fully understand our true pain points and introduce the best products to solve them."
- "People who demonstrate a strong competency. Develop solutions that help us win with our customers."

This is direct advice from Customers! As you can see, the customer is not just talking about their sales rep. It's everyone in the company. I call this "thought leadership depth." Your Customer wants thought leadership depth from your company. What is the implication for us as leaders? We have no choice. We must develop thought-leadership depth in our company!

If you are a small business CEO, you may be the only one in the company who deeply understands the Customer environment. This is an issue, especially if you try to sell the company someday. How do you expand the capability throughout the company and enable yourself to scale and take on more customers? I have solved this problem several times, and am now working as a CEO Coach in companies who are achieving just that. I am going to show you my own summary of how you can master the same through what I call the "3-Level Certification Program."

3-LEVEL CERTIFICATION PROGRAM

The first concept of the 3-Level Certification Program is that everyone in the company completes Level 1. The smarter your people are about your products, the industry and the customer environment, the more effectively they can help your company grow profitably.

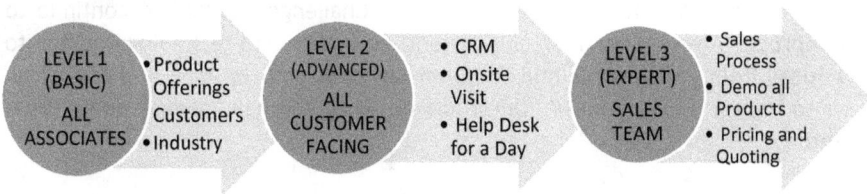

LEVEL 1 (BASIC) ALL ASSOCIATES	• Product Offerings • Customers • Industry	LEVEL 2 (ADVANCED) ALL CUSTOMER FACING	• CRM • Onsite Visit • Help Desk for a Day	LEVEL 3 (EXPERT) SALES TEAM	• Sales Process • Demo all Products • Pricing and Quoting

Every customer-facing associate needs to complete Level 2. Level 2 is a deeper dive, a deeper sensitivity, and a deeper knowledge about our customers and how we solve their problems with our products and services. This level includes an onsite customer visit and sitting on the help desk for a day! Additionally, it involves learning the CRM and how to find customer information. Equipped with this knowledge, your customer-facing team will begin to be grow as a stronger asset to your customers in their business! If your marketing and product management people cannot teach this level, they are the wrong people.

Finally, level 3 is targeted specifically for the sales team, who is spending the most time with customers. This is everyone involved in selling, not just the sales rep, like the sales engineer for example. This includes training on our sales process, the CRM, how we price and quote, and being able to demo. If the VP sales cannot teach this level, you have the wrong VP of Sales.

The challenges that I believe you must address to implement the Level 3 Certification Program is:

- Developing the content and the training curriculum and testing,
- Finding a champion to lead the project. The natural spot is your services leader, someone technical who understands the industry.
- Choosing the technology to utilize for the training and the progress. A Learning Management System (LMS) is ideal!

The 3-Level Certification Program can be implemented with current associates, and should be integrated into the new hire onboarding process. Videos are excellent in this case, and a Learning Management Systems (LMS) would be an excellent tool here to track who has completed which classes and defining what level of training is completed and still outstanding for that role.

The bottom line is that by better enabling your associates, you are going to make your team stronger and increase your company's performance with customers.

Leadership development includes you too! The CEO has to stay on top of the latest technologies and trends that are arising. Challenge yourself to continue to self-improve. Always stay fresh and current, especially with technology. Listen to new ideas from your people and try them out to stretch yourself and learn new ways to impact your business. Don't just do what you have always done. Beat yesterday!

To Get RAVING ASSOCIATES:
1. COMMUNICATE
2. HOLD
3. ENABLE
4. **ENERGIZE**
5. RECOGNIZE

4. ENERGIZE

We have learned already that strategy should drive structure and culture, but I will tell you something strategy does not drive: energy! How many times have you been part of a company or organization that takes a lot of time to set out a strategic plan, and then none of it gets implemented? It just sits on the shelf. This is very frustrating to associates, especially those who helped to come up with the plan. They want to see goals achieved, plans implemented, and dreams come true. So if you want to make them raving associates, you have to energize people around executing the ideas.

What can you do to start to improve your company energy? My first question is this: how did you do on the first 3 parts of CHEER? Do you have something going already? Have you changed anything in your company as a result of reading about the first 3 steps of creating CHEER? Will you? I am honored you are reading this book, but I would even be more honored if you took some of these ideas and tools and techniques and utilized them to advance your company! What is your plan, and when will you do it? This is how energized execution people think. If you do not have this focus, you need someone on your team who can help you drive programs to completion. You have to instill a philosophy of execution in your company.

Bossidy and Charan's in the book *Execution* did research that suggests people think of execution as the tactical side of business, something leaders delegate while they focus on the perceived 'bigger' issues. This idea is completely wrong. Execution is not just tactics – it is a discipline and a system. It must be built into a company's strategy, its goals, and its culture. As the leader, you need to be deeply engaged in it.

> *"Execution is about the discipline of getting things done."*
> —*Larry Bossidy and Ram Charan*

Utilizing Teams to Energize

I am a big believer in the use of teams to get things done. In fact, at our Quarterly team meetings, we have team leaders give updates to the whole company, and we have signups for new teams we are forming.

As an example, one of the teams I like to implement is a "Focus and Fun Team." Their mission in our company is to make sure we are living up to and becoming the culture that we desire, the culture that we had put on a piece of paper and voted on by our associates. This is a group of associates representing every department so they are the main channel of communication to associates in their area. The Focus and Fun team has two budgets to manage and programs to roll out:

1. **The Focus** – take responsibility to ensure our company focus areas are understood, being communicated, and working in every department.

2. **The Fun** – lead and conduct activities to ensure that our associates enjoy their colleagues from around the company. The team budgets and plans all the fun activities that we want to do (you may have an activity committee doing this for you today).

The Focus and Fun team is a way to involve your associates in rolling out programs affecting your front-line associates and their ability to service the customer.

This is one example of a very important team. Give your teams power, support them, attend their meetings, and stay involved.

The Roles You Assign to People
What would you tell me if I asked you what the top 2 strengths of your customer support manager are? How do those skills match the requirements of the job? Many times, this is out of synch because we want to stretch people, push people, and teach people. These are good to do once in a while, but many associates fail because we put them in a role that does not capitalize on their strengths. You can figure this out; there are some great tools available to evaluate core strengths. Some people are strategic, some are operational; some are financial, and some are relationship builders. If you want energized associates, quit putting people in roles that do not utilize their best strengths.

Systems and Project Management
People get energized when programs are being completed and executed. Focus on managing that! If I told you I had a project to complete and there were 95 steps to complete it, and some of the steps are dependent on other steps getting completed first, would you feel more comfortable if I tracked that in a system, or is it fine if it's manually tracked or tracked in an Excel spreadsheet? There are many projects in progress across your company. How are you and your teams managing them? Do you have a project management system where key mile-

stones are defined for executing the plan? Being a technology guy myself, I am a fan of utilizing technology to help accomplish our work. You will notice that I put thought to ideas for this throughout this book. There are many low-cost, even free, project management systems. It is great if it integrates with financial systems, and if project management is a revenue-generating business for you, you will need this. If not, just pick a tool and get moving. Require that the tool is used and do not attend a meeting where the project is not presented through the tool. Your team is probably duplicating efforts that could be streamlined. Get involved and check this out.

Stay focused on what's most important – Raving Fans and Raving Associates.
If you looked across your company right now – and if you could see everything that was going on – I bet you would find time being spent on projects and programs that you believe add no value and are unimportant to your mission. Like the old Eagles song, there is a lot of wasted time. As an example, let's talk about your competitors and how many resources you throw at understanding them better. Although it is very important for associates to understand the market, our competitors, and our customer environment, many companies spend way too much time worrying about competitors. I learned this from a wise company owner: focusing too much time on what competitors are doing can drain a lot of your company time and energy. She was right. Instead, focus on higher priority items first, like the customer, what they need, and how you are doing to meet those needs. Focus on your associates and what they need to be better enabled. Don't allow yourself to waste too much time on things that are lower priority.

Associate Performance Reviews
The Quarterly HDO (Hopes, Dreams, and Objectives)

Why is it that most people hate performance reviews? They are usually not energizing! Why is that? Usually because these reviews are only one-way, negative in tone, and have nothing to do with an increase in merit.

It does not have to be like this.

I developed and implemented a quarterly review process to tackle this issue. Over time, I have refined it and used it successfully. I call it "The Quarterly HDO," standing for Hopes, Dreams, and Objectives. That's right, we talk about hopes, dreams, and objectives! The team I have used it with have often taken it and used it with their teams as well. People respond to it. Here are the main tenants of the HDO program:

1. You should focus on 3 things during your meeting (tell them in advance you want them to bring ideas): Hopes, Dreams, and Objectives. Start with the hopes and dreams. These are fun and sometimes inspirational. Leave it open, and let it flow. Again, you must take an interest and be authentic as a boss, or none of this matters.

2. Of course, you have to cover the Objectives. During this portion, review the results on the objectives set during last quarter's meeting, and then work together to set your objectives for the coming quarter. Thank them for the results they achieved and successfully executed!

3. The quarterly HDO is only 45 minutes, 15 minutes on each of the topics. Keep it agile. If you have to fill out annual reviews for your company, then one of the quarters might take a little longer.

4. The annual performance appraisal should simply be one quarter in a year of quarterly reviews. It is the last quarter of 3 other similar discussions. It should be a typical discussion with no surprises. However, many times managers wait until the end of the year to have "the conversation." We all know this, but it still happens. If you can stay disciplined to do quarterly reviews, this will just be another meeting.

Maureen Metcalf of Metcalf & Associates is an expert in the area of leadership development. She has helped my teams with workshops in which she talks about the importance of being authentic as a leader. It's not only about you understanding who you are and your true values, but it's also about understanding the same things about your people!

The Mentality of a Startup
You want energy? Get your people thinking liking a startup. I have started up 3 companies myself in the past 3 years, and I coach other startup and small business CEOs to help them reach their potential as a company. We all know what the startup culture is like, right? The buzz. Staying lean and low cost while you build that new innovation that is going to change the game! Everyone is focused on the same goal. It's fun and there is camaraderie and excitement. Our associates all desire this environment in their career. As the CEO, the question for you is: can you create that culture within your company? If you can, that energy can provide a tailwind to help your business execute more effectively and efficiently! Sounds great, right? It does to your associates too!

One key skill CEOs must demonstrate is the ability to increase the speed with which things are done. Leaders can slow down and stifle execution simply by how they move and what they focus on. If you are dragging groups of people through multi-hour "review" meetings and issuing multi-page actions, then you are stifling your company. You are making it boring for your people! I know because I have done it. It may work in a big company at an executive level, but this does not help smaller companies whose main competitive advantage is speed and flexibility. As an example of something you can do to change your company, I will introduce you to a concept I invented at one of my companies. I have heard no one else use this term outside of development. It's called: "Agile Meetings."

Agile Meetings
Agile meetings are about keeping the number of meeting attendees down, the meeting length short, and the agenda focused. For example, I do pipeline reviews with the sales manager, the sales rep, and me. That's it – not a room full of reps all reviewing their pipelines together. It lasts 20 minutes. Take 3 accounts (that I pick), and focus on what we are doing to win! You can learn a lot in those 20 minutes – how we are managing the sales process, how that rep is being managed by their leader, and if we are really going to win those deals. You must stay focused and know what you want. You cannot go into this meeting waiting for someone to "serve up" information to you. You should get into the CRM yourself and look at the activity on the accounts and do some preparation. Come into this meeting prepared with very focused questions and areas of discussion. This approach can be applied to any department with their people in a lot of meetings, which may be impacting your execution by wasting time.

The key to "Agile Meetings" is for you to do a great job at preparing prior to the meeting! It's you – it's not "them!" Follow-up the meeting with a short, bulleted summary. If a more detailed review of a specific issue or opportunity is required, meet on that separately and only with the associates that are related to the issue. That's it! Keep it moving. Think speed. Instill the mentality of a startup into your company!

I hope you get the message here. As the leader, can you see the impact you have on the energy in your company by how you move and what you get involved in and make important? If you can get the team to execute, everyone is happy and everyone gets energized. You can see that successful execution, and good energy is mainly about you. It's about being agile as a company and developing your company speed; it's about putting people in the right roles and rewarding those who "do." It's about staying focused and following through on the most important

milestones. It's about digging into the details of the plans. And it's about building a start-up atmosphere that we're all in this fight together, and we are going to win!

To Get RAVING ASSOCIATES:
1. COMMUNICATE
2. HOLD
3. ENABLE
4. ENERGIZE
5. RECOGNIZE

5. RECOGNIZE

If you successfully implemented all 4 elements of the Raving Associate Success Formula, recognition and awards will be the icing on the cake, right?

Not always. Why? Because recognition is sensitive, complex, and sometimes a frustrating experience. We leaders sometimes forget a very basic principle that we all know: recognition is personal and everyone is motivated differently. What's the answer then? No recognition program? That is not going to motivate for sure, but if you roll out a program that isn't well thought out, you can actually demotivate the associate!

If we want to create raving associates, which we agreed we do, then your goal is to figure this out in a manner that works for your company and your people. You have to develop your program for your company, but remember that whatever recognition you choose is going to tell your people what is valued most highly in the company. Be thoughtful.

To give recognition properly to your team, you must understand what motivates them. This is possible by spending time with your people to genuinely ask questions and intently listen to them. What is gained from this alone is a huge gift for many leaders. It can unlock the key to the raving associate.

Many recognition programs are set up early in the year and based on targets achieved throughout the year. This is good because it will drive the behavior and results you probably need to hit your annual plan.

Some recognition programs are monetary, and in this case, they should be challenging yet achievable. The associate should be able to exceed 100% achievement. In this case, they may be more motivated to continue to push higher all the way through Q4.

I typically like to do an "Associate of the Quarter" that gets recognized at our quarterly company-wide meetings, and Associate of the Year, which gets recognized at our annual kickoff meeting where we also bring the family in to celebrate with us!

40

I recognize all teams. I give out innovation awards. I also invented an Award of Courage, which is the most prestigious award and focuses on associate's personal battles and displaying courage in the face of major challenges. We used an associate team to manage the nomination and selection process for all these awards. They built their own voting processes. The award was not chosen or influenced by management unless they needed a tie breaker. The team made the decision.

The final point is this: To recognize people, you have to take time to do it correctly, to shake someone's hand, to walk into their cubicle and say thank you, to give out a gift card that says, "Job well done," and to give someone some personal time or family time. This is how you say, "I care." I used to walk around and hand a personal card to everyone that was nominated for an award, whether they won or not, because being nominated by your peers is impressive on its own! None of these things take a lot of time or money, yet most leaders do not pull it off consistently.

HOW GARY HIRES AND ONBOARDS HIS LEADERS
A CASE STUDY WRITTEN BY A FORMER ASSOCIATE

There are many stories of how Gary demonstrated the great people leader that he is. I will start with sharing my first impression of Gary. I knew from the interview process that Gary was going to be the type of leader that would raise the bar – stretching me and pushing me to be more than I thought I could be.

He called me several times in between our formal interviews sharing with me challenges that he was experiencing with Customer Support and asking for advice. I knew he was testing me to see how I would react and if I had the capabilities he was looking for to improve the situation. In parallel, however, I felt valued and respected because he was calling me and asking for input.

For the final interview, he asked all candidates to develop a presentation around a particular article / trend in Support Services, our respective position on the trend and then describe our recommendations for improvement of support services and how we will go about implementing. He had me come into his executive staff meeting to present like I was a team member looking for buy-in. I could tell in that experience that he expects a lot from his team, he is inclusive in his decision making and thorough in his process.

Once I was hired, I experienced Gary consistently in the ways I had initially observed. He cared very much about the team, the Customers, and making the company the best we could be. Gary implemented teams within the organization to address some of the internal challenges the employees were particularly concerned with (some inward focused and others Customer impacting). These challenges came to light during an annual employee satisfaction survey which Gary instituted early in his tenure to get a pulse on employee satisfaction & engagement. Gary wanted the employees to be a part of solving the problem so they would feel included which means more likely to embrace and accept the new way of doing things to improve.

Gary treated Customer feedback similarly. He established and led a Customer Advisory Board (CAB) comprised of Customers who could influence their peers and positioned this CAB as an extension of the executive team. The exec team was advised to be transparent as we could be so the CAB could help us improve our methodologies to better serve our Customers. Gary created a culture that valued new ideas and collaborative problem-solving, that always put the Customer at the forefront and where accountability was expected in everything we did.

I knew my experience was going to be career changing and life changing the moment I was made an offer that was soon followed by a beautiful planter that Gary had sent welcoming me to the family. That is something I never experienced before nor have I ever since then but it is something that I have instituted in my own hiring practices because I remember how it made me feel.

To Get RAVING ASSOCIATES:
1. COMMUNICATE
2. HOLD
3. ENABLE
4. ENERGIZE
5. RECOGNIZE

LEADING THE WAY – FINAL THOUGHTS ON THE CHEER SUCCESS FACTORS

I hope you find the CHEER process unlocks the raving associate opportunity for you. They want you to be a great leader, and they will respond to you. Do not put everything we covered here in the hands of your HR leader and ask them to implement it. As the leader, you have to take the lead and stay out front. Your HR leader can help you and assist you, but do not step back. The associates want to see you in front, and they want you to commit to them and promise them that you will make these programs happen! Do not let them down.

If you are smaller than $10M in revenue, you probably do not have an HR leader. When you do get to this point and are hiring your HR leader, find someone who loves the CHEER process and will be passionate about it. They must be intimate with, sincerely care about, and want to help drive the business goals of the company. Yes, they do have to make sure to protect the company and its leaders legally, and that is important, but it's more about the people and the customer. It's more about how the HR leader can look at "what the business is trying to accomplish" and help us get there in a professional and legal path. I also like my HR leader to be strong with technology. Applicant tracking systems, learning management systems, gamification, collaboration, social apps, and automated expense reporting are technology that's vitally important to implement. These can affect your people in a very positive way! If your HR leader believes what you believe and wants to build what you want to build, I promise that you will have excellent chemistry. I know because I have been through this process myself.

"Teach your associates that nothing is out of our reach!
We can be the leader. We can be the best.
And we can beat bigger companies."

DIMENSION 1 WRAP UP – CREATING RAVING ASSOCIATES
So, there you have it. The key to unlocking the potential of the first dimension of The Growth Cube is the Inverted Pyramid, effectively implementing the CHEER process, and your continued commitment to this principle:

YOU AND YOUR COMPANY SUCCEED BECAUSE OF YOUR PEOPLE
AND WHAT THEY CAN ACCOMPLISH FOR YOUR CUSTOMERS!

The Inverted Pyramid
A Growth Culture Increases Company Value!

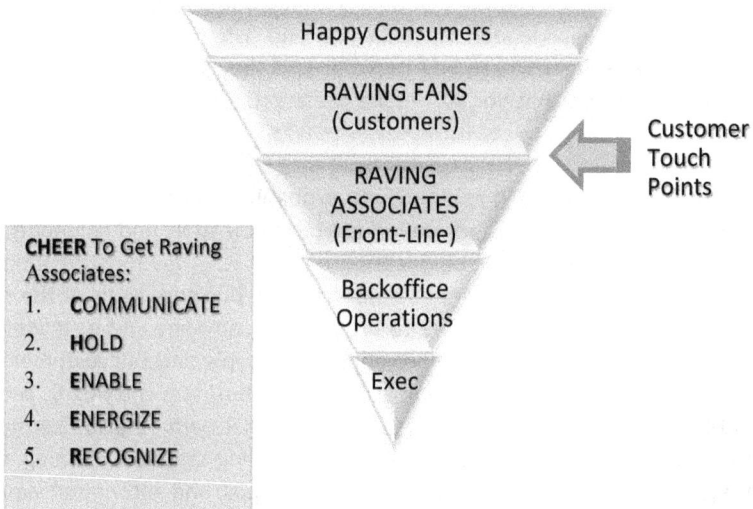

Happy Consumers

RAVING FANS
(Customers)

RAVING
ASSOCIATES
(Front-Line)

Customer
Touch
Points

Backoffice
Operations

Exec

CHEER To Get Raving
Associates:
1. **COMMUNICATE**
2. **HOLD**
3. **ENABLE**
4. **ENERGIZE**
5. **RECOGNIZE**

As we transition to Chapter 2, we will learn that raving associates are critical to creating Raving Fans. There is a reason that people are on the top of The Growth Cube. Putting your focus on your associates, especially those on the front-line, will help you win with your customers. You know what to do, and your people are hoping for it. Let's go do it!

CHAPTER 2 – CURRENT CUSTOMERS.
Creating Raving Fans.

"Our DNA is as a consumer company – for that individual customer who's voting thumbs up or thumbs down. That's who we think about."
—Steve Jobs

Early on in one of my companies, I formed a partnership with one of my customers, who I will call Jeanne. I went out and spent a few days at her offices to learn her business, meet her team, and see where we could assist. One of the things Jeanne did that set her apart is that she took me into a meeting with her boss and had me give a background on our company and listen to her boss' ideas. I was honored that she trusted me with her boss, and I really wanted to come through for her. I have to say I was very impressed with the operation as well. I thought our associates and our other customers could learn from Jeanne too, so I invited her to join our Customer Advisory Board, which she excelled at! I invited Jeanne to join us as a surprise presenter at one of our internal company-wide kickoff meetings. We developed trust, and we pushed each other. Jeanne wanted her company to be the best, and we were part of the solution! A couple years into our relationship, we helped Jeanne and her team develop and produce a "Future Vision" presentation that she successfully presented to the Board around how technology could help them reposition against their competitors. Their board loved it! We were a professional team and pushed each other's companies forward. We are still friends to this day.

Your customers and the relationship you build with them are critical to your company's success and your success as the leader. Did you know that according to *Marketing Wizdom*, the average business loses 20% of its customers every year simply by failing to attend to customer relationships?

There is a lot of focus today on customer advocacy. There is no better advertisement than a customer that stands up and promotes your product. We have gamification software products to help us manage this advocacy. This is good, but it is not enough on its own. The key to industry leadership success, based on my 17 years as CEO/President of public and family companies and organizations, is to build up an inspired group of customer advocates that I simply call "Raving Fans."

THE GROWTH CUBE™
Unlocking the Growth Potential of Your Company

You likely know what a raving fan looks like. Have you ever seen a rabid football fan in the fourth quarter of their favorite team's game? How about a soccer fan supporting Barcelona in the second half of the UEFA championship? What if our customers felt just as passionate about our company?!

So, this is the challenge of the second dimension of The Growth Cube. No matter what your business, it always starts and ends with your current customer and their belief in your leadership, your people, and your products and services, and of course the results they are getting from partnering with you.

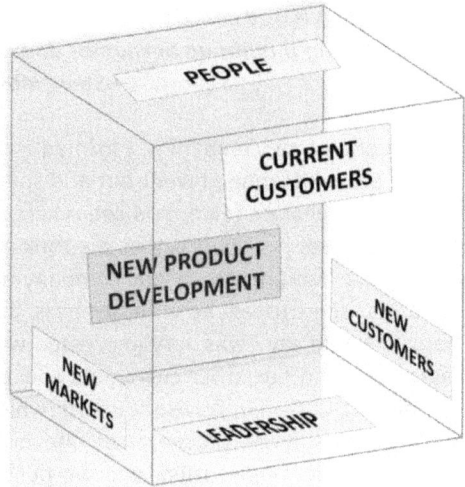

Are you an Apple customer; maybe one of your friends? Why is it that Apple customers want everything Apple? Apple has not invented technology, but they have been innovative, and they know their customers. They understand the importance of the consumer experience. I think we can all admit that Apple has developed a group of Raving Fans – customers obsessed with their latest products!

No matter what brand we are loyal to personally, Apple has been one of the most successful companies of our time at creating raving fans. Apple enjoys an unprecedented high level of brand loyalty. As of March 2016, there are over one billion actively used Apple products worldwide. Since the 2003 launch of iTunes/iPod, through the 2007 launch of the iPhone and ongoing success with mobile devices, Apple is the world's largest information technology company by revenue, assets, and market capitalization. Apple iTunes store is the world's largest music retailer. Do you think the employees of that company – 115,000 of them – are proud? Do you think their attitude, their innovation, and their energy helped win customers? Yes, a lot of them!

Apple's loyal customer base is revered by many, but they are the exception. With new digital technologies enabling customers to easily research and switch to a

48

competitor, brand loyalty is under ever-increasing pressure. Unless we are innovating and investing in better solutions for our customers – areas in which Apple has excelled – you risk losing your customers quickly.

Through my four roles as President/CEO of growing organizations ranging from $10M-$150M in revenues, we achieved a career retention rate of 99%. How did we do this? I believe the loyalty we achieved was directly related to the results our customers were getting from us. From the caliber of products, people, and services to our focus on being successful in all 6 dimensions of The Growth Cube!

Regardless of the industry, keeping customers is critical to you and your business. The loss of customers is called **Churn**. It is the opposite of **Retention Rate**. If our churn rate is 3%, our retention rate is 97%. A churn rate of 3% means we are losing 3% of our customer base annually. This is very good for most industries. However, if our churn rate is over 10% and higher, we have serious growth challenges. In addition, in some industries, unhappy customers may not leave just because it is not easy to do, so they stay but they remain unhappy. This is sad, and this is changing in some industries like software, where contracts and Software as a Service (SaaS) creates an environment where you change from one app to the next with ease of implementation and no financial or legal penalty.

Churn usually comes down to this: *your products or services, or God forbid your people, are simply not that great.* You have not built a unique and valuable company that is a thought leader in the space. The customer is deciding, and despite all the new fads and trends and technologies that have come and gone, it still always comes back to having customers who love what you do and why you do it!

"Don't confuse high retention with loving you!"

It is one thing to have acceptable or even high (95% plus) customer retention. It's another to have customers that love what you do! You can have high retention and not grow your company. Growth comes faster and is more sustainable when you have customers that love who you are and what you do for them.

How do you get customers to love you?

1. *Focus outward on the customer.*
   The relentless focus on creating a raving customer starts with the leaders of the organization deciding there is nothing more important. The customer is king – they are the reason we exist as a company. Why do some companies forget this?

   When I first started at one of my companies, things were so backward that I put a customer ombudsmen in place just so we could cut through the years of built-up bureaucracy that was preventing us from responding to the customer. The customer ombudsman reported to the president and had ultimate power to make things happen on my behalf across the company with the charter to create raving fans among our customers.

2. *Invest in great people.*
   Inspiring raving fans is largely dependent upon having raving associates who get support from their leaders through something like our CHEER process. As we mentioned in the first chapter, our associates and the products and services they develop are going to create the customer experience associated with our company, so we better invest some time and resources there. Our front-line associates and the products they make are touching our customers many times a day. When you walk into an Apple store, how are you treated? That is an Apple Customer Touchpoint. Those "Customer Touchpoints" are where you need to concentrate as a leader. Each Touch is both high risk and high reward. Excellent hiring, deep training, and building associate loyalty and enthusiasm directly translates to improved customer loyalty and enthusiasm!

3. *Invest in technology and R&D.*
   At all of my company's, my goal was to get support of the board to spend 5% of revenues each year on R&D, and we did it! This commitment helped to move us into an industry-leadership position within 3 years and significantly grow revenues coming from new products. If we want to inspire our customers into becoming raving fans of our company, we must continue to invest in the success of those customers through new technology, strong people, and key programs.

"It takes more skill to keep a customer than it does to win a new one."

Why do we all naturally accept that it is more expensive to win a new customer than it is to keep one? Is this even true? We cannot just magically create customer advocates. These days, unhappy customers can easily leave you for your competitor. In the long run, retaining customers takes a great product, great service, and a great solution to their problems. You get that through investment. What if you sold a product and never enhanced it, never supported it?

The table below shows the investments necessary to win new customers vs. keeping current customers:

ACQUIRING A NEW CUSTOMER (Investments)	BUILDING A RAVING CUSTOMER (Investments)
☐ People	☐ People
☐ Technology Tools	☐ Technology Tools
☐ Sales	☐ Traction
☐ Marketing	☐ Support
	☐ Customer Success function
	☐ Referrals / Advocacy
	☐ Education

New data supports an investment in current customers will generate new customer leads! In a recent Nielsen report on Global Trust in Advertising, "Recommendations from people I know" trounces every other type of lead generation program in terms of trust. This highlights the opportunity for growth of new customers when they are being referred by one of our current customers.

There was a recent study conducted by Bain & Company, in coordination with Harvard Business School, where they analyzed the costs and revenues that came from serving customers over the customer's life cycle. What they found is that, "the high cost of acquiring customers renders many customer relationships unprofitable during their early years. Only in later years, when the cost of serving loyal customers falls and the volume of their purchases rises, do relationships

generate big returns. The bottom line: Increasing customer retention rates by 5% increases profits by 25% to 95%."

These 2 studies highlight for us the importance of building an awesome product and providing extreme customer service to keep your recurring revenue streams going and get a healthy ROI on your customer acquisition cost.

> *"Increasing customer retention rates by 5%*
> *can increase profits anywhere from 25% to 95%."*
> —*Bain & Company*

If we can dedicate more of our leadership time into the areas that drive our customer's success and inspiration, and invest in the people and solutions that can help solve our customer's challenges, we will unlock the growth potential of your company. By making our company goal to "create raving customers," we set the tone with our associates that the customer's success is paramount. Get the whole company aligned in this direction, and we can inspire a new level of growth for our company or division and take it all the way to the top!

The Inverted Pyramid
A Growth Culture Increases Company Value!

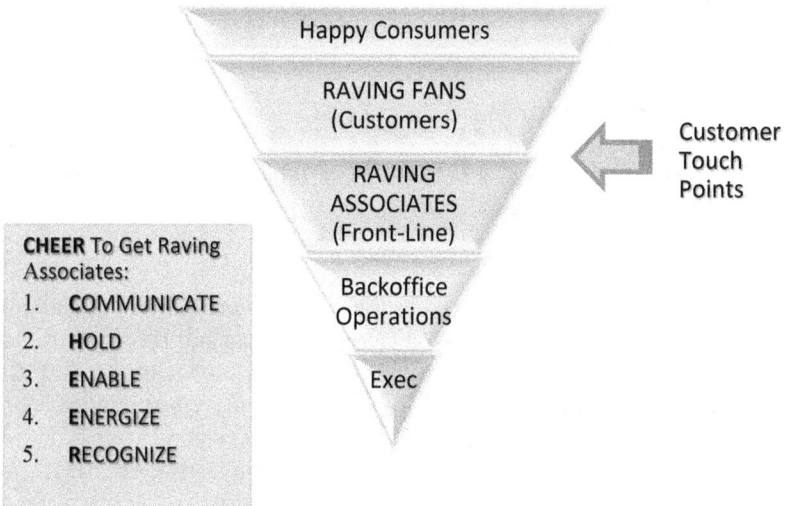

Happy Consumers

RAVING FANS (Customers)

RAVING ASSOCIATES (Front-Line)

Backoffice Operations

Exec

Customer Touch Points

CHEER To Get Raving Associates:
1. **COMMUNICATE**
2. **HOLD**
3. **ENABLE**
4. **ENERGIZE**
5. **RECOGNIZE**

The Inverted Pyramid.... Revisited
Speaking of "the top," we already learned that the customer is at the top of the Inverted Pyramid and that they should be the focal point of everyone in the company. Building associate loyalty and enthusiasm directly translates to improving customer loyalty and enthusiasm. Said another way:

Your success at creating raving fans is directly
related to your success at creating raving associates.

We also know that how we perform at the customer touchpoints – where your associates touch your customers – are critical for our company.

THE CUSTOMER TOUCHPOINTS
The question here is: how do we interact with our customer throughout the life of our relationship together? We want a long-term relationship, right? Then why do so many companies forget about the customer after they sell them something? They are missing a huge opportunity. If we agree that we want a long-term relationship with our customers, then what does that look like? When do we touch them, and when will they touch us?

We probably do not have visibility to all the times in a given day that our customers are being "touched" by people in our company – whether it's customer support, sales, product development, billing, various meetings, even when they get touched by one of our outbound marketing campaigns, and when they search our websites. All of these are touches and there are probably many, many more happening than you might first expect, which means there is opportunity to improve!

The sum of all touchpoints make or break our company. So, what are the touchpoints for your company? Are they pleasant for the customer, or are we disappointing the customer? If so, when and where?

Zappos, the successful online shoe retailer, created a point scale called the "Happiness Experience Form," which encourages their salespeople to make a personal, emotional contact and address any unstated customer needs. They are trying to create an interaction, not just a transaction. I love that, but it only covers one touchpoint. We need to do this at *all* touchpoints by putting the right people in

place and building the right processes. In this manner, we can create raving fans and help our customers win in their markets.

Map the Customer Journey to Identify Touchpoints

If I asked you to map out the customer's journey in terms of the "customer for life" relationship we want with the customer and our company, what would you draw? Would you draw your internal process, or would you draw the customer's buying process? They are both important, but they are distinctly different.

If we had to paint the optimal customer journey, we would want the customer to move from being a new customer, to implementing our product and loving it, and then getting more out of it and become a raving fan and advocate. From there, they would buy other products from us, and in the end be a very strong reference for us. Right? Isn't that what we want from our relationship with the customer?

Knowing the life cycle that the customer encounters with our company is important. We are touching them at various points, and we want them to be inspired. However, we need a way to organize our company around this. We should start with the customer buying process, and work through the life cycle of the customer relationship with us. In most companies, there are 5 steps to the customer's life cycle with our company:

1. They research your company and its products verse competitors
2. They evaluate and buy a product (hopefully yours!)
3. They implement and use the product
4. They optimize the product and its usage
5. The customer then pushes your company to new limits that results in us customizing the product and services in a special way that helps that customer compete and win in their markets!

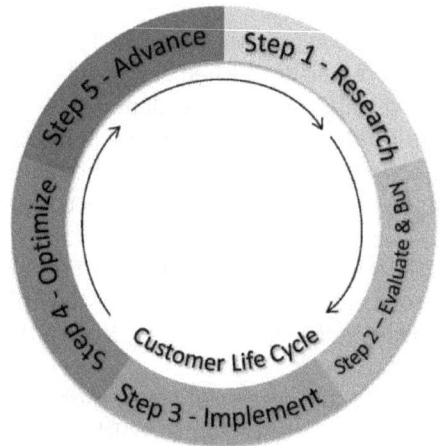

Customer Life Cycle — Step 1 - Research, Step 2 - Evaluate & Buy, Step 3 - Implement, Step 4 - Optimize, Step 5 - Advance

THE 5-STEP CUSTOMER TOUCHPOINT PLAN™

Note that we have outlined the customer's 5-step process, not our internal process. We want a map to the customer in order to best help them. Our internal processes for sales, marketing, and other functions should tie to these 5 basic customer life cycle steps. We want the best experience for our customer when they touch us at each of these 5 points.

We want to be able to show the customer that we have the skill and expertise to effectively guide them to a decision and improved results for their business by working with us. I have developed a model that will give you a roadmap to defining the touchpoints and developing your plan to create a raving fan at each touchpoint. This model is called the 5-Step Customer Touchpoint Plan™.

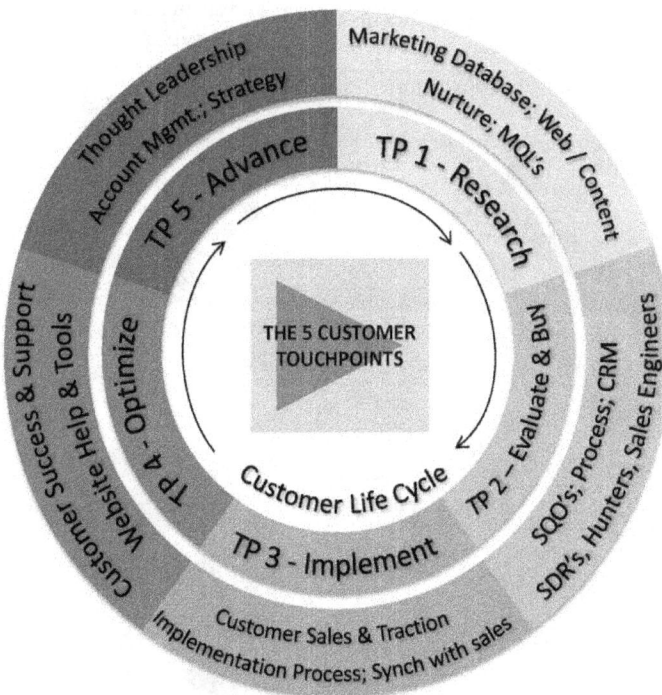

It is a model that I have used and refined for many years in real companies! Let's go through each of these 5 touchpoints in more detail, and keep in mind that at each point, we want to build an awesome experience for the customer. Each touchpoint is an opportunity for an associate to partner with a Customer; To fulfill

their desires and exceed their expectations so that the customer says 'Wow, this company is different. And I love it!

TOUCHPOINT 1 – RESEARCH

At Touchpoint 1, the customer is researching and learning about products and services available in the market. Because the customer is trying to learn, we want to educate them with great content and an intuitive and easy-to-use mobile and website experience. For the most part, the customer will not be talking live to a human at Touchpoint 1. They will be interacting with systems and online tools that we and our competitors and partners have built! If we invest in our technology and our technology development talent to make sure the online and mobile experience is top-notch, we will stand out in the market! I see a lot of companies cut corners here, but this is an opportunity that shouldn't be ignored!

> **TouchPoint1 (TP1)**
> The customer is researching so we want to educate with good content and an intuitive website. As customer gets more interactive and serious, we create a Marketing Qualified Lead (MQL)

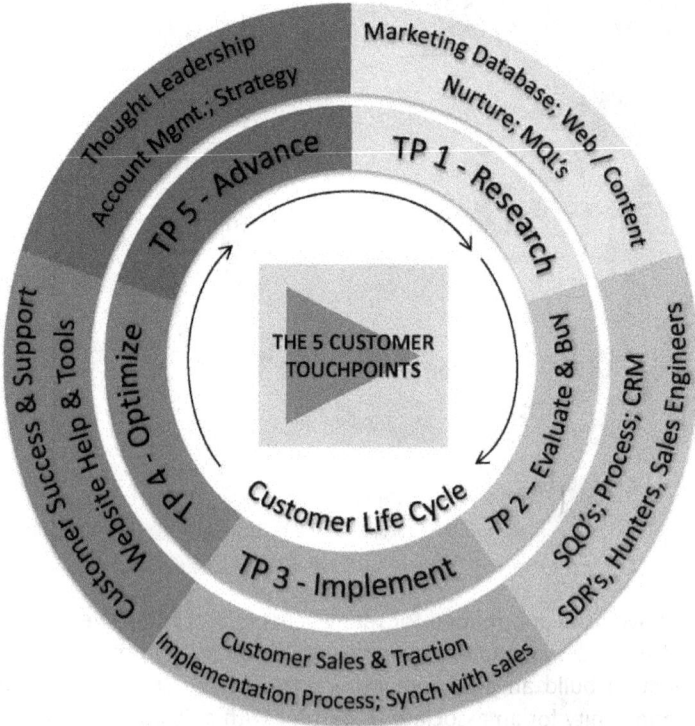

The development of thought-leadership level content is also very important at Touchpoint 1. This can become an organizational and competitive skill if you focus on it. Content development can be done by everyone in the company, and everyone in the company can use their social networks to communicate content. This is extremely valuable if a company can develop this kind of culture. We require that each technical and marketing person in the company develop one piece of content per month. When you add this up, it will be a great level of content to start with! If we are successful with Chapter 1 and have a group of raving associates who believe in the company, this will make it much easier to ask them to promote the company socially!

Video and training programs are also very valuable in this early stage as well. Many customers enjoy consuming this kind of information to broaden their knowledge. These tools can be valuable on a website and mobile devices, and they can easily be distributed through social networks. Through personalization techniques, you can present content relevant to the person visiting.

Outbound marketing and nurturing programs are also important at TouchPoint 1. These efforts make your marketing database, campaigns, and marketing automation systems very valuable investments. With strong tools, we can see customer activity and what interests them, and we can nurture them by providing additional content and education at our website. Customers will value us as not only a product or service provider, but also as a source of information that can be trusted to help them throughout their buying process. You should not only focus on having a strong website. Combining a strong website with omni-channel capabilities allows customers to have options to interact with your company through a variety of methods. This includes chat, phone, e-mail, social media, mobile devices, etc.

The goal of Touchpoint 1 is to provide information and knowledge from experts through newsletters, blogs, and other means, and ultimately to help the customer along their buying process at a pace that works best for them. It does no good to push a customer if they are not ready to move forward; you are just wasting your time and irritating the customer.

We will cover marketing in more detail in the next chapter, "Winning New Customers," but keep in mind that Touchpoint 1 also applies to existing customers who may have one of your products and are now looking at some of your other products. They research the same way as new customers, and we want to win that add-on business!

At some point in Touchpoint 1, the marketing team determines that this is a lead, typically referred to as a Marketing Qualified Lead (MQL). This determination can be very sophisticated, but you should keep it simple for small businesses. An MQL has to be qualified by the sales team before it is taken into the sales funnel. If it is taken into the sales funnel, we move to Touchpoint 2 with the customer.

TOUCHPOINT 2 – EVALUATE & BUY

Have you ever been fishing? When there is a fish is on your line, you are excited and nervous. You know that you have to handle this just right. You can bring the fish in if you use skill, patience, and your smarts. Your customer is not a fish, but you get the idea! The customer is now a Sales Qualified Opportunity (SQO), and they are actively evaluating you and your competitors. If you perform well as a company, you can win! It is a team effort, and everyone needs to work together to define what the customer needs, help them evaluate us and our products, and win their business if we can get the job done!

The SQOs are being managed through defined stages in your CRM. The sales rep is the quarterback and should bring in the resources as needed. At Touchpoint 2, the customer is interested in learning more than what they can find on their own. They want to see specific products, get demonstrations (if the website does not provide them), and/or get a quote. Sometimes the website / chat experience may allow the customer to immediately buy. This conversion ability is a key metric, and it is extremely effective where it is achieved. The more we allow our customers to touch and taste our products, and see that it can help them in their business, the better chance we have to win their business. Whether this is through online try-buy products or through a demo, this can make or break the customer experience at Touchpoint 2.

For more complex sales, outside "hunter" sales reps can be deployed on site, and for more complex deals, your company can include sales engineers or SMEs (Subject Matter Experts). It's "all hands on deck" as we try to bring this opportunity into focus through a strong Statement of Work and a sales rep who is trained in the process and leading a team. The salesperson should get involved to help the customer! The sales team should be trained on the customer buying process and adapt to that. Our goal is not to sell a product. Our goal is to understand the customer, their industry, and their challenges, so that we can help them win with their customers! It's not about us – it's about them and their success. Customer Centric Selling (CCS) is an example of a sales process that maps the customer buying process. Another process that I have found successful is the Buy Cycle Funnel from Mark Sellers. Before I hire an outside sales rep, I look for this: is the sales rep trained in a sales process? Within my companies, we also have onboarding and certification programs that reinforce this.

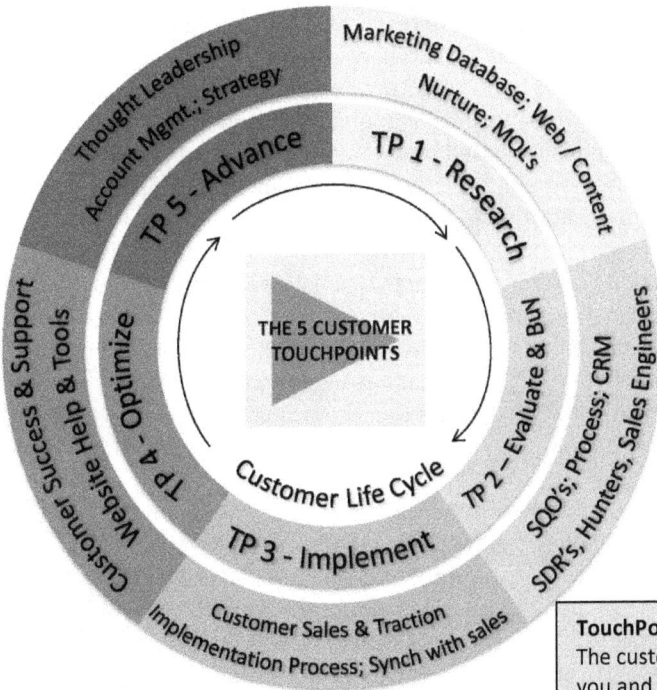

The Customer Relationship Management (CRM) system is a tool that should be customizable to the buying process, and the steps to move through the process should be defined and completed prior to moving to the next stage. A CRM tool is critical to efficiency and effectiveness make sales, and I find many CEOs let their sales team run without sales discipline here. If they just manage it better, the CRM is right in front of them!

TouchPoint2 (TP2)
The customer is evaluating you and your competitors. They are a Sales Qualified Opportunity (SQO) and are being managed through stages by your sales team, and utilizing your CRM. Your team is into discovery and defining the SOW. Allowing the customer to touch and taste your product can give you a great chance to win their business.

In the next chapter, we will talk more about how to organize the sales team to win new customers. We will discuss the difference between "Farmers" and "Hunters." Since this chapter is focused on creating raving fans out of your current customers,

let's focus here on the farmer. A farmer is responsible for current customers – making sure they are satisfied, getting results from your solution, and aware of and hopefully purchasing other products and services you may offer to their market. The farmer is a team builder that is responsive and knows the customers' business. They can speak at industry conferences about that vertical. They are a thought leader. They know how to pull together company resources to solve customer problems. They work with customer support to respond to escalated issues. The farmer's compensation plan is based on retention of customers and recurring revenue growth within their accounts. They should do anything they can to prevent the loss of a customer (churn).

We discussed certification programs in Chapter 1, and we will even detail it further in Chapter 3. Certification programs are something I like to use as a way to deeply train our customer-facing teams on our products and the customers' business. Partners should be certified in a similar manner. Someone in the sales team – channel manager for example – should own the responsibility for partner training, certification, and performance.

At some point in Touchpoint 2, we win the customer's confidence, and as a result, we win the contract! We spent a lot of time and effort to achieve this, and it is cause for a celebration. However, the work of creating a raving fan, which is our goal, has just begun. How well did we define what needs to be delivered to the customer? Will we deliver to the customer's expectations? We have now moved to Touchpoint 3 where the customer begins to experience our implementation team and our implementation capability more deeply.

TOUCHPOINT 3 – IMPLEMENT
The diversity of the people reading this book will vary from those of you who have a very complex on-site implementation process, to those who have automated try-buy products that convert to contracts without the need for a personal sales discussion, and everything in between! For those of you who have mainly one-time project business, your challenge will be to figure out ways to stay involved through online tools, other projects, managed services, and other recurring ideas. In any event, you try to make these concepts work for your business. There is a process where the customer or you implement your solution, and you have to make sure it sticks, that they love it, and if it is a product with ongoing use and an ongoing stream, we want them to stay with us. We strive for all this traction. If you have traction, your customer is fully utilizing your product and will be unlikely to leave you (churn). That's what we want! This is why the Implementation Touchpoint is so important.

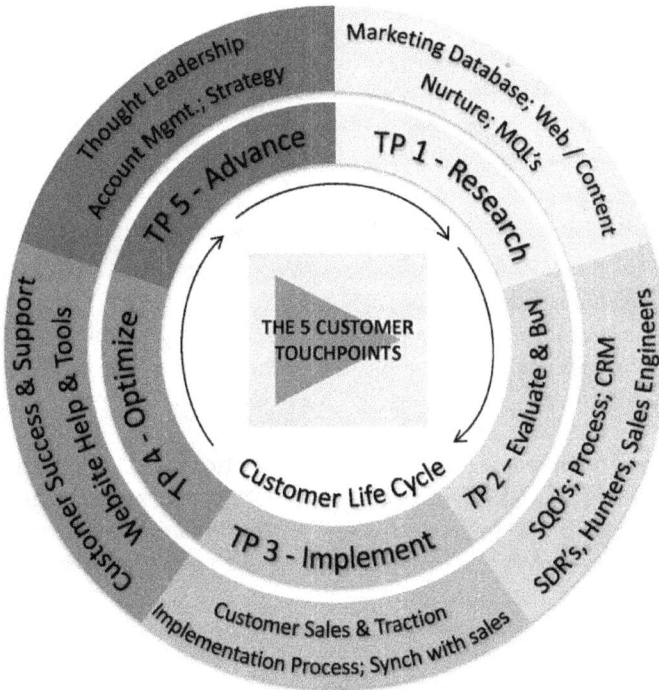

THE 5 CUSTOMER TOUCHPOINTS

TP 1 - Research — Marketing Database; Web / Content, Nurture; MQL's

TP 2 - Evaluate & Buy — SQO's; Process; CRM, SDR's, Hunters, Sales Engineers

TP 3 - Implement — Customer Sales & Traction, Implementation Process; Synch with sales

TP 4 - Optimize — Customer Success & Support, Website Help & Tools

TP 5 - Advance — Thought Leadership, Account Mgmt.; Strategy

Customer Life Cycle

TouchPoint3 (TP3)
This is about implementing the agreed SOW, making sure the customer loves what they bought, and getting traction and an ongoing relationship going with the customer

Implementation is the door to the long-term relationships we seek, and as such, we should move quickly into a 3-step process:
1. Implementation
2. Making sure they are a raving fan and completely satisfied
3. Making sure we have traction.

1. Implementation	2. Satisfaction	3. Traction

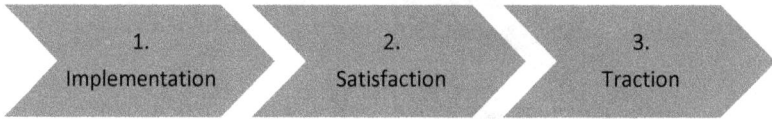

Many companies fail on the handoff from sales to implementation. This can be because we have a backlog of orders and take too long to get to it (which subsequently delays revenue!). Other times, it is due to us making mistakes during the sales process in defining the scope of work accurately and in enough detail. You have to focus on this or your business will have profitability issues.

The key here is the handoff of a detailed Statement of Work (SOW) that will truly enable you to meet (and slightly exceed) the customer expectations. So many times, the details from all the conversations and notes during the sales process are lost and not brought over and included in the implementation process. The companies that figure this out and do it seamlessly have a significant competitive advantage. A CRM with all the relevant attachments and notes is critical to the implementation team.

If the implementation team can get involved in the late stage of the sales process, at least for large projects, this will help dramatically. You can even have an implementation planning meeting as part of your late stage sales process. This is costly if you bring the implementation team in too early, but it also is very beneficial. They can add value and pick up the requirements earlier, and they can see potential pitfalls and help develop a strong proposal. If you can afford to do it, get your implementation team involved in the sales process. It will pay off in the long run!

Having people trained in Project Management (PMP) is critical during the implementation process. Managing projects is a skill set, and throwing your top technical people in this role without project management training is not good for them or the customer. You also need to make a commitment as a company to manage your projects through an online collaborative tool that can be accessed by the company and the customer. Everyone can see the project and where we are, and this can be used for regular project update meetings. Setting up a common site that can be accessed eliminates e-mailing schedules to everyone. Why not just go online to the live version?! I am impressed by the Bain Collaboration room, and by the tools and techniques utilized by Impact 21, a strong professional services company who does a great job at this!

There are many project management tools available, and for smaller companies, many can use the free tools! Don't let your people blame the tool – it is usually a lack of project management discipline, and not the tool, that causes the project to go off the tracks. Without a tool, I guarantee you will have projects do just that!

In terms of ongoing offerings and maintaining traction, many companies have discovered the value of managed services to the company and the customer. Managed services include providing the customer with ongoing support, usually from the same team that implemented their system. You can provide block hour agreements where the customer gets x number of hours each month to dedicate to help the customer get projects completed that are in the backlog. This is an additional revenue opportunity for your company, and it is also an awesome way to stay involved in the account and make sure that the solution is providing the results the customer desired.

You might have an automatic customer renewal process in place, and an escalation process if the customer was not renewing. This is not enough anymore. For many of you, customers can leave your company very easily. They can switch to another vendor with little friction and effort. This means that you should get involved with the customer early in their implementation. Make sure you are getting traction, that your product is sticking, and that the customer is seeing results. The title I assign to the person doing this and leading these efforts for your company is the Customer Success Manager (CSM). First of all, that's a great title! The CSM role will vary in different companies, but the concept is that the CSM gets involved very early and stays with the account, along with the sales farmer (sometimes the CSM *is* the farmer), and helps the company keep that customer for a long, long-time.

There are a couple techniques you can deploy to help with traction:

1. Customize the system for the customer, so it fits like a glove and works for their process. There must be some things you can build into the scope that is unique for that customer. That will delight them!

2. Get the customer users involved in the sales process. If you involve them early enough, not only will you learn what they really need, but you will get more buy-in when the system gets implemented.

"Each customer Touchpoint is an opportunity to partner with your customer."

TOUCHPOINT 4 – SUPPORT

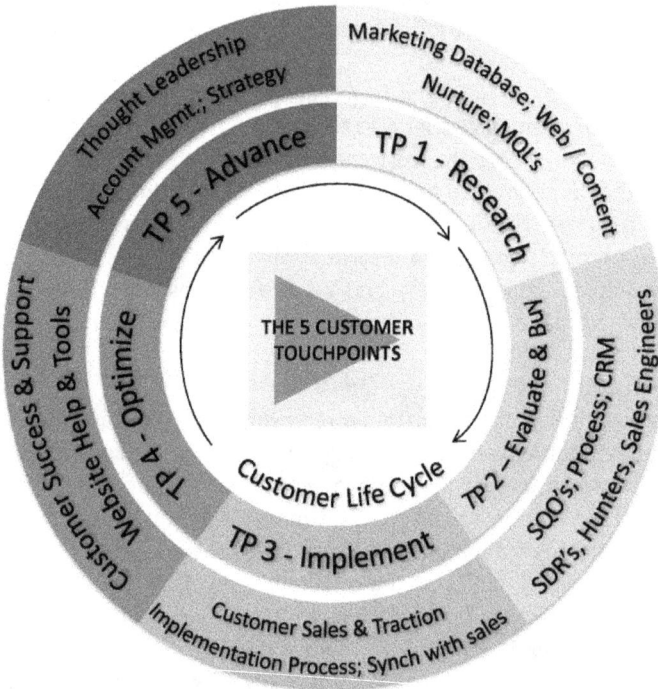

TouchPoint4 (TP4)
The customer is contacting you for help, ideas, and may even be frustrated. Your team's ability to respond to this over and over again effectively will ultimately determine whether you keep that customer.

The implementation is complete, and the customer is live with your solution. What do you do now? If your goal is to never lose them, you need to build processes that ensure there is traction, which means the customer is using and loving your product. That means that the CSM needs to stay with the account and never let go. At the same time, your support organization should come into play and start to reinforce and support the CSM efforts. Once again, the handoff between implementation (Touchpoint 3) and support (Touchpoint 4) is another focus area for your leadership team. Most likely, there are some outstanding issues generated during implementation that have not yet been completed. At some point, those "open tickets" need to be assigned to support from within your CRM. This should be tracked and managed in the same CRM that the sales team and the implementation team are using. Do not get discouraged, though. Most companies are not one system, but if you can pull it off, you will differentiate yourself in the market, have 360-degree visibility of your customer and their activity, improve your customer satisfaction, and improve your profitability. I think those are enough reasons for you to spend some time evaluating what you can do here!

The customer is contacting support for help, ideas, and maybe to alleviate frustration. Your ability to respond to this effectively will determine your ultimate result in keeping that customer. For the support team leader, it's all about responding to and resolving customer issues. That's it. To stay on top of this, have your support team take ownership of providing metrics on a daily, weekly, and monthly basis showing performance by customer against goals for major items like response time, resolve time, resolved on the first attempt, resolved within 24 hours, and the aged backlog (tickets that are not resolved). These metrics should be very visible in your company. With one of my recent consulting clients, we put together and made visible a customer satisfaction dashboard – showing key CSAT metrics and our current performance, programs, and leaders driving our improvement! This was made visible to the whole company via real-time electronic dashboards in the office.

You should challenge your support team to provide omni-channel support and be able to report on it from each channel. By omni-channel support, I mean that you have integrated systems and tracking so that no matter how your customer wants to communicate issues to you (phone call, e-mail, chat session, social media, etc.), you are on it! Track it and solve it all in one system.

You should make sure that your support team gets the training and technical strength required to resolve problems themselves. It is not just about customer services skills, but also technical skills. Keep pushing more and more training and

certifications for your people – differentiate yourself! Customers will love calling if you have a team that has the skill and the attitude to serve them. Be careful of setting too many tiers in customer support. The customer will not be happy waiting for a call back and will be a raving fan if you solve the issue on the first attempt!

I love hanging around customer support departments. It is such a critical customer touchpoint for the company during the lifetime of your relationship. As you are learning, where the customer touches us is where I like to hang out as the CEO. The customer is touching you a lot in customer support. This is where the customer questions, requests, and issues start, and you should have a customer support leader who is so passionate about helping the customer that you cannot stop them. They should have an intensity about helping them resolve these issues and get the most out of your products and services.

An example of a very successful program the customer support leader and I initiated together was our Escalated Accounts meeting. It is a weekly meeting at one of my companies that focuses on 3 major account escalations. It can be an account that I have escalated from my view, or it could be an account the support leader escalated. They are typically major accounts that are unhappy that we had action plans for, and this meeting would focus on that by providing a forum for all departments involved to come together and do what we all wanted to accomplish: drive new process changes that would help create a raving fan!

TOUCHPOINT 5 – RAVING FANS

So you have a strong customer support department, and you have an excellent Customer Success Manager involved in your accounts. You are focusing on traction, open tickets, escalations, and on new products your customers may able to use. Still, something is missing. The relationship with your customers is just not where you want it to be as a company. Do you know why this bothers you so much? I can tell you: your customers are not raving fans of your company!

TouchPoint5 (TP5)
The customer has been using your product and services but wants more. They want to customize your solution to better fit them and help them win. If you succeed, they will become raving fans and visible advocates for your company.

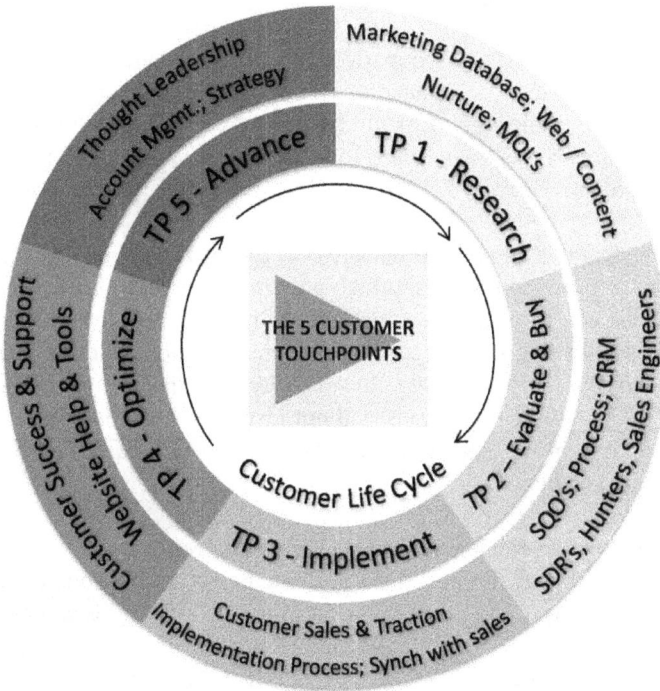

The ultimate goal of your company is to deliver a solution that excites the customer, that enables the customer to succeed in their markets to the point that they stand up and enthusiastically and genuinely (not because you asked them) advocate your business. We call this customer the Raving Fan. Just think about ourselves as consumers. What is the best product or service you own as a consumer? Your watch, your grill, your car, your lawn care product, your network provider? Do you ever tell your friends about all the features you like about your phone? Are you a raving fan for some product or service you are receiving today? The answer is probably yes, but there are also surely some products that you use in which you are not impressed.

The reason we all focus on management of current customers is because we not only want a customer to continue using our company for business and to create a long-term relationship, but if we are successful, we can grow our company and increase company valuation! Current customers provide a much-beloved recurring revenue stream. If they leave (churn or turnover), recurring revenue and reputation decline, and if a significant number of your current customers churn, you have major growth and survival issues.

According to the Gartner Group, 80% your future profits will come from 20% of your existing customers. As leaders, we chase big, new customers like they are going to take our business over the top. However, the fact remains that statistics do not support that. If you want to grow, you have to spend more quality time with current customers.

For the customers of your company to be raving fans, it means that they visibly advocate for your company and high potential to provide leads to your company by referring you to their colleagues. Raving fans regularly come to you with ideas and suggestions to make the company better. They tell their board that your solution is providing a competitive advantage against their competitors. These reasons are why having raving fans and not just repeat business is so important. To get there, one of the key strategies you can deploy is to focus on Customer Account Management.

Customer Account Management and *The Raving Fan Triangle*[TM]
First, account management is not about one person or how one department manages the account. It is a company-wide commitment. This is where many companies miss the mark with their customers. Customer account management is about how an entire company manages the relationship with your current customers. The account manager – what I call the Customer Success Manager – is the quarterback, but it takes so much more dedication and commitment over a period of time to be successful.

Your company's foundation is built around being able to deliver a great product – something we focus on more deeply in Chapter 4. Your product must be cool, smart, creative, intuitive, easy to use, and it must offer the customer improved performance. Once the customer makes in investment in your product, the question we ask is, "Is that enough?" Customers are not static. People change, organizations change, direction changes, mergers happen. Many areas of your customer account are evolving. With that, there must also be change within your company.

How do we stay on top? How do we make sure we evolve with them? We create innovative solutions that keep our company relevant as a key customer partner!

In some industries with complex products, an on-site account management function is needed and wanted by the customer. However, account management does not have to be an expensive on-site cost for your company. The key is to determine what level of account management you need for your company to stay on top and involved with the customer – to be part of their team. In some cases, the account can be managed remotely and costs can be kept down. Be careful, though. There is an investment required here *beyond* the customer support department, which is simply battling to respond to tickets and issues arising out of an omni-channel world.

I believe you have to seek a deeper relationship with your customers than your competitors. You do this by employing the concepts I am sharing with you throughout this book, but it starts with a passion and a philosophy that you are going to be more than just a supplier that has good products. That is important, but it does not set you apart. Other companies have good products. You have to be committed to move from supplier, to partner, to teammate. By teammate, I mean you are helping your customer win in their markets! Yes, you put resources behind helping them compete!

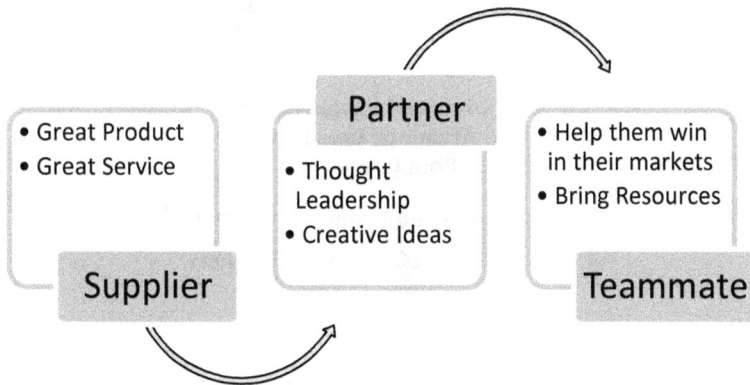

Supplier
- Great Product
- Great Service

Partner
- Thought Leadership
- Creative Ideas

Teammate
- Help them win in their markets
- Bring Resources

It's a simple concept, but most companies cannot pull this together and make it happen. This is one of my top secrets to success! The step-by-step plan to get there is outlined in The Raving Fan Triangle!

The Raving Fan Triangle

When you succeed at establishing a Raving Fan culture, the result will be low churn and Customers who are interested in all your products. The formula to succeed is by mastering what I call *The Raving Fan Triangle*, a process that I have developed and evolved in my companies as CEO/President for the past 17 years. It involves a focused evolution of the company through 6-stage progressive process:

The Raving Fan Triangle™

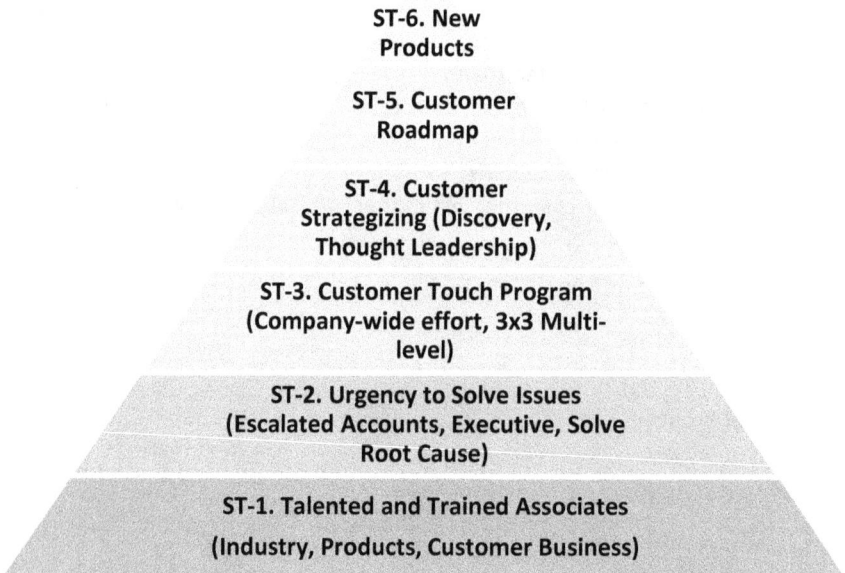

ST-6. New
Products

ST-5. Customer
Roadmap

ST-4. Customer
Strategizing (Discovery,
Thought Leadership)

ST-3. Customer Touch Program
(Company-wide effort, 3x3 Multi-
level)

ST-2. Urgency to Solve Issues
(Escalated Accounts, Executive, Solve
Root Cause)

ST-1. Talented and Trained Associates

(Industry, Products, Customer Business)

ST-1. Develop Talented and Trained Associates.
Understand the Customers Business.
Stage 1 is about you and your company doing one thing very well: understand the Customer's business. Their industry, and their goals and problems – and help develop a plan to help them solve those problems and reach those goals. If you are not involved in those discussions, you need to be.

Your Customer Success Manager, your Support department, your executive team – everyone in the company – should be pushed to become knowledgeable about the industries we are serving, and how our products and services help our Customers. We should understand the competition and how we might be different and better. Many companies call this thought-leadership – but was does this mean? You should define this in more detail for your company. A lot of companies want to be thought leaders and say they are thought leaders, but they do not execute on this vision. We help our Customer succeed by going beyond the operation of their business and focusing on the Customer's Customer. The questions you should brainstorm with your team is: What are we going to be the thought leader of? How can we help our Customers win with their Customers? What special skills/tools/expertise do we have that can help with this?

You should make it a goal to establish a compelling vision of where you want to go. And to be the thought leader of that space. You will have to develop and build a leadership team that focuses on this and is respected by Customers and industry partners. Do not take this lightly or accept mediocrity. Building value and delivering results is not going to happen without a top-notch staff that is motivated to succeed, and who is respected by leading Customers.

When I first joined one of my companies as president, I realized that the team did not focus outwardly on the customer's business. They focused on what we did internally. I bought a book for our associates called *Only the Paranoid Survive*, by Andy Grove, CEO of Intel. The concept was that each industry has inflection points that create opportunity and are also high-risk moments for our company. As leaders, we need to recognize them. I had everyone in the company read the book because I wanted to get us all to look outward at our customer's business and understand the inflection points. The lesson is that if we did not move and evolve with these changes, we would be left behind.

Through the inspiration of that initial foundational philosophy – and many of the concepts you find in this book – we began to successfully change the company from a stagnant operation to one that could effectively create raving fans and win

71

in the marketplace! We became recognized by our customers as "innovative" and "market leaders." This is a crowning achievement for any company.

At Stage 1 of the *Raving Fan Triangle* we need to be communicating consistently and openly with customers. At a bare minimum, we should invest in a vibrant, fresh, and thoughtful content development and communication program. We should work with our marketing team to utilize our website, newsletters, mobile app, social media, blogs, webinars, and other methods to keep the communication open and flowing with our customers.

One of the key events during Stage 1 is the Annual Customer Conference. Every company should have one of these. If people cannot attend in person, there are still many ways they can participate. Anyone involved in using our product should be invited. This is a chance for you and your team and your customers to share industry trends, new product ideas, and a venue for customers to mix it up and learn from each other. Customers and internal experts do the keynotes (these can be streamed to remote attendees), and the breakouts are jointly run by your staff and one of the customers. Customers get a real chance to meet your team and get closer with them. At several of my customer conferences in the past, the final segment of the agenda included our leadership team sitting on chairs in front of the audience and taking question over an open mic. Most of the time, this is a non-event if you have regular communication throughout the year. It is a great symbol to show your customers that we are all in this together and want to learn and evolve to help them!

ST-2. Instill an Urgency to Solve Customer Issues
Stage 2 involves customer issues within your company. Before you can go out and talk the customer about their goals and strategize with them, you must make sure that you are excelling at responding to and fixing their current issues. Are there open tickets? What is the age of these tickets? Are their suggestions the customer has made to people in our company that we have not acted on? A good CRM (Customer Relationship Management) system can help capture customer input in one easy view. Your customer support leader can help you in this stage, but you must get involved yourself! At my companies, I have implemented a program with the customer support leader where we conduct quarterly Key Performance Indicators (KPI) reviews with our bigger and most strategic customers. The meeting would include only me and the head of customer support. That's it. Agile and lean!

ST-3. Build an Expansive and Consistent Customer Touch Program
Once you have addressed the customer issues and are truly helping your customers, only then do you earn the right to expand the conversation. At this point, you should work with the management team and the current customer sales team to develop a multi-level customer touch strategy. I call this our Customer Touch Program. As the CSM and the company make progress with account goals and actions, the quarterback (CSM) should prepare and make professional presentations, establish rapport with the people at their target account, and write detailed reports that not only define your plans with your customer but help educate your associates in the company as to what is needed to create a raving fan! The Customer Success Manager can lead all of this, but every department can be part of these improvements! This is the beginning of going out to capture the customer add-on opportunity!

Your target is to get 3x3 in every major account. You should define what "major" means for your business, but 3x3 means taking your one point of contact at that account and expanding to other relationships. Find two other people at their level, and find 2 more above and below them. Get to know them, find out what they need from your product, and develop a relationship with each of them. Go as high as you can go, of course! However, the goal as Customer Success Manager is to have you and your colleagues within the company to have relationships developed within your account at 3 levels high and 3 levels wide!

ST-4. Get Involved with Tour Customer. Strategize Together.
If you've gotten this far – congratulations! You have established programs with your current customers to:

1. Implement executive touch into our top accounts
2. Get meetings with high-level leaders within our customer accounts
3. Build more in-depth account plans
4. Set up meetings to do more thorough onsite needs analysis
5. Position the CSM in the quarterback role and support the heck out of them!

To get to this point with your major accounts is a critical step in the evolution of your company and your relationship with your customers.

If we have built credibility and trust with the customer through the prior 3 stages, they know that we are experts in their industry, that we are responding to their issues effectively, and that we have an open communication program where they

have access to our people. It is only when we have this credibility that we begin to take the conversation to the next level. We should not run to Stage 4 too fast. Customers have to trust that we have their best interests at heart, and we do this by nurturing relationships at various levels of their company and ours. Being open and honest about the company's business policies and programs and being consistent over time are two key success factors. Trust will compel the clients to remain loyal to the company, even if competitors offer a better price or product.

Strategizing is not simply about going to the customer site and having a strategy meeting every once in a while. It's about getting involved and working together on the challenge at hand. It's about investing resources and time into your customer's business success! The Customer Success Manager needs to drive this and be the quarterback in setting-up, implementing, and managing their customer strategy activity, including defining the customer strategy and how our solutions fit into that picture and timing. There are excellent online analytics, research databases, and robots that can allow us to quickly and immediately access detailed information on our customers, their recent news, and industry activity that affects them.

One of the events I found to be successful to stimulate Stage 4 is to host our own industry conference. This involves hosting a trade show where you can invite customers and prospects. It is a thought leadership program that is not designed as a sales effort, but is instead educational in nature with customers and partners participating in panels and speaking roles. The trade show is supported by our marketing and sales team, and our partners are actively involved and contributing to the whole event – and can even pay to be part of it if you would like to do that. It should be good enough that your customers would be willing to pay – whether you charge them is up to you. They will pay it if it is good! Be a thought leader. Provide avenues for your customers where key leaders can network with peers and gain insight into market trends to develop long-term strategies. Leading customers are presenting. Your top company thought leaders are presenting. Side meetings are set up with customers and your top leadership on their ideas and goals. If successfully planned and implemented – and this takes some time – this will enable you to get deep into customer needs, industry trends, and pressing issues, and it is a fantastic learning ground for your employees.

If you can bring your customers to your home office for this, it allows them to meet all your associates and keep costs down for your company. However, we have also taken this concept on the road. We call it a "Road Show." This includes a bus concept where we have a crew of experts and systems we can demo, and we pull up to the customer's office to show them our current and future products in action. The advantage of going to the customer site is that it is easier to have more of their decision makers in attendance, as all of them may not be able to travel to an Industry conference at your HQ. You will learn a lot more about your customer by going to their office too.

"Gary gets to know the customers, gets to know the markets we are in,
and looks for ways to move the company forward."
—One of Gary's former VP Direct Reports

ST-5. Deliver on a Roadmap for the Customer.
At this point, you have held serious strategic discussions with your customer. Congratulations! Now you must bring business insight, an understanding of your customer's competitors and industry trends, and the ability to identify new areas of growth and opportunity.

Stage 5 involves taking what you have learned in Stage 4 and putting it together in a thought leadership plan that makes them turn their head and say, "Wow, these guys know our business!"

Have you ever achieved this stage with your customers? They want you to get there, but so many companies stop at Stage 3 or 4, and thus, they miss the opportunities. If you manage Stage 5 well enough, your customer will present your plan to their board. This clearly takes you to another level in your partnership!

At one of my companies, we were very successful at putting together a 5-year strategic plan that the customer used internally to gain commitment and investment. This gave us excellent exposure at higher levels within our customer accounts. We developed this 5-year plan along with our customer. This includes offering and education them on new products/services based on what we see happening in the market. This is thought leadership. The plans should be specific to each customer. Developing a plan that the customer likes, and that their boss likes, can go a long way to securing retention of that customer for a long time!

"80 percent of your future profits will come from
20 percent of your existing customers."
—Gartner Group

ST-6. Develop an Ability to Launch Vibrant New Products

Many sales teams run to Stage 6 right away without ensuring that we have succeeded at the prior 5 stages. This is a mistake. Running to Stage 6 too early can hurt your company credibility. By understanding and responding to every day customer needs and issues, building trust and industry expertise, thinking strategically about your customer's future, and establishing rapport, you now have the privilege and respect to present your other products and services, and develop completely new and innovative solutions with the customer. This is true teamwork. You both are working together, and you both have a lot at stake. We will cover the keys to a successful "New Product Development Process" in Chapter 4.

Successfully delivering on these 6 Stages of the *Raving Fan Triangle* is not easy, and you will try to cut corners, but if you don't, you will unlock the key to your success with your current customers.

Being able to deliver on all 6 stages of the *Raving Fan Triangle* will not only keep your customer close to you for a long-time and buying your various products and services, but it also generates referrals that can help you win new business in the future.

What you can see in all of these 6 steps is investment. Investment in time, in people, in systems – all to build a strategic relationship with your customers. If we can dedicate more of our leadership time into the areas that drive our customer's success and inspiration, and invest in the people and solutions that can help our customer's work with us to develop their own *Raving Fan Triangle*, we will unlock the growth potential of our company and take it all the way to the top!

"A customer can never be too happy or too satisfied."

I love customers. Always have. Always will. It is so interesting to work with customers hand-in-hand, as a true partner, to help them succeed, and to see them get excited about what we do. Utilizing a framework like the *Raving Fan Triangle*, we begin to specifically understand how we can go above and beyond to create raving fans!

SOME FINAL POINTS ON CUSTOMERS

Customer Success Leader Role on Executive Staff
Although everyone in the company must focus on creating raving fans, one of the most effective steps you can take is to assign a dedicated resource to the Customer Success Leader role! I have seen the power of this in multiple companies that I have led. Give them the power to cut across departments. Include them in your staff meetings with a Customer Success Report. They should lead customer KPI reviews. They should report on retention and churn, and they should report on customer traction. In a small company, the head of customer support could assume this role.

The Raving Fan Triangle™

ST-6. New
Products

ST-5. Customer
Roadmap

ST-4. Customer
Strategizing (Discovery,
Thought Leadership)

ST-3. Customer Touch Program
(Company-wide effort, 3x3 Multi-
level)

ST-2. Urgency to Solve Issues
(Escalated Accounts, Executive, Solve
Root Cause)

ST-1. Talented and Trained Associates

(Industry, Products, Customer Business)

Customer Success
The Quarterback

Move up – but not too fast!

Other areas the Customer Success Leader can help you is with systems and analytics. Specifically, how do we get a 360-degree view of the customer within our company? How can we utilize the existing CRM – or buy a new one – to aggregate

data from the various touchpoints that we discussed earlier, to provide one snapshot of our how our customer is doing across all departments and all key metrics. Your Customer Success Leader can help you drive this within the company.

Impact 21 CEO, Lesley Saitta, assigns an analyst to every customer and works with analytics to help the customer find and solve issues and generate financial savings. These analytics offerings from Lesley compliment her core business solution. They are making sure the customer gets a ROI!

Measuring Raving Fans
So how do we know if we have raving fans? To get a gauge on this in your organization, I recommend you do both satisfaction surveys and Net Promoter Score (NPS) ratings. You can simply add one question to your customer survey for NPS, and you got it. Commit to me, and yourself, that you will sincerely push to the top of the score range. This is what your customer wants! Why do you pat yourself on the back when you are slightly above average or even average? A customer rating you as average in satisfaction will leave you if something better comes along. You know that, right? We said customer retention and churn were important – we have to walk the talk. If your satisfaction score is "satisfied," you must continue to push to be above "very satisfied." Also, if your NPS score is 7.5, you must continue to push and invest to get above 9.0 or higher, to the point where a customer commits that they would be extremely likely to recommend you to a friend.

For some industries, notably software and services where I hang out, it has been shown that Detractors (score 0-6) tend to remain with a company and Passives (7-8) leave. This is clearly an issue! Because the satisfaction / NPS survey is a leading indicator, it should be implemented as a discipline to stay in front and on the pulse of customer growth issues. You want a raving fan? They will rate you as 9 or 10 on the NPS, and as "Very Satisfied" in the satisfaction survey. This is the goal we must commit to.

THE ELEMENTS OF VALUE – Bain and Company

Three executives from Bain and Company wrote a piece in Harvard Business Review recently on the Elements of Value. This concept of value supports many of the concepts we have in our book in terms of creating raving fans and innovating. Bain's argument is that the more elements of value you can provide with your products and services, the greater the customer loyalty and the higher your sustained revenue growth.

Their study found that:
- Companies that performed well on multiple elements of value have more loyal customers than the rest. (They used Net Promoter Score (NPS) to test loyalty.)
- Companies that scored high on four or more value elements had recent revenue growth four times greater than that of companies with only one high score.
- Some elements do matter more than others. Perceived quality affects customer advocacy more than any other element.

How do we apply Bain's value principles to our company?

1. We should start with a survey of current customers to learn where the company stands on the elements it is (or is not) delivering. The survey should cover both product and services, because examinations of the two may yield different insights. For example, the product itself may deliver lots of value, whereas customers have difficulty getting service or technical support.

2. Asking customers what they feel is valuable is one thing, but the next step is coming up with new concepts that require anticipating what else people might consider valuable. I like design research to help with this – as it focuses on the user experience and the user process – and identifies opportunities with your target customers.

3. Combined with the survey data above, you can then conduct an ideation session with your internal customer-touch people. This is a way to ignite your team, generate ideas and get people involved. We had fantastic results in doing this with our recent Startup company as it helped us better define the business requirements for the development team!

4. Through this process, you will identify the top elements that have the greatest effect on customer satisfaction and loyalty in your business. Now build a competitive advantage with them. The elements of value work best when a company's leaders recognize them as a growth opportunity and make value a priority.

5. Although many successful entrepreneurs have instinctively found ways to deliver value as part of their innovation process, that becomes harder as companies grow. The leaders of most large organizations spend less time with customers, and innovation often slows. We can continue to produce innovation if we are working directly with customers and partner, and pushing our team to continue to improve our understanding of their business!

QUANTIFYING THE CUSTOMER GROWTH OPPORTUNITY

"You can double the size of your company just by
focusing on growth with your current customers!"

At one of my companies, we went through an exercise of quantifying all the opportunities for growth within each of our customers. We wrote the customer names down the left-hand column and identified and sized all the growth opportunities if we were to be successful at 100% penetration. Do you know what we found? We determined that we could double the size of the company by just focusing on the customer base. Without one new customer! Can you believe this? Think about what this would do for your company! What would your business feel like – and what would it do for the value – if your revenues and profits were double what you had today? I showed this analysis to a private equity firm, and they were immediately engaged. They had never seen an analysis like this and committed that The Growth Cube process would be part of every company they acquired in the future. By doing a detailed analysis, we also had a detailed plan and hit list for each account that our sales team was assigned to go after!

Look at a company like Zappos, a high-growth online shoe retailer that was acquired by Amazon in 2009. Zappos uses a loyalty business model and relationship marketing that has resulted in 75% of its customers being repeat buyers, and repeat buyers who purchase 2.5x more than single customers. This effort to improve the less easily measured, but far more personal aspects, of service contributed to a 5% improvement in the company's overall Net Promoter Score. The high level of customer retention that Zappos could achieve was the main reason why service became their biggest asset and their main "marketing" strategy in reaching new loyal customers.

The opportunity within your current customer base is huge! But how do we go after it specifically? Sales plans, compensation plans, and sales teams are a sensitive and fragile package to synchronize.

Bad things can happen if we do it haphazardly.

The 2016 case of Wells Fargo should be required reading for sales executives and those trying to motivate sales teams. For more than 15 years, "cross-selling" more products to current customers was a driving force of Wells Fargo financial success, but like a drug, in the end you want it so bad that it can eventually spiral out of control. Federal regulators and the Los Angeles City Attorney's office are now involved and recently announced that Wells Fargo opened as many as two million deposit and credit-card accounts without customers' knowledge! Leadership was aware of the issue as it was happening and reportedly did scold the team, but it still kept happening across 6,000 branches. Branch managers routinely monitored employees' progress toward meeting aggressive sales goals – sometimes hourly – and sales numbers at the branch level were reported to higher-ranking managers as many as *seven times a day*. Can you imagine that sales environment? All of it built to capture the opportunity within the current customer base. They knew it was important, but their strategy and implementation were flawed. They were a company with a respected brand who was known for their sales process success, and they were many times emulated by others – but not anymore. Wells Fargo had a highly-respected sales team and process, and they severely damaged their brand and violated the trust of their customer. This will be tough to recover from.

What should we learn from this? First – get in the right mindset. It is great to have aggressive sales goals. You should push to grow the company, but not at the expense of the customer. You need to establish a philosophy in your company that selling is always about taking care of the customer. Giving them awesome products and services that help them compete more effectively.

The second lesson is that to achieve your goals of current customer growth, you have to deploy the proper tactics within your sales team and other departments. As a leader, you need to stay close to implementation plans and monitor them. Listen to employee and customer feedback, and know what's going on in your organization.

Let's now move back to your strategy and take a deeper look at how you will approach the current customer opportunity in front of you in the coming year. I want to help you not only quantify the opportunity, but also to develop a specific plan for success. One of the unique philosophies we have with The Growth Cube process is that after you have completed your planning, you will have an executable, quantifiable plan to implement. Your plans will not sit on the shelf!

There are companies who tout the importance of "upsell-cross-sell" opportunities within the current customer base. They have the right idea, but to me, we have to dig deeper to get to a specific plan. The upsell-cross-sell philosophers talk like there are only 2 opportunities: the upsell and the cross-sell. The truth is that there are bigger and more detailed approaches than this implies. Also, I am not crazy

about the tone of how this sounds. It sounds like we are more focused on us selling something and less on helping the customer. A lot of people I meet are confused by the "upsell-cross-sell" philosophy and how it translates into real revenue in their company.

I believe there are 6 specific growth opportunities within your current customer base that you should analyze, quantify, and develop plans for. I call these *The 6 Windows to Growth with Current Customers*.

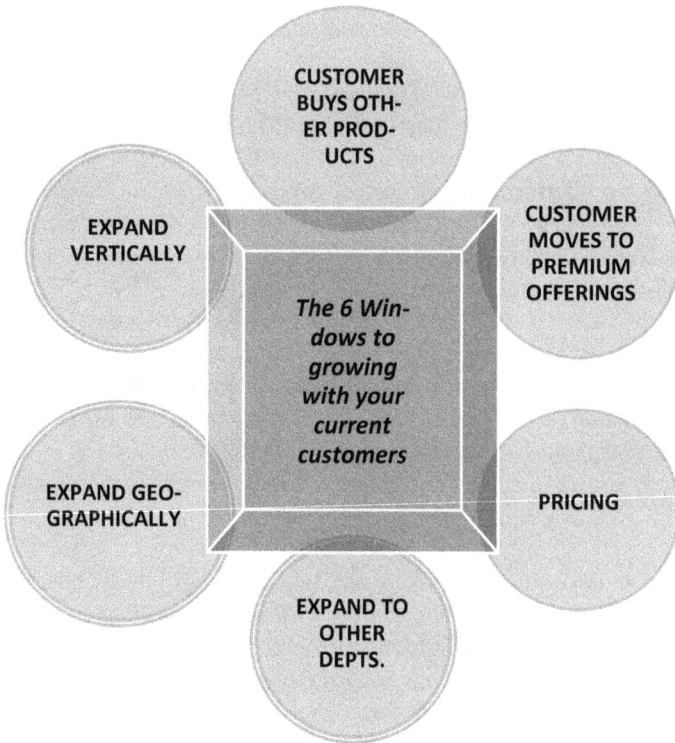

1. Customer Wants Your Other Products

Imagine the opportunity if all your current customers purchased all your products. In fact, don't just imagine it, quantify it!

You can do this by simply putting all your customers alongside the left edge of your worksheet. Add a column for which sales rep is assigned to that account. Now across the top and to the right, put all your products and services. Underneath each product, put an average price.

Now find out which products each customer has purchased already and fill that in the appropriate cell. If you have the contract value or revenue to put in that cell, that would be great. If you total the revenue in your worksheet, this should tie to the current customer revenues in your financial system.

Now look at the blank cells without revenue in them. By multiplying by the average price, you can arrive at a figure for potential by customer (and by rep) if the current customers bought all your products. This is the potential within your current customer base if your current customers bought all your products. Now this will never happen nor do we want it to – we want to provide the customer with what they need – but for planning purposes, let's size this opportunity and detail it.

2. Customer Decides to Move to Premium Levels

If you think about some of your music streaming services like Pandora or Spotify, or your storage products like Dropbox or even Amazon Web Services (AWS), all of them offer levels of service. The lowest level is free for a reason, but there is a segment of buyers that will stay at that level. However, there is another group of other buyers who want more. They like the service so much that they are willing to pay more to get more. You should design offerings at these higher levels that provide strong value for the investment. If you do not continue to provide value for their investment, customers will leave, so put some thought into this design, and stay with it. In this manner, you will be on your way to improving your performance in this area!

The potential here within the current customer base is based on if all our current customers upgraded from their current level of service to a higher value / higher cost premium level. What is the potential of this current customer base opportunity? You can take the same worksheet used above and now add your various price levels, based on basic, enhanced, and premium offerings. By multiplying the delta between the customer's current price, and the price at the premium level,

you now have the revenue opportunity if all customers moved to the premium level. More specifically, you should now understand which customers in your worksheet offer the largest opportunity, and which rep is assigned to them! This should be built into the sales team targets for the year.

3. Customer Accepts Fair Price Increases

Pricing increases need to be handled carefully and fairly, and they should always be part of your annual planning process. The goal is not to gauge the customer that's for sure. Within some companies, recurring streams, which is what we should be focused on, and related price increases at renewal for example, are acceptable. This needs to be thought through and managed, of course. If there has been heavy discounting to get the original sale, it is also acceptable to most customers to get them back toward a standard list price over time. Changing your product's price is risky, but it is an opportunity to grow, and that is what this book is about. As long as you continue to make enhancements to your product, communicate with your customer upfront, and manage price increases strategically and fairly, these revenue gains will drop right to the bottom line – no other growth program you can come up with will do that!

4. Customer Helps You Expand to Other Departments

The opportunity to move to other departments within the same company is not as easy as it sounds. Typically, from my experience, it takes a new product and really should be viewed more like a new product launch. However, there is at least a relationship there to build from, and that's what you should try to leverage. There are many ways that an expansion to other departments becomes an opportunity. It could be your current customer driving it or maybe you partnered with or acquired another company and this brought in a new product to your company where the buyer is different than your current buyer. How do you move across the customers' company and find success?

We will talk about this more when we get to Chapter 3, but you may be surprised to find that your product is already up and running in another department at one or two of your customers. The key is to identify those active customers who are different – where you may have expanded out to another department. You can easily quantify the potential of this opportunity by using the same worksheet we have been talking about for the first 3 opportunities and adding a column for a new product and an estimated price. Identify if all your customers are potential opportunities for this or if it is a segment of current customers; you will be on your way to pursuing this opportunity!

5. Customer Helps You Expand Geographically

If you are only involved in a portion of the USA and want to expand nationwide, or if you have the USA and you want to expand globally, this should present a nice growth opportunity. Many times, this will be a different decision maker than your current customer contact today, and you will need their help to make these connections. Make sure your sales team identifies the geographic expansion potential within their accounts during your annual planning. What is the size of this potential? For each major account, you can build a worksheet that has the various geographies across the columns on your page. Make each of the rows the title of the person you are talking to. The first column(s) of data would list your key contacts at your current geographies. The challenge for you and the sales team is to fill in the names and build relationships with the contacts identified in the other geographies!

6. Customer Asks for Your Help in Expanding to New Verticals

I recently did a project for one of my customers where I helped them think through how they could expand to other verticals. As they do this, they grow their business. When they grow their business, you grow too! This opportunity needs to be handled a little differently – in your strategic discussions with your customers. You can help them think through a move to a new vertical, and ultimately, how your company can help them.

You now have 6 specific, actionable programs to incorporate into your current customer growth planning! By combining these 6 views together, you will uncover what I learned by doing these same steps within my companies. You can double the size of your business just by focusing on your current customers and the opportunity available with them! It takes time... a lot of time. But other growth programs do too. It's not going to just come to you. You have to go after growth if you want it!

You can also use the analysis that you did above to look at sales team assignments and workload. You will be able to see the potential by assigned customer reps. You can start to analyze workload and territories by customer rep and determine if changes should be made. When you are finished, you will have defined strategies by account and by rep to increase your revenue. A key metric for you is revenue per customer growth, and revenue per rep growth.

None of this going to be easy! You are going to make mistakes, but the venture is important for the growth and success of your business. Steps 1 and 2 are straightforward, and your current customers will love it if you have a lot to offer them

here. However, be careful with steps 3 through 6, especially if those involve contacting other decision makers beyond your current customer point of contact. Your current customers will be nervous about this, and it can be sensitive and risky if you do it without your current customers help. See the information box below for some tips I have learned that will help you navigate these waters!

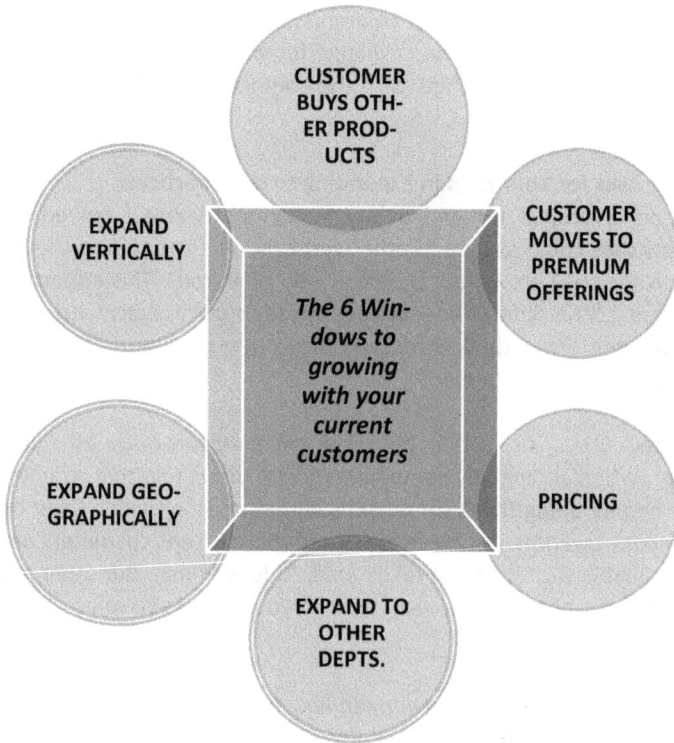

CUSTOMER BUYS OTHER PRODUCTS

EXPAND VERTICALLY

CUSTOMER MOVES TO PREMIUM OFFERINGS

The 6 Windows to growing with your current customers

EXPAND GEOGRAPHICALLY

PRICING

EXPAND TO OTHER DEPTS.

WHAT CURRENT CUSTOMERS SAY ABOUT GROWING IN THEIR COMPANY

I have gone out to my current Customers at my companies and asked them about what it would take to expand our business to their colleagues in other parts of their company. This is what they told us to focus on:

1. CURRENT CONTACTS NEED TO BE RAVING FANS FIRST!

If the people in the department that you are serving today are not happy, you should not be expanding elsewhere within the company. This is the bottom of the Raving Fan Triangle™. Do not move up too fast!

2. PREPARE TALENT AND TOOLS IN ADVANCE OF APPROACHING

Your Customer contact's name is on the line when they introduce you to their colleagues, so you better nail it. You better be able to demonstrate expertise with the new contact you want to meet. Have a story, understand the space, and be able to reliably demonstrate ROI. You should develop a steady flow of relevant content targeted to this new audience and demonstrate the breadth of your subject matter expertise in this new department's area of the business. Finally, develop a list of referenceable companies who have successfully expanded their internal footprint with our products.

3. PREPARE PRODUCTS IN ADVANCE OF APPROACHING

If you have a new product for a new department or geography, make sure it has been thought through and developed. You need validated, competitive and clearly defined value propositions for each of your products. I know in some cases we want that Customer to be a pilot, but for all the others, you should follow this script to succeed!

4. INVEST IN MARKETING

Finally, the 4th key to success from current Customers on expanding within their account is to get more exposure within the analyst community. If analysts are not talking about you, they are talking about someone else! Analysts are key influencers. So, when that department head goes to their industry conference, and they ask their peers about your company – do they give a positive response. It's about expanding your brand recognition and credibility.

DIMENSION 2 WRAP UP – CREATING RAVING FANS

We have learned the first two dimensions of The Growth Cube. It starts with our commitment to creating a company with raving associates, who will build a customer base of raving fans. We have given you tools that you can use to make this happen: In Dimension 1, the Inverted Pyramid philosophy and the CHEER process provides the glue to keep your team inspired, including our Level 3 Certification Program. In Dimension 2, the 5-Step Customer Touchpoint Plan can help you optimize the experience when your customer touches your company, and the 6-Stage Raving Fan Triangle program will guide you in building closer, long-term customer relationships. We have also outlined the 6 windows to growth within your current customers, which if done well, will put you on the way to doubling the size of your company!

If we were to do all this successfully in your company, I am sure you would be the leader in your industry, and possibly achieving what many leaders search their whole careers to reach! However, we cannot stop there. To unlock the true growth potential of your company, there are more steps to consider, evaluate, and take. One of those is to build our capability to win new customers, the focus of our next chapter.

CHAPTER 3 – NEW CUSTOMERS.
Helping <u>Them</u> Win.

"Right at this moment... Somebody, somewhere is looking for a product just like yours."

When I first joined one of my companies, I went out and visited a bunch of our customers and spent a few days in their offices to see what they were doing and how they were utilizing our products and services. I then went to a competitor's customer and met a great leader I will call Joe. He was not even a customer at the time, but he invited me to visit his office anyway! So I went! I was new, and Joe took me under his wing and taught me what happens at our customer environment. I learned a lot by spending 3 days on the front line with Joe and his team. He and his staff still talk about how impressed they were that the president of a company did this! And they were not even my customer. After 2 years passed, they left their previous vendor and came with us! 3 years later Joe was president of his industry association and a recognized thought leader in the space! We are still friends today because we built a relationship. It was more than a vendor providing a product.

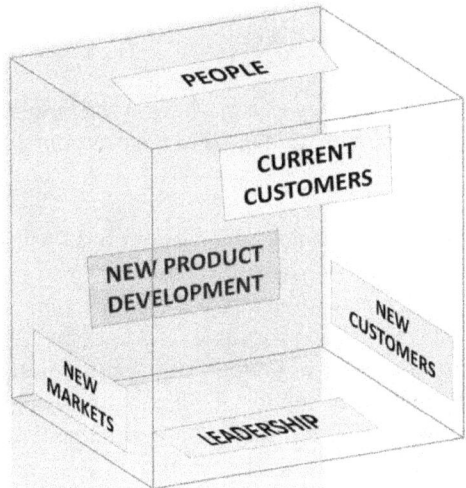

Winning new customers is vitally important no matter what your business entails. Somehow, most leaders I meet are not happy with their company's results in capturing new customers. It is one of the top 6 strategies of your company, so we focus on it in this 3rd dimension of The Growth Cube to help you develop a roadmap to change your new win trajectory. After successfully improving new customer wins in my last four leadership roles, and now with several companies in

my current coaching business, I am going to share with you what I have seen succeed in real companies that I led!

HOW ARE YOUR CURRENT CUSTOMERS?

If you have succeeded at making your current customers raving fans and your churn rate (attrition rate) is low (<5%), then congratulations! You are succeeding at the first half of the formula to win new customers!

Some of you will not let that point register, and you will fly by what I just said and keep reading. However, it is one of the most important points for us to remember:

> *"To succeed as a business in the long-term, the pre-requisite for winning new customers, is to have current customers who are raving fans."*

I ask that you think deeply about this. Ask your leadership team what they think. Be honest with yourself. I have seen it so many times with CEOs – the focused and elusive quest to win new customers supersedes the current customer who is already sitting at your table, and yet you still do not give them attention. For the future of your business, I beg that if you have not mastered Chapter 2 and have the metrics to support it – if you are having trouble keeping your current Customers – go back to Chapter 2 and work on it for a year before you start Chapter 3. If you do not, you will be wasting all your money winning new customers while the existing customers run out the back door. The result then is no growth at all!

THE ROADMAP TO WIN NEW CUSTOMERS

My goal in this book is to give you tools, models, techniques, and step-by-step plans that you can take and execute. It's about execution. Winning new customers is no different. The road to winning new customers involves executing 4 steps successfully:

1. Defining Your Strategic Plan
2. Defining Your Marketing and Sales Strategy
3. Generating Sales Qualified Opportunities with Your Marketing Team
4. Winning the Sale with your Sales Team

| 1. COMPANY STRATEGY | 2. MARKETING AND SALES STRATEGY | 3. GENERATING QUALIFIED LEADS | 4. SELLING TO WIN |

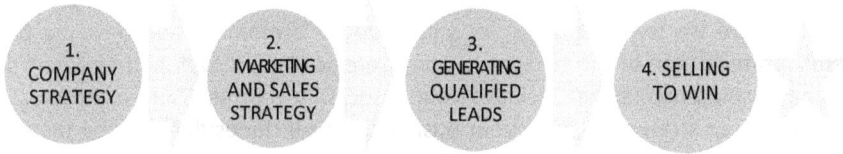

As we know, it is easy to show these steps and this graphic, and then it can all fall apart in the execution. That is why so many CEOs I meet are frustrated with the level of new wins they achieve. Stay with me and stay focused, and we will get there together. Let's work on the details of making these 4 steps happen for you!

1. THE STRATEGIC PLAN

I was the President in a Fortune 500 company, and I remember this moment like it was yesterday. In a group planning meeting with all the executives in our company, I looked up and there was our group president. He ran a $2B business. He asked all of us to come up to the front of the room and form a circle around him, kind of like you see on the football field when the team comes together around one of the team leaders right before the game. He was in the middle of the circle of all us executives. He then abruptly yelled out as loud as he could: "Where are we going?!"

We were all kind of surprised and looking at each other, but before we could even think about it, he directed us to yell, "Up!" So we did. And we did it 3 or 4 times. "Where are we going? UP! Where are we going? Up!"

That moment has stayed with me my whole career. Here was a leader trying to rally his team around the direction we were going. It is exciting and stimulating to see a group of pretty tight, white collar executives let it loose and show some passion! We did want to go up. We wanted to grow. Of course, in order to achieve that goal, we need to define what "up" is and how we will get there. We were good at that. We were highly respected. We had a great leadership team, and we knew how to plan. I was trained in that environment, and it was impressive. However, we did have some issues with execution, both with achieving organic growth and acquisition growth. In our case, the problem was not the plan. It was the execution. I have learned that a commitment to The Growth Cube process fixes this. I know because I have done it as a company leader – and you can too!

Execution starts with defining the plan that you want to execute, so before we get to winning new customers and asking ourselves the question, "Specifically which customers are we trying to win," let's back up for a moment and describe the overall strategic plan of the company. The strategic plan – developed as a part of a teambuilding process that includes your associates, partners, and customers – will define your strategy to grow your business. This includes defining the market segments you pursue, who your customer target is (persona), your product/service offerings, what differentiates you from everyone else going after that same thing, and a few other very critical items!

If you polled your team on these topics today, would they all have the same answers? No. Do you know why? Because you have not defined your plan as a company. That's an issue. Being clear on the answers to these questions are fundamental to your team having focus, and as such, spending your time and money on the most important initiatives. If you do not do this, you are going to waste marketing and sales dollars and not get the ROI you want from your marketing and sales investments.

"Where are we going?"

Your Associate Is Thinking This

The place to start – with your team.
You know what your management team is going to say if you tell them you want to develop a strategic plan? It won't be good. We have all been part of planning processes that are a total waste of time. Months of work in planning sessions making sure your words are just right and your charts flow, and it only to ends up sitting on the shelf or on the planning drive on your server.

Do you know why this happens? Because the CEO and his/her direct reports did not make the planning a team effort, did not really take it serious, and in the end, they did not inspire everyone to implement it! He/she did not hold people accountable. Your associates want you to hold them accountable to the plan. They are praying that you invest the time and resources into the programs that you all identified. That's all everyone wants! To execute the plan that you all agreed was important! But too many times, other "fires" take priority, and before you know it, another year goes by without executing the plan. How much credibility and enthusiasm will you have if you try to do strategic planning again next year? Think of all the time you spend on plans that do not get implemented. You do not have enough time in your day? You feel like you are swamped, but what you may not realize yet is that you have not prioritized and focused what you and your team are working on. These are the reasons. It does not have to be this way. You need to commit to yourself and tell your team today that you will not let this happen!

"Look at strategic planning as a teambuilding opportunity!"

So what is your role, and how do you lead this effort? The first step is for you to get involved from the beginning of the process and stay with it all the way through execution. I am sure you have built a team that knows more about each of their specific disciplines than you do. If not, you have not hired and trained the team effectively. You should learn from them, but also guide them; you should go with their ideas, but enhance and refine them. If you think you can develop this plan by yourself and not involve your team, trust me when I tell you that will not work.

I was recently at an event where a major company executive was explaining how their CEO went on a remote 10-day vacation on a mountaintop, wrote a 30-page strategic plan for his company's future, then came back and asked the company to implement it. I can tell you right now that this plan will probably fail. One of the key secrets of doing strategic planning with all of your associates is that it is an opportunity for teambuilding. The meetings do not have to be long. I believe in agile meetings that are rapid, small, and to the point. Your entire team must talk and work on this together, so you do have to meet. The discussions, the negotiations, the frustrations, defining things more clearly, the arguments, the late nights, these are all something you vitally need – a team that is fighting together and building relationships and covering each other. The planning exercise can help you do this! This will bond your team. Do you agree with me that the implementation and execution of the plan will go a lot smoother if we include people in the planning?

You can make it creative and fun and insightful all at the same time. You do not have to take a lot of time doing it. As an example, I send an all-employee survey every year with 7 questions about our company innovation. What current growth programs should we put more resources behind, and which current programs should we kill (these are interesting answers!). Which new products should we be adding to our roadmap and developing? It takes each associate 5 minutes to complete this. Put together all these ideas, from all your people, and you have the

basis of something that can significantly change the growth trajectory of your company! After receiving the feedback, we would analyze it and then take some ideas to our quarterly town hall meetings to conduct breakout sessions around them, dig deeper, and develop the ideas out further! Involving everyone in the process is the key!

We sometimes even involve customers in the process. Your Customer Advisory Board will love to give you input on where you should focus and grow your business. All you have to do is ask them and be disciplined in following up with them to prove you listened and acted on their ideas! If you are not going to do this, do not ask them.

Key points to remember:

1. *Get personally involved and engaged.*
2. *Approach the strategic planning process as a teambuilding event.*
3. *Include everyone in the company in the process.*

All in all, the development of the strategic plan will require a team effort (if you want buy-in – and I know you do!) and will be a team-building exercise for the company as you coalesce around what you are going to become and how you will do it. In the process, you will develop a deeper understanding of your markets, your products, and your services, and you will see more clearly what you can do to help your customers' business!

Let's Build a Strategic Plan!
Building your strategic plan is a 3-step process of defining where you are today (Point A), deciding where you want to be (Point B), and defining the execution plan to get from Point A to Point B. It's really that simple. What I recommend is that you build the plan around the 6 dimensions of The Growth Cube, where you would define these 3 steps for *each* of the 6 dimensions. The plan will be excellent if you utilize The Growth Cube framework!

POINT B
Target
Position

The Execution

Plan

POINT A
Current
Position

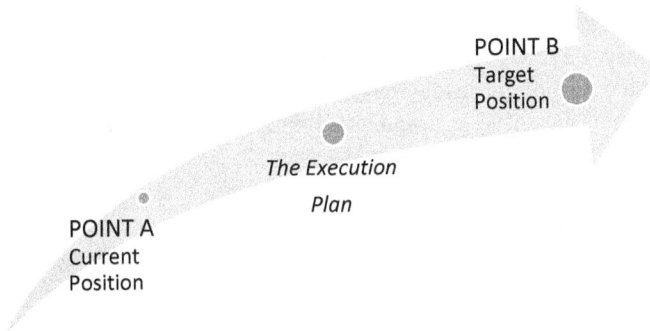

We are going from Point A to Point B

STEP 1. DEFINE POINT A.
Where are we today? What is our current position?

The Growth Cube 6

When I first go in and coach my clients, I initially help define the current position, Point A, around all 6 dimensions of The Growth Cube. Imagine 6 rows (one for each dimension) and in that first column (Point A), you are going to tell me all about your current team, your expertise, your products, your markets, your leadership, your customers, and your target customers. Add some of the key metrics that represent current performance in each of those areas, like revenues and profitability by product, customer churn, and growth rate of recurring streams, to name a few. To help you get started, try pulling together some of your people and kick around these questions:

1. What does your company do? Tell me in one sentence. (Your "elevator pitch.")
2. How would a customer describe what you do?
3. How does "what you do" help your customer win in their business?
4. What is the one thing our organization did best this year?
5. Ask your customers to tell you in 2 words what your company represents. You can do more extensive research of course.

We begin our planning by gathering all the facts about how we are doing across each of the 6 dimensions.

Thought Leadership and Brand

The second area I recommend you focus in your planning of your current position is your brand and thought leadership area. I don't want you to worry about the vague question, "What is your brand?" Instead, tell me from your heart what your business passion is! Up to this point, we have discussed "what you do," but now we want to know "why do you do it?" Why do you and your team get up every morning and put in all the time, day and night, for your company? Why are you doing it? What passion is driving you to do this, over and over again, most likely for many years in a row?

I am currently a CEO of a startup company called Med-Compliance IQ (www.medcomplianceIQ.com). We are launching our first product, called WoundWise IQ, which we believe will actually help to save someone's life! Can you imagine working for a company that has that kind of opportunity? Does this make you get up in the morning and race with the gazelles!? Not every company has this potential mission. There is only so much you can do if you make soap (I think). What I am trying to draw out of you is what inspires you and your people about your company! Simon Sinek says, "The goal of the business is not to do business with people who *need what you have*, but to do business with people who *believe what you believe!*" I love that.

Ask a small business owner why they started their company, and you will find this passion. Nearly all the small business CEOs I work with have a dream and a drive. The beauty of this is that it can inspire your team – and your hiring – if it is compelling and authentic!

> *"Strategy is about shaping the future!"*
> *–Max McKeown*

When it comes to the area of thought leadership, do you know that there is a consensus among researchers that being a thought leader can make a very significant and positive difference to the success of your company? This sounds like something we should look at more closely, doesn't it? I recently read an article in *Forbes* that said this: "Companies that embrace *thought leadership as a strategy for growth* represent the essence of market leadership, corporate accountability and changing the rules of client engagement." This makes sense to me.

A thought leader, according to *Harvard Business Review*, is a person or organization who everyone in the industry – including competitors – goes to learn about their area of expertise. Including competitors! Imagine that. Additionally, it says something similar in that thought leaders are the go-to people in their field of expertise.

If you know your thought leadership area of expertise, you can begin to evaluate and build solutions and share best practices, tools, and techniques with others. Thought leaders are trusted. Envision your company leaders inspiring people with their innovative ideas, and then turning those ideas into action for your company, while at the same time supporting the growth of your industry!

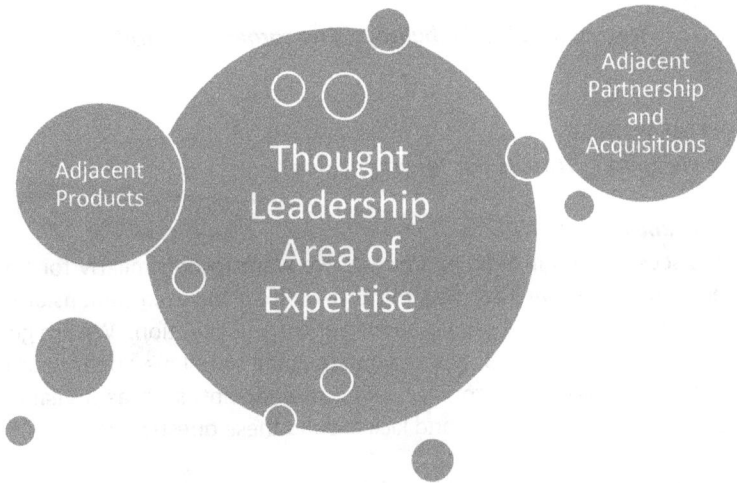

So tell me, what is your company's thought leadership area of expertise? Because if we know that, we need to defend this turf and then build out from it. This will be the seed from which you will grow your company successfully! Some people call these core competencies. Every business begins and grows around a set of core competencies, but there are almost always additional core competencies that you'll need to acquire or develop over time. You can never stop.

To help you get started, try pulling together some of your people and kick around these questions:

1. What makes you different?
2. What is unique about your business versus your competitors?
3. What keywords (or phrases) would you use to describe your business?
4. What are the customer benefits of your products or services (i.e. how do you help people)?
5. Have you received any awards, recognitions, or accreditations that are relevant in your industry? This may be an area where the industry experts are seeing something special about you.

If you find that you are not a thought leader today, you need to move now to Point B: What are you going to be the thought leader of!?

"You cannot hit the bullseye if no target is set up!"

STEP 2. DEFINE POINT B.
Where are we going? What is our target position?

The Growth Cube 6
Just as we discussed about defining Point A, we want to do similarly for Point B. Remember your worksheet that had the 6 rows (one for each dimension). The first column (Point A) now has details about our current situation. We are going to add another column for Point B, where you are going to tell me about your target situation and your target performance. Pick an endpoint, such as 3 years. Now pull together some of your people and kick around these questions:

1. Where will our customers' businesses be in 3 years, and how can we help them get positioned to win?
2. What important problems can we help our customers solve that we are not solving today?
3. Who will your customers be? What types and sizes? Where will they be located?
4. How many products, and which products, will you be selling in 3 years?
5. How many people would be working in your business, and which are the most critical positions?
6. What does our board and other owners want us to accomplish over the next 3 years?
7. What would success look like in 3 years in terms of target metrics and key financial metrics?

The Point B planning process can take some time and discussion, but it is obviously critical. By using The Growth Cube framework, you can challenge your team to think broadly and creatively about what you can become while also building the details in a logical, all-inclusive manner across 6 vital dimensions. The more clarity you have about where you want to be at a specific time in the future, the easier it will be for you to create a solid plan that will enable you to get from where you are today (Point A) to where you want to be (Point B). Some people refer to this as the "As Is – To Be" model.

> *"Good positions don't win games; good moves do."*
> *–Gerald Abrahams,*
> *chess player and author*

STEP 3. DEFINE THE EXECUTION PLAN.
How will we get from Point A to Point B?

To be honest with you, this whole book is about execution, so this section is going to be short. Do not think for a minute this is not important. In fact, execution is the secret sauce. It is the step many companies miss altogether. Most companies who put together strategic plans do a great job at Point B, and they might do an average job at defining the current situation, Point A. Still many, many companies (and I have seen them and I am sure you have too!) simply forget about or out-right ignore this third step in which we develop an execution plan. The plan sits on the shelf and eventually the pressure of making the month or the quarter takes our attention. All the strategic planning time, and all the ideas, eventually die. This is totally unacceptable.

If you were growing at the rates you wanted to grow, you probably would not be reading this book. Whether you are a startup or an established company leader, I am assuming you are currently being challenged with growing. You may be frus-trated with your past performance, and you want to figure out new and different ways to get to higher levels. If that is you, I want you to trust me on this. I have been in your shoes! Let's develop your execution plan with your team. We will go back to our Growth Cube™ planning worksheet where we have defined columns for both Pont A and Point B. Now I want you to add another column labeled "Exe-cution Plan," where you are going to tell me, at a high-level and in a bullet point format, the keys to execution across each of the 6 dimensions. To help you get started, pull together your team again and discuss these questions:

1. What held us back last year in terms of getting to our goals?
2. What are the critical constraints or limiting factors to growing our company faster?
3. What additional knowledge or skills are needed to make us more effective in our execution?
4. What additional resources do we need to achieve our Point B goals?
5. What leadership and culture obstacles do we have to overcome to grow faster?
6. Of all the problems or obstacles standing between you and your desired future outcomes, what are the most important?
7. What are the steps that we must take now to create our targeted business 3 years from now?

"Execution is all about what you actually end up doing,
not what you say you are going to do in the future."
–Larry Bossidy and Ram Charan

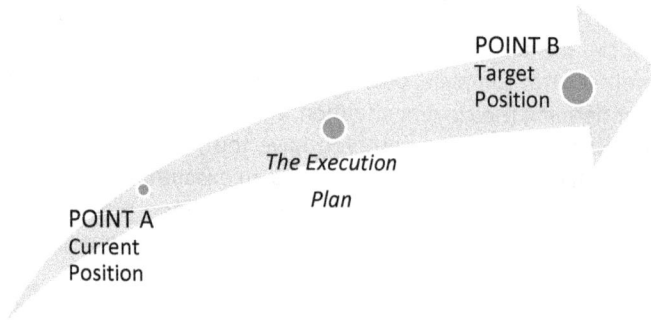

POINT B
Target
Position

The Execution

Plan

POINT A
Current
Position

The Growth Cube Report that you will finally complete with your team will be your strategic plan. When you complete it, you will have defined where you are (Point A), where you are going (Point B), and the execution plan to get there! Do you have that today for your business? Well then let's get it done!

One last point I want to leave with you:

I hope the "Strategic Plan" part of this chapter was reinvigorating for you! These are all my own ideas that I have found successful. I have made mistakes in planning, and could have done better many years, but I am sharing with you the end result of my learning and what I have seen succeed! You have to develop a strategic plan for your company, and it does not have to be 100 pages. Completing your next strategic plan can be a rewarding experience for you and your team. I compare it to playing chess. I love the game of chess. The goal is clear – capture the king. However, you have a competitor who wants to not only defend their king, but also aggressively capture yours! During the execution of the game, you have to evaluate risk and reward and make moves to win. It is exciting to me. Your strategic planning process can be the same way. If you can create enthusiasm around your strategic plan and inspire your team that you can achieve it, and then back it up with the details that need to get done, you will lay the foundation for your company investments to pay off, capture your competitor's king, and take your business all the way to the top!

> *"To win, you have to have a fighting spirit;*
> *You have to force moves and take chances."*
> –Bobby Fischer, World Chess Champion

MARKETING AND SALES STRATEGY

This 3rd dimension of The Growth Cube is about winning new customers. Although we have proved that you can grow your company significantly just by creating raving fans within your current customer base, you still need to win new customers. If you are not winning new customers, that is a big red flag to me. Is there a shift in the market that we are not aware of? Who is beating us and what products and service do they have that are different? Are we getting passed up by new technology? These are major issues. We have to be engaged and aware.

COMPANY STRATEGY	• Strategic Plan • Thought Leadership Area • Teambuilding • The Growth Cube™ 6

MARKETING AND SALES STRATEGY	• 5 Customer Touch Points • The Big 4 Assets • Analytics

PT B

Execution Plan

PT A

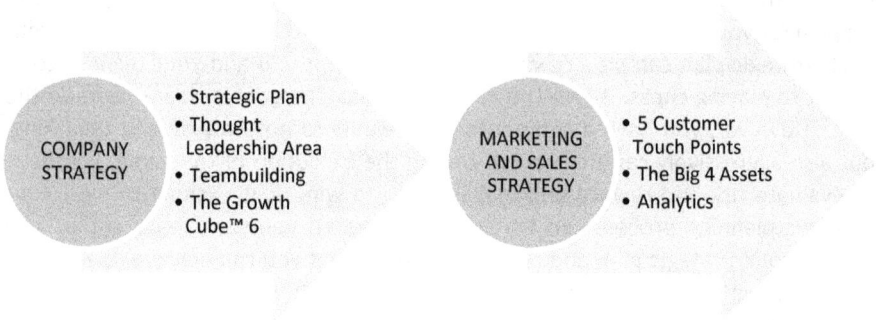

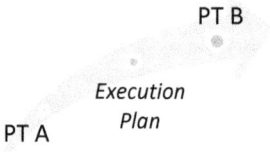

So to win new customers, the next question is what marketing and sales resources do we invest in? More specifically, which programs and channels do we invest in, and where do we set our focus? We will attack this next!

MARKETING STRATEGY
You will not find the term "sales and marketing" in this book. I always say "marketing and sales," and that is because, "Marketing is the engine of the company," as my good friend and mentor Bob Yopko used to say. Since marketing is the engine, we will cover that first.

I have to share a frustration with you at this point, though, and you will probably agree. There is so much confusion today around what to build into a marketing program. I know because in my current coaching practice, I work with these very smart, very innovative entrepreneurs. Yet, they are still confused. They want to implement marketing programs to build their brand and generate leads and invest in the programs that will make the biggest impact, but they get confused when they talk to marketing companies. It seems that every marketing company has a different expertise and a story about why their expertise and their ideas are the smartest to invest in. Some promote lead generation, some talk about demand generation, others claim it's all about inbound marketing, while others emphatically push social media channels or SEO and PPC strategies. The small business owner cannot do all of these things at the same time, but they would be open to a step-by-step process if it made sense to them!

I wanted to write this section of the book to clear things up for you as the leader of the business. To give you an easy way to look at your marketing tools, the assets you may not even realize you own, and how you can make this marketing cost result in qualified leads that you can close! I am going to show you how you can focus your marketing investment and not just to create a lot of buzz and activity. We must accomplish what we set out to do here in the 3rd dimension of The Growth Cube: win new Customers!

> **TouchPoint1 (TP1)**
> The customer is researching, so we want to educate with good content and an intuitive website. As the customer gets more interactive and serious, we create a Marketing Qualified Lead (MQL).

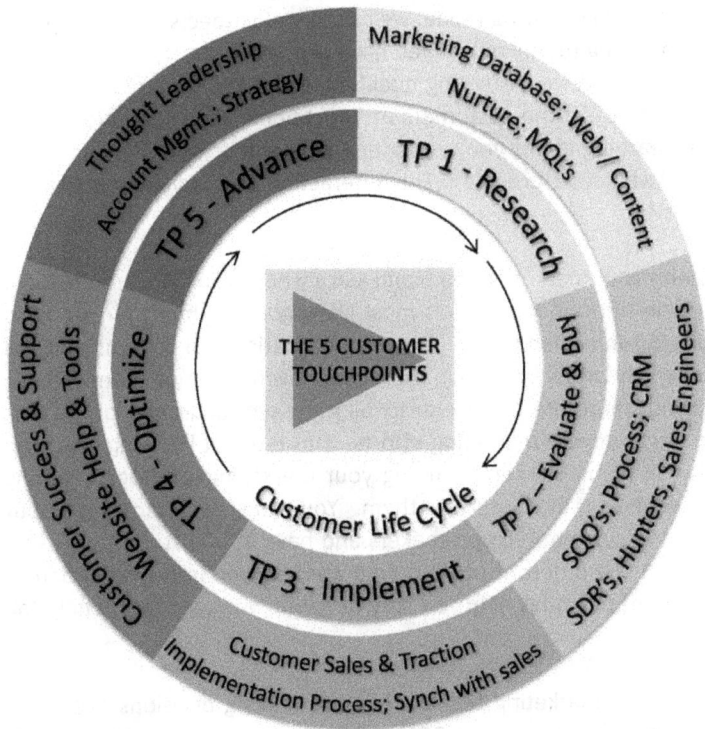

THE 5 CUSTOMER TOUCHPOINTS

TP 5 - Advance — Thought Leadership; Account Mgmt.; Strategy

TP 1 - Research — Marketing Database; Web / Content; Nurture; MQL's

TP 2 - Evaluate & Buy — SQO's; Process; CRM; SDR's, Hunters, Sales Engineers

TP 3 - Implement — Customer Sales & Traction; Implementation Process; Synch with sales

TP 4 - Optimize — Customer Success & Support; Website Help & Tools

Customer Life Cycle

TOUCHPOINT 1 – When the Potential Customer Is Researching Products

Remember we talked in the last chapter about Touchpoint 1. At Touchpoint 1, the customer is researching and gathering data about products, services, suppliers, and pricing. From our standpoint, it is about making sure that our company and our products are recognized as a respected and viable solution. For those of you who have a sales force, we have to make it through this first screen in order for our sales team to even have a chance. How do you optimize that this happens?!

If you are running a business, you know how important it is to get the word out about your company's products and services. If you don't do this, you will have a difficult time winning new customers. In addition, if you have your outside sales force chasing leads that are not qualified, you are wasting time and money.

The customers at Touchpoint 1 are evaluating and narrowing down their choices. They are doing research themselves both online and through their networks, prior to making decisions on finalists. If they are not in buying mode, we call them Suspects. If we know they are in buying mode, we call them Prospects. The prospects are leads in your marketing funnel only if you have captured their e-mail and company name. They are not yet a marketing qualified lead (MQL) to be screened by our sales team. In any case, the customers at Touchpoint 1 are in fact touching your company and learning about you, evaluating you, and comparing you. They have an interest in what you provide. This interaction and touch is vitally important to your growth.

You should work with your marketing team and learn who is your most predictable buyer. Build a profile of the buyer who is most likely going to buy your products and services. With this information, develop communication and content that will interest them. Keep them coming back and attract even more of them. These people are called your target *Personas* – describing the typical profiles of the persons you want to target in your marketing efforts. This is about knowing your customers, how you will segment them, refining your messaging, and personalizing your online experience so that it interests them. You can start by analyzing your current customers and current decision-makers and have a brainstorming session with your team about the different profiles who are involved in buying products like yours. These target personas help you stay targeted with your marketing dollars!

This is managed by your marketing team. They are making decisions every day that are impacting your brand and your ROI, and you need to be aware of what is going on and understand the detail of the marketing activities and costs and help in establishing priorities.

There are 3 main principles I want to detail for you further in regard to Touchpoint 1:

1. **THERE ARE 4 ASSETS IN MARKETING THAT YOU NEED TO INVEST IN AND WORK HARD AT NURTURING**: Your online customer experience (website, mobile, and app), your content, your CRM, and your marketing database and other social followers. We will reference these assets throughout this book.

2. **INBOUND MARKETING PROGRAMS are about drawing *prospects in*,** helping them find you and become aware of your capabilities, and what you can do for them!

3. **OUTBOUND MARKETING PROGRAMS are about *going out to prospects*** and making positive impressions. You are pursuing targeted segments you outlined in your strategic plan, and making them aware of your capabilities and what you can do for them.

THE BIG 4 ASSETS OF MARKETING

We are going to be talking about these 4 assets throughout this chapter because they are critical investment areas for you as the CEO. By investing in these areas and putting resources behind their success, you are going to create more value in your company. The BIG 4 assets of marketing are:

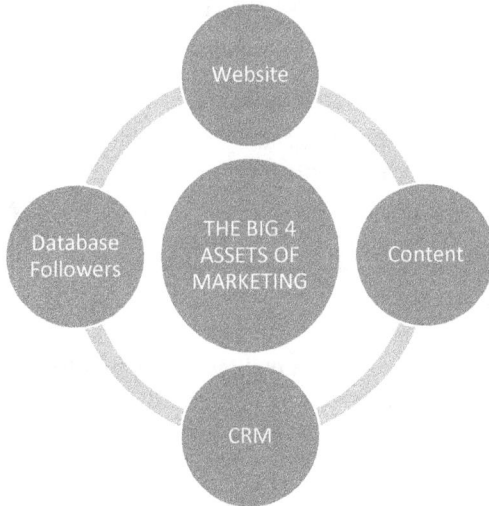

Website

Database Followers

THE BIG 4 ASSETS OF MARKETING

Content

CRM

THE GROWTH CUBE™
Unlocking the Growth Potential of Your Company

1. *Your database*, including your social followers, and your ability to segment and learn more about and communicate relevant messaging to specific personas and segments.

2. *The content that you create.* Is it helping the customer in their decision-making to run their business more effectively? Is it showing the customer why your product can be useful to them in that quest?

3. *Your website and mobile online and app presence.* Is it a great user experience and intuitive and easy to use?

4. *Your CRM has the history of activity by customer,* and hopefully a 360-degree view where you can see all customer activity from the beginning of your relationship all the way through their implementation and support issues and activity, and their billing and financial transactions. If you can also see profile information on your key contacts at each account, that is also a big plus.

INBOUND MARKETING (Drawing Them IN)
With inbound marketing programs, we are targeting those people who are actually looking for products and services we provide. We are trying to *draw them in* and eventually lead them to our website where we have all kinds of content and calls to action (CTA) that will generate leads for the company.

The idea of inbound marketing is that you target a core audience by providing useful and quality content to entice them into finding out more about your products or services. You are giving suspects an opportunity to share and consume your content (which better be interesting!) and eventually get them to click on a CTA to learn more, follow you, ask for a demo, test the product, or maybe even try to buy! If you can generate a lot of followers in your social network, you can use your social and web presence to ask these suspects questions about your products and services.

Inbound marketing is a pull technique that leverages 3 of your 4 assets: an effective online presence, your database of social followers, and great content!

1. Website – ONE OF YOUR BIG 4 ASSETS!

All roads lead to mobile access of your online experience, which today is centered around your website. For this reason, development of a strong website and associated mobile and app experience is a key strategic investment. Think about the design and customer experience of the site and what your strategy is. Your website is not the only way prospects contact you, but it is the key source. You should also discuss strategies in your company for providing omni-channel access to your company, where the customer can interact with your company through a variety of methods (chat, phone, e-mail, social, mobile, etc.). If you are transacting on your website, you will need to additionally invest in an ecommerce solution to drive revenue and profit on your site, focusing on optimizing online conversion rates.

2. Content Development – ONE OF YOUR BIG 4 ASSETS!

Development of valuable content is a key to inbound marketing. We are trying to generate interest and demand (Demand Gen) by giving away content freely (in most cases) to build awareness. The goal is to provide information and knowledge from thought-leaders in your company through whitepapers, infographics, blogs, and newsletters (that suspects sign up for). We are also talking about all your website content. Unless there is a strategic reason, blogs should be organized together at your company website (rather than a separate site). Of course, the key to success is to have awesome content that the suspect is actually interested in and finds value in to the point that they actually share it with someone else! Determining proper and valuable content preferably customized to your various personas (content marketing strategy) is key to your success here! What is your thought-leadership? Develop content around those topics and go on offense. Lead the way for your industry, and be the go-to source for information and direction.

SEO and Keywords

If a potential customer searches in Google for a product like yours, does your site appear on the first page of the Google search results? If not, you may need to invest in Search Engine Optimization (SEO). If someone goes into Google and is searching for your products and services, what do they enter? What words or phrases do they type? These are called keywords, and they are vital that you develop and optimize your content for SEO. This is a skill in itself and no one (even the marketing expert companies I have talked to) can figure out what Google is doing and how their algorithms

work or change over time. You can invest in Pay Per Click (PPC) ads that initiate when your keyword is entered for quick results, but in any event, your content (including web pages) should be developed with your keywords in mind so that when the suspect is searching Google or similar search engines, your company and your content will emerge. For small businesses, help in this arena is often difficult to justify and budget for.

> *"Go on offense with your thought leadership content.*
> *Be a leading voice in your industry."*

Once you determine the type of content you want, you should develop a content calendar for your company to have consistent releases of this thought-leadership content. There should be a strategy for each piece. In addition, you should unleash all your associates to contribute by developing content and sharing in their social networks. One of my companies we built monthly content development into the job descriptions of certain associates. Clearly having a group of raving associates who believe in the company makes it much easier to ask for them to promote the company socially!

3. Database Social Followers
Speaking of social sharing by your associates, through social media sites, blogs and ratings/review listings, your prospects are talking with your customers, friends, and strangers about price, service, selection, and satisfaction. They are asking for their referrals! You may be surprised sometimes who you are connected with socially and what responsibility they have. You should have company pages where your customers are located (LinkedIn, Twitter, Facebook, etc.) and hopefully frequent for knowledge and marketing promotions. How many followers do you have on these platforms? Which platforms are most important to your company's success? Your company and your associates can join LinkedIn groups for example, and they can engage other people in the groups as well. You can also encourage customers to post on the company's Facebook wall or website, comment on blogs, or take part in contests. When they participate, they become invested and engaged.

Whatever the future social platforms may be, your goal is the same: communicate socially where your potential customers hang out. You can also advertise to get to even more targeted and specific audiences, but the idea behind inbound marketing is that you draw them in, and they take the step forward to you. Unfortunately, there are no guarantees, and in general, it is difficult to calculate ROI from inbound investments.

MARKETING MODEL FOR GENERATING SQO'S

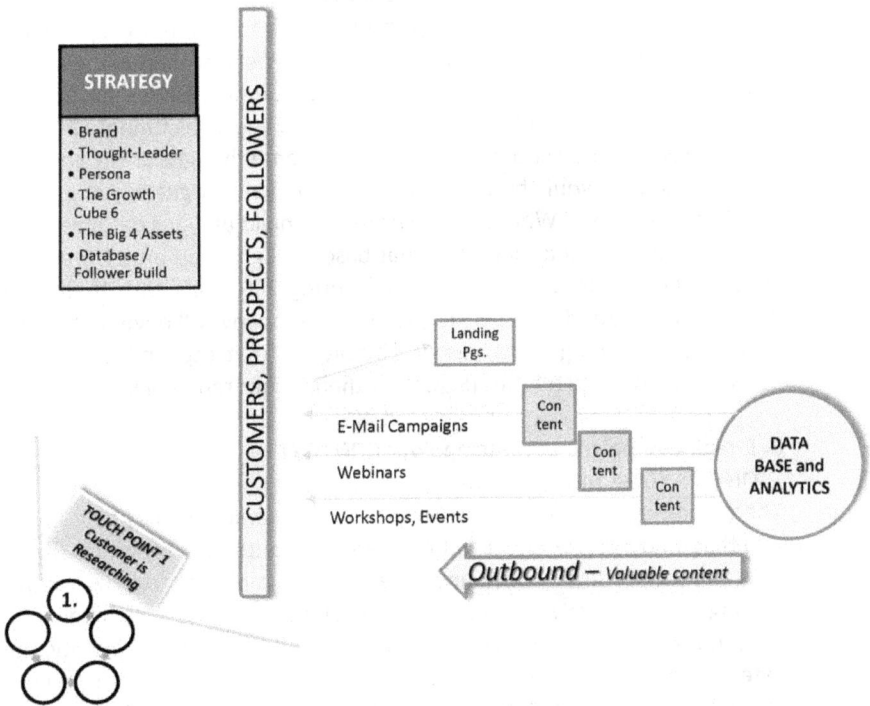

OUTBOUND MARKETING (Actively Going OUT)

With outbound marketing programs, we are actively going **OUT** and pushing our products and services to suspects even if they are not looking for those products or services. It's a push technique to generate leads (LEAD GEN). The techniques can include direct mail, events (webinars, workshops, trade shows, etc.), and advertising/PR through many different types of media. The beauty of outbound marketing programs, and the key to managing the outbound marketing expense, is to target specific segments and prospect groups with specific targeted messages

111

that should relate to their needs. ROI can be fairly easily tracked on outbound campaigns through click through on landing pages and event attendance.

In addition to the content development already mentioned above, my top 3 outbound marketing investments are the lead database, e-mail campaigns, and educational webinars/workshops:

1. Database – ONE OF YOUR BIG 4 ASSETS!
The leads in this database are in your marketing funnel, but they are not yet qualified to be pursued by a dedicated sales person. This is the secret sauce. This is a company asset. The marketing funnel should be tracked and managed as diligently as you are managing the sales funnel. Assuming you have a good list of names, if you put some thought to the content being developed, your thought leadership, and your target personas, you should find success. What is your strategy to build up your database and nurture, segment, and market to that base? I'll give you a trick we have used: all newly hired sales reps should bring 200 leads with them and load them into our database. In return, the company will develop specific outbound marketing programs specifically for that rep and generating sales qualified opportunities (SQOs) for them! Your reps will love this!

2. E-mail Campaigns Leveraging Your CONTENT –
ONE OF YOUR BIG 4 ASSETS
The marketing companies who favor inbound marketing are going to tell you that inbound is where it's at now, and that outbound programs like e-mail campaigns do not work anymore. This is simply not true. As of this writing and per *McKinsey*, 91% of US consumers still use e-mail daily. In addition, although e-mail activity is giving way slightly to social activity, the rate at which e-mails generate purchases is not only estimated to be 3 times higher than social, but the average order value is 17% higher. The bottom line is that you still need to be investing in e-mail campaigns. Content development, newsletters, and new product launches are some of my favorite initiatives for making successful e-mail campaigns.

One of the beauties of outbound marketing is you have a database of leads and the analytics around their activity. You can have active and consistent e-mail communication with this group (who can unsubscribe if they do not feel what you are sending fits them). At one of my companies, we developed a dashboard report around the marketing funnel activity and progress month-to-month. You can also get excellent analytics on campaign results from Constant Contact and Mail Chimp, and more sophisticated (and expensive) marketing automation programs like Hubspot. There are other players, and they will change over time. What you have to remember is what you are trying to accomplish, and then find the right partners and applications that can you help you accomplish your goals.

3. Webinars and Workshops

I like webinars and workshops because they reinforce our focus on providing thought leadership to our target personas. (See how the strategic plan is helping us now!?) Education and training programs are very valuable at Touchpoint 1. Customers often enjoy consuming this kind of information to learn. The content developed for these events can be repurposed on the website and distributed socially as well! I love repurposing content to increase ROI on content development!

We mentioned that content development is not only one of our 4 marketing assets, but is also crucial to outbound programs, and now you can be begin to see why. At the end of the day, we have to keep outbound and their analytics in perspective. The clicks and open rates on e-mails are tracked desperately as key measures, and they are, but we also must remember that this is only the first click in the journey of the buyer. We have to focus on where the potential customer goes next to consume our content – to the landing page, the website, and the event. We must ensure that this is supremely informative and valuable to them. The more we can customize the customer experience when they touch our company's website, the more our message will fit their needs and the more they will feel at home with us!

The most important marketing question the CEO should be focused on is: "When my customer experiences my product or service, do they love it?"

CUSTOMER EXPERIENCE MARKETING
We have talked a lot about the customer in this book already, so you know how important your current customers are! Showcase them more through content that you develop about them, like case studies and customer stories and video testimonials. Market these to other customers like them through techniques like personalized newsletters.

THE GROWTH CUBE™
Unlocking the Growth Potential of Your Company

Referral programs are excellent, but take it a step further with gamification and advocacy software, which can be great tools to utilize with your current customers. Led by the marketing team, advocacy tools are an asset as we give our customers a way to interact with each other, with potential new customers, and with the company in a very positive, fun, and supportive way.

A recent report from *Forrester* predicts that in the next year, more business-to-business marketers will organize their efforts around individual clients and less on broad marketing of their products and services. *Forrester's* research found that 37% of marketing decision-makers said improving customer experience is a critical priority, second only to growing revenue! Challenge your team to come up with creative ideas beyond the traditional customer-based marketing techniques to feature your current customers and what they are doing to succeed utilizing your products and services.

MARKETING ANALYTICS
You now realize that marketing has a funnel just like sales has a funnel. Have you looked at the analytics of your sales funnel? I bet you have! You should be doing the same with your marketing funnel! The marketing funnel has your Touchpoint 1 leads. They require nurturing by your marketing efforts. Marketing automation products can help you organize and gain visibility to activity and results. Analyzing and nurturing your marketing database and your marketing funnel will enable you to make your marketing process more effective and efficient, resulting in more sales qualified leads (SQOs) going to your sales team!

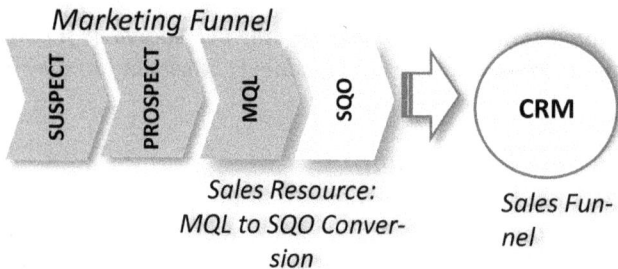

Marketing Funnel

SUSPECT PROSPECT MQL SQO CRM

Sales Resource: MQL to SQO Conversion

Sales Funnel

Let's review some of the key analytics in marketing at Touchpoint 1:

1. Suspect.
The total number of names in your database, including your social followers. Although the database is a company asset, it needs to be nurtured and communicated with. It should continue to grow.

2. Prospect.
A prospect is a suspect that is active. They are possibly attending a webinar or downloading content, but activity is still low. In my experience, 25% of your suspects should be active. So, if you have 30,000 suspect names in your database, 7,500 should be active and therefor considered a prospect.

3. Marketing Qualified Leads (MQLs).
A prospect is defined as an MQL after they have demonstrated a defined level of activity. MQLs are actively learning and consuming content. They are on the hunt for something and are moving towards buying. Depending on the company and the product, this could move fast, so you should move fast too once an MQL has been identified. MQLs should be tracked in the CRM, but they should not have a money value until they are qualified, otherwise they will over-inflate your view of the sales pipeline opportunity.

4. Sales Qualified Opportunities (SQOs).
When someone tells you how many leads were generated last month, you need to clarify what is meant by a "lead" in your company. To me, a qualified lead that goes into the sales funnel – an SQO – is what counts. Although the marketing activity and MQL generation is good, and the investment is needed, it is the SQO result that we are looking for. Because of this, you need to develop a process in your company to get the MQLs qualified by a telesales / e-mail rep whose sole purpose in your company is to convert MQLs to SQOs.

To qualify for SQO, the sales team must accept the lead from marketing, verify the following, and add the SQO to the CRM sales funnel with a potential cash value:

1. Budget – does the prospect have the budget to buy?
2. Authority – does the prospect you are talking to have the authority to buy?
3. Needs – will your solution offer the prospect value?
4. Timeline – when will the prospect make a decision?

Some products convert to a sale right on the website and do not require the intervention of a sales person, and that's great for those businesses. But what if the prospect is interested in learning more than what they can find on their own? The prospect wants to see specific products, get demonstrations (if the website does not provide it), and get customized cost information around their specs. That sounds like a qualified lead, but it's not until those questions above can be answered, so keep your telesales SDR (sales development reps) on it until it is converted to an SQO.

So you can see now that the SQO is the most important result of a successful Touchpoint 1 – a touchpoint which is essentially led by the marketing team in your company. If you want to pay an incentive to the marketing team, it should be built around SQOs generated, and if you can track it, preferably SQOs that close! For your planning purposes, per *B2B Marketing Zone*, 15% of MQLs become SQOs and move to Touchpoint 2. Touchpoint 2 is where the sales team takes the lead. If you are not generating enough SQOs per month, work your way back and look at your MQL generation and how you can improve quickly!

You should be tracking and reviewing reports monthly on the following metrics:

1. SQOs being generated by month. We certainly want our SQOs increasing each month.

2. Calculate the cost per Sales Qualified Opportunity (SQO). Make sure to separate this calculation for partner-generated leads versus your own marketing generated leads. The calculation is to take the marketing and sales investment and divide by the number of SQOs generated over that same period.

3. SQO lead source. You should be tracking your won business in your CRM and looking at the source of the lead. For those you have won, where did the lead come from? Invest more of your marketing and sales budget there!

MARKETING MODEL FOR GENERATING QUALFIED LEADS

Okay, you did it! Through a smart and focused set of marketing initiatives that we call the "Marketing Model for Generating SQOs," you have started generating a consistent flow of qualified leads for the company! Now that we have taken you through it step-by-step, if you want a graphic model of the Marketing Model for Generating Qualified Leads, please go to www.thegrowthcube.com/resources and you can download a copy!

RESET AND QUICKSTART APPROACH

I am sure you have a lot going on in your marketing activity today. You probably are not sure if it is all effective. You have the right instinct. When you look at this graphic and see all of the time and effort and programs, it becomes apparent that marketing is a big expense area for your company. So the CEO needs to get involved and understand the intricacies of the programs being implemented, the results the programs are delivering, how customers and prospects feel about how they are being touched, and how the team is performing. If you feel like it is a black hole right now, you should seriously consider scrapping it all and starting over. I am serious. Restart with your strategy and your thought-leadership focus, and Touchpoint 1. Follow the steps we have outlined in this chapter! Take control. Marketing to win new customers and marketing to current customers should be a team effort with your head of marketing taking the lead, and they should be able to explain things so you understand them. If they are confusing you, then it's time to make a change.

Once your company's strategic plan and marketing and sales strategies are defined, here is a reset and quick start approach I would recommend:

1. Build Your Asset Strategy

You can now see how the website, your content, your database and followers, and the data in your CRM (coming up in the next section) are all big assets of your company! These need to be treated as such in your business. Investing here is an opportunity to build the value of your company and protect and build the future of your business. Sticking to disciplined processes and management of these assets will maximize your success!

MARKETING ASSET SCORECARD

	SITUATION TODAY	ACTIVE PROJECTS TO IM- PROVE	STAFF ON IT TODAY	TOTAL	POTENTIAL POINTS	%
WEBSITE	2	4	3	9	15	60%
CONTENT	1	1	1	3	15	20%
DATABASE	3	2	1	6	15	40%
CRM	3	3	2	8	15	53%
				26	60	43%

The Big 4 Assets   *Grade each cell from 1 to 5*

Try building a chart like the one above. Grade yourself on your Big 4 Assets. In this example, there is a lot of work to do – they graded 43%. How do you look?

2. Start Outbound Programs
Get some outbound programs going toward your current customers, and then add your new customers into the program. Customers will appreciate the communication. Make it fun, informative, and consistent, and you will find the beginnings of success!

3. Start Inbound Programs
The inbound programs are a little more nebulous and the ROI is not as tight. Although important, I would prioritize and start with outbound and move to inbound next.

Final Thoughts on Marketing Strategy
We all know marketing strategy is critical, but sometimes bridging that strategy to the execution of marketing programs can be expensive and fail to deliver a clear ROI. Rightfully so, this can make CEOs uncomfortable. If you approach the Big 4 Assets like assets on your balance sheet, find a great marketing leader to drive things, and you get involved and learn, you will find the clarity you are looking for.

Marketing is about building a relationship with your customer and being a resource to them. There is a reason there is always a long line at Starbucks. Do your customers show this much loyalty and commitment to your products and services? How would you rate your company at winning new customers and creating raving fans out of them? Do they want to experience you again?

I had the opportunity to hear Dennis Schiraldi and Mike Pontikas speak recently about marketing and their predictions for the coming year, and they did an excellent job outlining marketing trends coming at us. Not only does Google evolve and change, but even bigger shifts will occur with artificial intelligence (AI), machine learning, and robots. It is an exciting time! As these technologies continue to evolve and change the marketing landscape, and offer you and your team more data and analytics, keep the fundamental Growth Cube™ concepts in front of you. These concepts are what counts. At the end of the day, if you do not have an awesome product, customers who are raving about you, and associates who are fired up, then all the marketing investment in the world will not make a difference.

The question you and your team should be relentless about getting right is: *When my customer and potential customers experience my product or service, do they love it?*

SALES STRATEGY

If you look at your sales activities today, there might be a lot of moving parts and lot of things happening, but the first question is: *Is it all resulting in closed business at the levels you want?*

If the answer is "No," I am not surprised. After all, you are reading this book. You want more. And I am sure you are agonizing over it as any leader would be. You might be asking yourself:

- Is the sales team activity… the right activity?
- Are people in the right roles?
- Is the team fully trained and equipped to win?
- Is our strategy all messed up?

These are all natural questions every CEO faces at some point, but how do you go about addressing them without making it worse? Managing a sales team is a delicate balance of art and science. It gets more complex when partner channels are added.

I can help you.

Again, being successful at sales is both an art and a science, and so, I am going to build around those two central themes to lay out my recommendations for your sales strategy and improving your sales performance.

1. The Science: Organize your team and build sales discipline in your processes and systems

2. The Art: Figure out the best way to motivate your sales team to win!

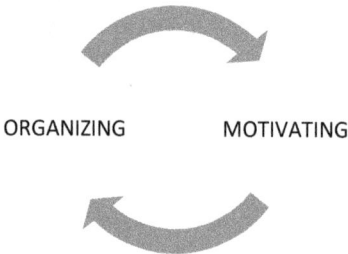

ORGANIZING   MOTIVATING

1. ORGANIZING AND MOTIVATING TO WIN!

Everyone wants great salespeople. It is sometimes difficult to find them. Sometimes when you do, in many respects it is like the NFL draft. They look good on paper or maybe at one company, but when you get them, they are not successful. Why is that? Is it because they were not a good sales rep in the first place, or is it that you somehow did not help them be successful with the role, training, and compensation plan that you gave them?

When I first joined one of my companies, the company had one sales team performing both hunting and farming duties. We weren't winning new customers or growing our customer base. However, the sales team was achieving its quota by just selling to the installed base. One of the first steps we took was to separate the teams into hunters and farmers, and along with that changed the compensation plans accordingly. We also hired a VP leader of the hunters and a VP leader of the farmers. The leaders' compensation plan was the same as the people they managed.

It worked! The hunters started bringing in new customers to the company at record rates! And the farmers (who we called Customer Success Managers) became beloved by the customers for their attention, involvement, and focus on them and their needs. Some customers told us later that assigning dedicated farmers to their accounts was the best thing they loved about our company!

You can achieve this success too!

What I want to share with you are the results from my 17 years of experience in trying to organize and motivate sales teams to win, keep, and grow customers. I have led companies with direct and partner sales teams, and I get very involved in the sales efforts. (Remember I like to hang out on the fault line where the company is touching our customer!) To help you get started with your decision-making, let's revisit something we already have committed to in Chapters 2 and 3. Something you are already comfortable with: *The 5-Step Customer Touchpoint Plan*.

ORGANIZATIONAL STRATEGY AND THE 5-STEP CUSTOMER TOUCHPOINT PLAN

We already learned that this strategy should drive the structure and culture in your company. We will follow that same model in looking at the marketing and sales team and how we want to structure there.

As I reflect on all the great sales performances I have seen, and the ones that have failed, one of the biggest issues I have seen is role mismatch – both defining the right roles and then matching the right people to them. So I want us to focus on successfully implementing two strategies as they relate to how you organize your team.

A. SALES ORGANIZATION STRATEGY – Define the Roles

If you have a strategy defined for the company, you probably know the products that are being developed. You know your sales by product from last year and the road map for this year. And we have our customer Touchpoint model that we can use to better define our marketing and sales operational plan, including how we want to organize your sales team. This takes some thinking, and you may want to engage with a coach, but it is important that you build your sales organization around the customer's life cycle, the 5 Touchpoints, and the products and services you have in your arsenal to provide.

ORGANIZING
SALES
• Define the
Sales Roles

MOTIVATING
SALES

The customer's life cycle includes 5 major touchpoints and your sales team needs to be there all the way, at each touchpoint, for the life of the customer. When you are thinking about sales strategy and organizing your team, I want you to think through these 5 steps and how you will organize your sales efforts accordingly. I want you to define your sales strategy by starting with what kind of sales roles you need, and the associated product sales opportunity, at each of the five Touchpoints.

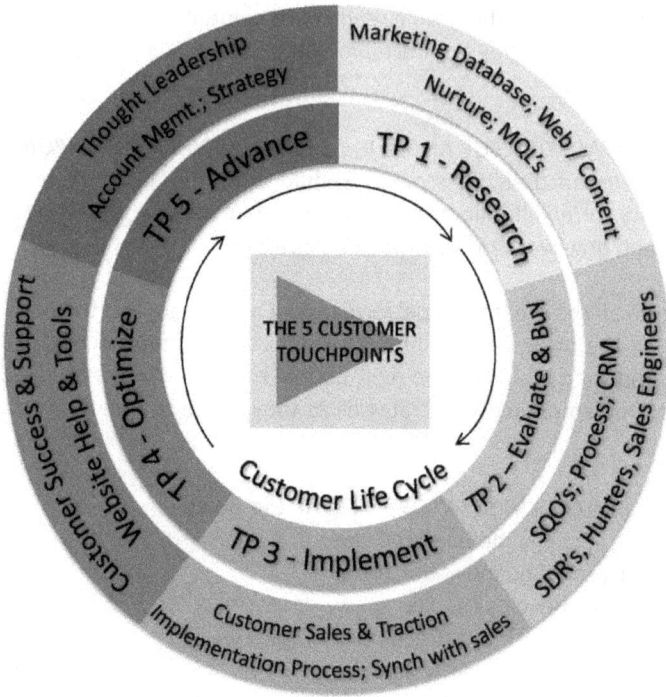

The outside band in the graphic represents the marketing and sales programs and resources you will deploy at each Touchpoint. In smaller companies, you may not have the resources to add all of these positions, so you will leverage the CEO and potentially one or two sales / customer service people across all 5 touchpoints. The main point is that you need someone to take accountability and own each of the 5 Touchpoints.

Let's talk further about the potential roles at each Touchpoint:

TP 1 – Research
In the research stage, most of this can be accomplished through great tools afforded to us by technology, including a strong website, relevant content, smooth mobile access, try-buy offerings, online demos and video learning, chat help, and much more. The sales resource here should engage as the customer increases their level of activity and interest. You will need to determine at what point this happens. Telesales reps, Sales Development Reps (SDRs), or other e-sales resources are useful here as the customer becomes more serious in their research.

Your sales team should help the customer learn, but they are also hunters that should be able to evaluate very quickly whether this customer is going to stay at Touchpoint 1 or move to Touchpoint 2 in the near future. This is an unqualified lead at this point and is not in your sales funnel, but things can sometimes move very quickly.

"Do not lose connection with the customer at any point in their life cycle – utilize everyone on your team to make sure this does not happen!"

TP 2 – Evaluate and Buy
When the customer reaches this stage, they are an SQO. They are qualified, and this is your hunter team's sweet spot.

The Hunter and Their Team
If you are big enough to support both a farmer and a hunter team, I believe this is the best way to organize. For smaller companies, they will have to work their way toward this model. The hunter is responsible for winning new customers. We all know this is not easy. It takes a special skill, and because of this, the hunter is paid a higher commission *rate* than a farmer because it is hard to get that new account and many times the initial order is smaller than the potential of the customer since they initially may be trying out one product. The farmer will pursue the add-ons later.

If you want to win new customers, you need to only pay the hunters on the new wins only – not recurring streams. I know you may want them to stay involved sometimes, but this should be by exception. If you open the door and pay them for ongoing streams, you risk growing your new customers. Most CEOs know this, but I still see them do it anyway. They may be persuaded by their hunters, or it may be something else, but the result is still the same. In the long run, the new sales will not come at the rate you want because you have no one dedicated to just that mission!

The hunter should utilize a team approach to cover the SQO opportunities that are in their funnel. Sales engineers and SDRs can be very helpful in making the hunter reps more effective and hit higher numbers than they could on their own. The SDR can focus on qualifying leads for the hunter, and/or they can support the hunter in their selling efforts.

The Secret Weapon: The Sales Engineer

At all my companies, we added sales engineers to the sales team. At one company, we called them Solutions Consultants. In a small company, this could be the CEO if they have technical product and marketing skills. You have to decide who this will be, but someone has to play this role or you have a major hole in your selling arsenal. It is amazing how many companies miss on this key resource to the sales effort. The sales engineer provides the sales team with a technical expert who can talk at a level with a big-customer technical VP. Also, someone who knows the customer business as well as they do, and where it is going in the future in terms of technology and competitive landscape.

Remember your customer is at the evaluate and buy stage, and you can help them if you have talented people on your team. Technical people in your customer account may want to talk with technical people in your company. They may not want to deal with sales people, no matter how good the sales rep is! To the customers point, the sales rep may not have all the technical skills needed to answer their questions. Supporting your sales rep with a strong sales engineer is the answer. What should they do? They should be a star in your trade show booth, doing demos, defining the Statement of Work (SOW), be a key speaker at industry conferences, and their compensation can be significant when tied to a successful sales performance. In the technology industry, many companies have a ratio of 2 sales reps per 1 sales engineer.

TP 3 – Implement

When you are implementing your product/services with the customer, clearly the focus is on traction – getting the customer initially comfortable and utilizing your product to help their business. Do not underestimate the effort and importance of traction. A customer success manager should be assigned to the account. They will work hand-in-hand with the implementers to make sure we have a great handoff from sales to implementation, and they will stay involved. The customer success manager does not have to be a quota-carrying position. Their job is clear. They are responsible for working with the customer and our products/services to ensure customer success.

TP 4 – Support

Once the customer is implemented and on your solution, the support team in the company should take lead responsibility. During the support process, the customer success manager should stay involved. Here we are concerned with traction and happiness. The renewal process should be incorporated in here as well. You can complement the customer success manager with someone from contracts who can help make the renewals happen inside the company, and you can also implement automated renewal systems to reduce the overall cost. However, the customer success manager has to escalate and respond if you want the customer to stay with you, and you want to jump on escalations, and you want the customer to love their experience with your products and your people. This is especially true if they do not already love your people and products.

"Everyone can sell!"

TP 5 – Raving Fans
When the Customer loves your current product, they will look forward to your next product. This will pave the way for upsells and add-ons, but these are earned because of the resource you have become for your customer. You have to earn this status, and the Raving Fan Triangle is the way to earn it.

The Farmer and Their Team
People know what you mean when you say someone in sales is a "farmer" or a "hunter," but they are really internal terms and should not be used with customers. The title of the farmer is typically a "Customer Success Manager," and this job title easily clarifies that their focus is on the customer's success! In the last chapter, we talked about current customer growth opportunity, and the *Raving Fan Triangle* as a process for you to systematically manage the growth of your customer relationships. The customer success manager is responsible for leading the organization's effort to make that customer successful with our products and services, and for customer retention, keeping traction, and adding on products that they might need. The customer success manager is typically also incented to build the recurring revenue streams in your business. They should love your customer's business and be striving to learn more and want to be a thought leader. This energy and drive around the customer's business will excite your customer!

Your whole company should be focused on creating raving fans, but the customer success manager is the quarterback. In small companies, the farmer and the customer success manager can be the same person. As a company grows, a farmer rep can be quota carrying around these upgrades and add-ons. Sales engineers and product managers can help drive the growth of new or target products, and they can be given bonuses or commissions also.

I have utilized a saying in my companies that is a very important message to influence your culture around these Touchpoints and making sure we have them covered. The message I communicate to my teams is, *"Everyone can sell."* What I mean by this is that no matter what your role in the company, you should be talking with customers and representing our company. You should know what we do and the products that we offer. Some will understand the customer environment intimately. You do not have to be a sales person to have a quality conversation with a customer. Not everyone is a salesperson, and we do not expect that, but everyone CAN talk with our customers about our performance and how we are improving. We all represent our company! The customer will feel it if your whole company is made up of raving associates that are involved and enthusiastic. Do not lose connection with the customer at any point in their life cycle, and utilize everyone on your team to make sure this happens!

Compensation Plans
The detail required to put together the sales compensation plan and to establish sales quotas and budgets is really not the focus of this book. Still, it is a critical skill in the *art* of leading the sales team. As you go through the exercise above, put together a rough outline of the compensation you envision for each role and your sales forecast by product. This will lead to a budget and ROI. This should all be agreed with key leadership in advance of hiring or putting people in roles. Start with a clean slate. Do not get bogged down with current roles and current people's skill sets. Assume you are a startup or building from scratch, and let's see what you can put together by utilizing some of The Growth Cube concepts!

Channel Sales and Sales Partners
Building partnerships should be a key growth strategy for your company. A partner sales channel needs to be managed as diligently as a direct sales force. Partners should be certified in the same way as your direct sales team, and someone in the sales team – channel manager for example – should own the responsibility for partner training, certification, and performance. Partners can also lead you to new markets that you were not in before! We will look forward to discussing partnering in more detail in Chapter 5, "Expanding to New Markets."

B. SALES ORGANIZATION STRATEGY – Fit the Best People in Each Role
How does this happen in some of the biggest and most successful companies:

ORGANIZING SALES
• Define the Sales Roles
• Fit the Best People in Each Role

MOTIVATING SALES

With great expense, we hunt and hunt for a sales rep for our business, never really finding exactly what we hoped. So eventually we pick the best candidate and bring them on, train them extensively on the product, the company, and the customers – for months. Within 2 years, they are gone. The sales never did increase the way we wanted, and all that time and all of that cost – and it's over.

This happens way too often, and it's usually not because of desire, talent, or personal interviewing skill on the candidate or the hiring party. The biggest reason is that the role we hire for does not match the skill set of the sales rep. I call this "Role Mismatch." I'll give you a classic example you will relate to:

Putting a sales hunter into a current customer relationship role (or putting a customer success rep out hunting new accounts). There are exceptions, but this is usually not a good fit. A sales hunter, a rep that pursues and closes big new accounts, in many cases is not going to do well nurturing a current customer who may have support issues escalating and no new sales activity for the past 6 months. Do we really want a hunter doing this anyway? That type of account may be better suited to the skills of a farmer who will fit better with the need for relationship building and customer service.

"Managing a sales team is a delicate balance of art and science."

This is a role mismatch I see all the time. I have had it in my organizations too. Many times you inherit this as a leader. Sometimes it happens because of pressure. Yes, the pressure to hit sales numbers sometimes pushes us to make unusual decisions that we normally would not make! We know better, but we overlook it and push our hunters to be farmers, and our farmers to be hunters. Inevitably, we end up disappointed. It's a role mismatch that can totally be prevented, but pressure from several down sales months happen, and then these kinds of ideas slide onto the table. Organizational and people decision making without thinking through the fit leads to mistakes that make it worse for company revenues and the morale of the sales team.

There are two steps you can take to prevent role mismatch and improve fit:

A. Define the Role through a Sales Role Worksheet

Adding a sales rep is so critical, yet many times we run into HR and tell them that we "need to hire a sales rep," and that's all the direction we give our hiring team. Answer these questions for me: What kind of sales resources do you need? What will they each be responsible for? How do you want to compensate them? If you want to get the right person in the right role, you can help yourself by thinking about the ideas we have been sharing in The Growth Cube process. What is your strategy and your need, and how will that drive the skills you want to hire?

In a small company or a startup, where people play many roles, you may have to combine two roles into one or be creative in your approach. For example, you can hire a candidate who compliments the skills of the CEO (e.g. if the CEO is a hunter, your first hire is a farmer).

I am going to give you an easy tool to help you lay out the role more clearly: The Sales Role Worksheet. It will help you think more deeply about the *Role*. Before you go to HR or your board and move to interview, complete the Sales Role Worksheet to help you define the role even more clearly! Try this out for your next sales hire need:

SALES ROLE WORKSHEET		*Check one answer per row*
☐ Support sales team	vs.	☐ Have their own quota
☐ Telesales	vs.	☐ On-site sales
☐ Renewals	vs.	☐ New customers
☐ Thought leader	vs.	☐ Generalist
☐ All sales	vs.	☐ Marketing and sales
☐ On road	vs.	☐ In office
☐ Full time	vs.	☐ Part time
☐ Base, bonus (no comm)	vs.	☐ Base, commission (no bonus)

B. Hire the Rep Utilizing a Disciplined CSF Hiring Process.

When you start to interview, you have to stay focused. Sales people can be especially great interviewers, and you can find yourself walking out of an interview saying, "That guy was impressive," when in fact they did not have the right skills that you need! This will not matter if you stay disciplined and grade the candidates objectively against the skills that are most important to the success of the role – the Critical Success Factors (CSFs).

We talked about CSFs in Chapter 1, so you have a good idea already what I mean, and now we are going to put it into application as we define the CSFs for a sales role. Make sure to get your CSFs completed upfront along with the job description and the Sales Role Worksheet. Get that package around to the interview team. First, take time with your team (30 minutes) upfront and define the 5 skills that you need to hire to make the candidate a good fit for the open role. Once you begin interviewing candidates, have the CSF worksheet with you, and score the candidates as you interview them. In the worksheet, column 1 includes the CSF list, column 2 and 3 might be your score against all of those 5 factors, and your related notes. In column 4 and 5, it will be one of your colleague's score and notes, and so on. By using this format, we make sure to hire objectively based on the skills we need, and you are asking and probing questions related to those important factors during the interview. The scores should be on a scale of 1-5, with 5 being high. Here is the most important point to remember: a candidate cannot be recommended unless they are 4 or 5 on EVERY CSF! Do not give in on this criterion or you will hire the wrong person for this role.

For example, a CSF for the hunter role would be: do they have demonstrated ability consistently winning new customers? If they have not done this, move on. They do not have the CSF requirement! I am emphasizing this to you because I see it happen so often, and I want to help you succeed in this very critical and costly hire. Here is an example CSF scorecard for you:

INTERVIEW VIA CRITICAL SUCCESS FACTORS

Position: Sales Consultant

Critical Success Factors	Completed by: Gary		Completed by: Ann	
	Rating (1 - 5)	Comment	Rating (1- 5)	Comment
Have formal Sales Process training, Planning / Organizing skills	5	Reason for rating	4	Reason for rating
Have worked under and beat quota's over $1M in the past	4	Reason for rating	5	Reason for rating
Great presenter including awesome Communication skills (Verbal / Written)	5	Reason for rating	4	Reason for rating
Demonstrated excellent Computer and CRM Skills	5	Reason for rating	4	Reason for rating
Deep knowledge of the products used by our customers	2		3	
	21		20	

Must have a 4 or 5 on all CSFs to be hired

C. TRAIN AND CERTIFY – Have a Formal Program

I believe that if you have great products and a great sales team, you have an excellent chance at company success. However, there are great teams in sports that do not win the <u>championship</u> despite having awesome talent. Why don't they win? Often, it is because they do not put in the practice and training as individuals and teams that it takes to beat other talented teams. The same is true for your sales team. Defining roles and hiring talent is important, but if you do not train them, you will risk your ability to hit the growth rates you want! The sales team has a key role in the customer relationship, and our ability to win and create raving fans as well. So how do we help them succeed, and what do we train them on?

ORGANIZING SALES
- Define the Sales Roles
- Fit the best People in each Role
- Train and Certify

MOTIVATING SALES

First, remember that our goal as a sales team is not to sell products, although we should know everything about our products. Our goal is to understand the customer, their industry, and their challenges so that we can help them win with their customers, hopefully by utilizing our products and services! It's not about us. It's about the customer and their success. Your company and its people must learn and become experts at the customer's business and how your products and services help them compete more effectively. If you can just do this one thing I am telling you right now, you can differentiate yourself from 70% of the competition who are focusing only on their products and features.

We talked about thought-leadership in Chapter 1. We introduced you to our Level 3 Certification Program, and we gave you specific steps on how to build your own program for your company. If you recall, the first 2 levels of the program involve training everyone in the company to get deeper knowledge about our products, the industry, the customer environment, and how we solve customer challenges and goals with our products and services. Level 3 of certification, however, includes only the sales team, and giving them deep training on our sales process, the CRM, and other sales technology, being able to demo our products thoroughly, and becoming efficient at pricing and quoting yourself as a rep or other customer-facing associate.

I will tell you a real story about the sales process!

THE GROWTH CUBE[TM]
Unlocking the Growth Potential of Your Company

A friend of mine was at their annual company-wide sales meeting, and they gave out an award to the top sales person in the company for the prior year. They called the woman who was number one up on the stage with all the executives to show everyone else in the room what the number 1 sales person looks and acts like. The CEO turned to her when she arrived up at the podium, shook her hand, and said, "If you had one thing to tell these sales people out here – these up and coming sales leaders – what would you tell them?"

She yelled out (and I am not making this up), "Fxxx the sales process!"

As you can imagine, that did not go over well.

But the point is that not many reps get excited about following a sales process. They will not cheer when you bring it up. I would also bet that this leading sales-person you just read about has a process they are using and do not even realize it! Some sales people simply do not understand how valuable a formal process can be for them and their income! A study conducted by *The National Sales Executive Association* showed this:

- ✓ 2% of sales are made on the 1st contact.
- ✓ 3% of sales are made on the 2nd contact.
- ✓ 5% of sales are made on the 3rd contact.
- ✓ 10% of sales are made on the 4th contact.
- ✓ 80% of sales are made on the 5th contact.

It's not until the 5th contact that the vast majority of sales are made, which means you have to stay with it! You need a plan for staying in front of the customer and guiding them in an organized way. In addition, is it possible the way you organize your sales process might allow you to speed this up and close the sale on the 3rd of 4th contact on average? This will enable your sales process to actually turn into a competitive advantage!

I have a lot of information and experience with sales processes and implementing those in my companies. From that experience, I can tell you this: it is vital to your sales success that you spend time understanding what your sales team is doing. Further, it is important to make sure they are following the process you have agreed to use within your company. If you hire reps whom are formally process trained, this will help you because they will understand the value of what you are doing. You should develop your own sales process training and certification program for onboarding and ongoing sales training. You should also make sure that your CRM has the sales process integrated into how you pursue sales opportunities, so that opportunities cannot advance from one stage to the next unless specific boxes are checked and accomplished with the customer first!

Here is an example of a draft sales process:

5 STAGE SALES PROCESS (EXAMPLE)

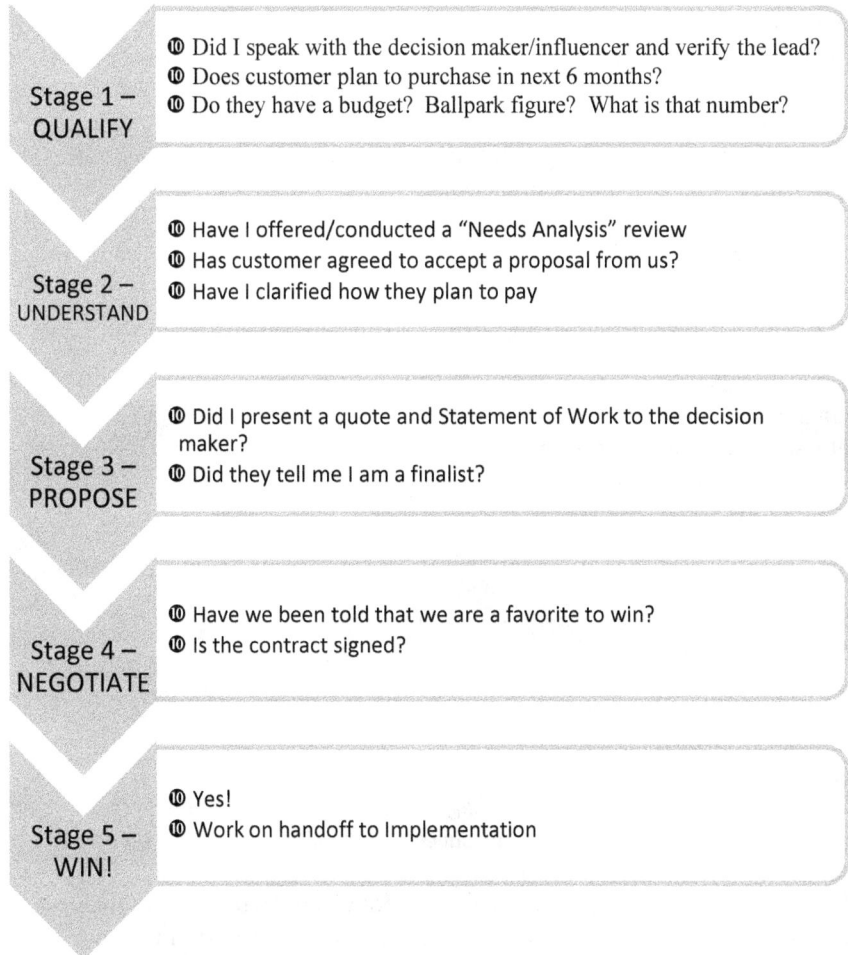

Stage 1 – QUALIFY
- Did I speak with the decision maker/influencer and verify the lead?
- Does customer plan to purchase in next 6 months?
- Do they have a budget? Ballpark figure? What is that number?

Stage 2 – UNDERSTAND
- Have I offered/conducted a "Needs Analysis" review
- Has customer agreed to accept a proposal from us?
- Have I clarified how they plan to pay

Stage 3 – PROPOSE
- Did I present a quote and Statement of Work to the decision maker?
- Did they tell me I am a finalist?

Stage 4 – NEGOTIATE
- Have we been told that we are a favorite to win?
- Is the contract signed?

Stage 5 – WIN!
- Yes!
- Work on handoff to Implementation

Once you check those boxes off, you can move the opportunity to the next stage

Start by drafting something like this with your sales team. Implement this sales process formally into your CRM and manage it. Of course, you can get more complex and more refined in your approach, but the main point about sale process is that you have to define yours, train your associates to use it, and be disciplined in your commitment to stay with it!

Organizing your sales team is about getting the right people in the right roles, but it is also about formally training them. This training program should be developed and viewed with prestige. You should certify your sales team like your HR person is certified for SHRM or your finance person is certified as a CPA. Those people are proud of their certifications – your sales person should be too. Certifying your sales team to your company standards will give them a key skill set that will improve their careers, success, and income, and it will ultimately have a positive impact on the company and its customers!

MOTIVATING THE SALES TEAM!

If organizing the sales team is the science, motivating the sales team is the art! For centuries, leaders have been trying to motivate sales people. This topic has been studied and tested by some of the greatest minds. Many companies have tried a myriad of different techniques and theories to help improve sales performance, yet it can still be very elusive. From my experience and the people I talk to who lead sales organizations, it seems that motivating the sales team can still be a challenge. I am going to give it my best shot in an effort to give you a clear path forward based on my success with sales teams.

ORGANIZING SALES
- Define the sales roles
- Fit the best people in each role
- Train and certify

MOTIVATING SALES

When you think about the most important motivating factors to the sales team, your first inclination is to think that money is the most important motivator. That may be the case. You certainly should take time to put together a win-win compensation plan that can get your reps to the income level they want. Beyond money, what is required to inspire your team? As the leader, where should you focus to fire up this very important team?

A. MOTIVATING SALES – Qualified Leads

If you put resources and money behind getting the reps qualified leads, you will get better sales results and happier reps. Note that the sales team does not want leads – they want *qualified* leads. So how will you setup your resources to get those leads from MQL (Marketing Qualified Leads) to SQO (Sales Qualified Opportunities)? First, the marketing team has the lead and the accountability to generate qualified leads through aggressive and targeted inbound and outbound marketing efforts. Some organizations put in Sales Development Reps (SDRs), who are baby hunters that screen and qualify MQLs and receive bonuses on effective SOQ generation. In small companies, this could be outsourced. Some small companies use their hunters to qualify leads, but this is not really where you want your top hunters spending their time. They need to be out working on active proposals with qualified customers.

ORGANIZING SALES
- Define roles
- Fit the best people in each role
- Train and certify

MOTIVATING SALES
- Qualified Leads

In my companies, we require newly-hired hunter sales reps to bring at least 200 contacts with them and load them into our CRM database so we continue to build that company asset. After we do that, we start to strategize how we can market to the segments of the database. In terms of generating MQLs, the most successful reps do not sit and wait for SQOs. They work with the marketing team to put on targeted webinars, workshops, campaigns, and events. We also ask our reps to get social themselves (inbound marketing) and to develop a strong social profile related to our industry – not just sharing and networking, but positioning themselves as a thought leader in our space. We do not hire new outside hunter sales reps whom have less than 500 LinkedIn connections, for example. The point is that the rep is active in networks and working together with marketing to generate SQOs themselves.

The sales team wants qualified leads. You need to adequately staff and invest in marketing to help make that happen, but the reps are expected to actively assist in helping to generate them!

B. MOTIVATING SALES – More Selling Time

A recent study by *Pace Productivity* suggests a sales rep spends only 23% of their time selling. Administration (21%) order processing (14%) service (13%) and planning (5%) are taking this away from the sales team actually selling! That's 77% of the time they are not selling! The sales rep wants to quote quickly and effectively. They want to have contracts signed rapidly so they can generate commissions,

ORGANIZING SALES
- Define roles
- Fit the best people in each role
- Train and certify

MOTIVATING SALES
- Qualified Leads
- More selling time

but all these other activities, albeit important, are bogging down and frustrating the sales rep. This should be an opportunity and an area of focus for you, as the leader, because not only will it motivate your sales team, it will most likely result in more sales for the company!

If I was you – and remember I was you at one time – there are 3 areas you should focus that I believe will enable you to get your reps more selling time:

1. *Meetings*
2. *Support Resources*
3. *Technology*

Meetings

I focus on eliminating excessive and wasteful meetings within my companies, at least meetings where people are not totally engaged. At one of my companies, I had the whole staff in my first week actively working on their computers during our staff meeting! I stopped the meeting in the first 15 minutes and said, "Why are you all working on your computers?" They were actually doing work! It was a bad habit they had learned to do from their prior leader, and he allowed this to happen. This is disrespectful and non-productive. We stopped it.

I eliminate meetings that do not produce anything. I add meetings that I believe will push us forward. I started "agile meetings." When we talk about managing sales team performance, we have all been part of the 2-hour weekly pipeline reviews that have all the reps locked into a room – most of the time listening to the VP of Sales chastise the worst reps about why their pipeline is so small. So much time is wasted, and it certainly doesn't inspire anyone. I changed this format and focus of pipeline reviews by implementing my agile meetings philosophy, and I even gave them a cool name: War Room meetings. It's a 15-minute meeting once a week with a sales rep, their manager, and me. Only 3 people. Only 15 minutes. We cover two key accounts (that I pick in advance) from their funnel (that I study in advance). If we need a follow-up discussion around a specific topic, we can schedule that. But that is it. You would be surprised what you can learn (and help with) in 15 minutes. Keeping it rapid and focused with an upfront agenda and doing your own upfront research, you can eliminate the long 2-hour pipeline reviews with a room full of reps and give your reps more selling time! This is not only time savings but also cost savings, and at the same time the War Room is very intimate and static-free with only 3 of us, and gives you hands-on, direct interactions with your sales reps. This kind of approach can be adopted in every department!

Support Resources
We have talked about sales support resources throughout this book. Sales engineers and SDRs are two great examples of investments you can make to support the reps and drive more sales. Of course, there are other departments outside of sales that can impact the sales team performance. I'll give you an example. When I first joined one of my companies as the President, I walked around the office the first week and into the sales department, and I asked the sales team what they needed most to be more successful. "Contracts," they told me. "Fix the contract process! It is way too slow, and we are getting a poor reputation with customers!" Can you believe that!? It was not the compensation plan, adding new products, better pricing, etc. It was the contract process! So, we focused on it with a cross-functional team effort, and as a result, we ended up greatly improving that process and helping the sales effort! Wouldn't it have been great if the CFO would have seen this issue in advance and started putting together a team effort to fix it without having to even get the CEO involved?

As a CEO, when you are hiring your CFO and HR Director – two positions that have big impact on sales motivation – you should look for and emphasize that supporting the marketing and sales effort is a priority. If you can get your HR and finance leaders to become sales supporters and sales enablers – instead of being anti-sales, which I have seen in way too many cases – you will unleash an unbelievable increase in selling time for your sales team!

THE GROWTH CUBE™
Unlocking the Growth Potential of Your Company

Technology

Technology aided opportunities go hand-in-hand with processes. With that same contract process team we talked about above, we implemented an electronic e-signature product that dramatically improves turnaround of legal documents between attorneys and customers, significantly reducing sales cycle time late in the funnel! Another example is the certification program we discussed earlier. This program includes significant training on the use of technology: CRM, mobile devices, contracts, quoting, and other customer-facing and customer impacting technology that we want the sales person to learn in order to be effective. These are just two important examples where technology in sales is making a difference. You can find them in your company just by talking to your team. The question you must ask is: how can we utilize technology and/or process changes to streamline and make things more efficient for our sales effort?

One area you should surely focus is on the CRM technology you put in place to support your sales, marketing, and customer service process. Salesforce has 3 different modules for those 3 different applications, and they all leverage the same database. The CRM should show what I call "a 360-degree view of the customer," as mentioned in Chapter 1. This is hard to achieve, but it is an important goal. For example, the help desk should be able to pull up customer information when they are talking to them on the phone or online (chat). Another example are Scopes of Work (SOW) that define how the company will meet the customer expectations. The SOW should be attached to the customer record in the CRM and be utilized by the sales, finance, implementation, and customer success teams responsible for implementing your successful solution! How about a CRM tool that is integrated with marketing campaigns so you know which contacts in your funnel are interacting with your marketing content? These are just a few examples of how an investment in CRM technology can become integral to the success of your sales (and marketing) efforts, and to giving your sales reps more quality selling time instead of hunting through folders and databases for all of this information!

Think about this:

Assume a sales rep spends 23% of their time selling today, and they are generating $1 million a year in sales revenue. I If you were able to double the amount of their selling time by freeing up another 23% of their time, you can double your company revenues!

138

By focusing on these three opportunity areas – meetings, support resources, and technology – you can be on your way to making this happen!

> *"To make your customers raving fans and to get the attention of new customers, your products have to be awesome."*

C. MOTIVATING SALES – Great Products!

The third area you should focus on to motivate the sales team is making sure you have great products and services coming out of your company! There are two aspects to focus on here:

1. Making sure your current products are awesome.
Can you tell me if your customers love your current products? Are they unique in the market? Are you digging into the support calls so you understand the issue areas, and do you have a process with your support team and development team to fix high-priority items?

ORGANIZING SALES
- Define roles
- Fit the best people in each role
- Train and certify

MOTIVATING SALES
- Qualified Leads
- More selling time
- Great products

Remember the Raving Fan Triangle we discussed in Chapter 2? If you do not pay attention to your products, and you have quality issues, your farmer reps are going to be stuck in the bottom of the triangle. You and your reps will find yourselves constantly dealing with unhappy customers due to product quality issues. Your reps will not only be demotivated, but your sales to the current customer base will be stalled until you fix it. You cannot let this happen!

2. Implementing a vibrant new product development process.
You can create a lot of buzz within your sales team, and with prospects and customers, by a continual release of exciting, innovative, and high-quality products. This is an investment area. We will show you how to do this in the next chapter, but it is clear to me that becoming an innovative company that remains successful

at new product development is a competitive advantage. This also ensures your reps remain successful with customers.

Here is an example of the impact we had with innovation at one my companies – direct from a customer!

PRODUCT INNOVATION AT GARY'S COMPANY
DIRECT FROM A CUSTOMER

When I came into my role, Gary's company was widely regarded as one that was not on the cutting edge of new technology and had become stagnant. I found in Gary a kindred spirit, someone who constantly thinks outside the box and is never satisfied with the status quo, wants to understand the business and market he is working in, and is always looking for new services or products to offer. He wants to know his customers, and asks questions until he understands. By listening to the customers, the ones who were actually using the company's products, Gary not only gave customers a sense of empowerment but also took many ideas we gave him and turned them into improvements and enhancements of the products offered.

Gary gets results. By the end of his tenure, Gary's company had developed a new reputation as a cutting-edge technology leader, and their solution is now a model in our market.

So there you have it! Want a more motivated sales team?

1. *Get them qualified leads*
2. *Get them more selling time*
3. *Get them great products*

The converse is also true. You can demotivate the team (and I have seen it) by doing the opposite of these things: not getting them qualified leads, taking up their selling time with non-selling activity, and delivering low-quality products to the market.

SALES ANALYTICS

All of this effort that we have taken as leaders to organize and motivate the sales team is very important, but it is also is very costly. It is a major company investment that we want results from. The results we are achieving in winning new business can be tracked. Based on my experience in growing sales, here are the top metrics you should be focusing on:

ORGANIZING SALES
- Define roles
- Fit the best people in each role
- Train and certify

MOTIVATING SALES
- Qualified Leads
- More selling time
- Great Products

New Customers Won versus Prior Periods ($ and #)

The goal is to win new customers. Are you improving your new customer wins each month when compared to prior periods? I like the number of customer # measure better than the customer $ measure because the quantity of wins tells you the depth of your success, but they are both important, because you want to win large customers also.

Sales Pipeline

We should be tracking total pipeline value, along with the value of each stage of the pipe. The pipeline versus quota x-factor is also important to track. If you have a longer sales cycle, your pipe will need to be larger than those who have a short sales cycle. Calculate the amount of time each SQO takes in each stage to determine your sales cycle. Based on my experience, most company's average a pipeline that is 5x the quota target, but it can change depending upon the product and the industry.

Average Contract Value (ACV)

Your top reps should be going after the larger deals. What is your ACV. It is going to be different for new versus add-on versus renewal, so please cut it this way before analyzing. Another area to investigate is how the average sale price (actual) compares to the list price.

Customer Acquisition Cost (CAC)

The CAC Ratio tells you the amount of money it is taking you in marketing and sales investment compared to the profit you are generating from sales. You could

be closing business, but are you doing this efficiently? Another way to look at this is sales closed per rep. Is your rep force able to close more business year over year with the same resources? If they are, it's a clear sign that they are getting better, smarter, and training is paying off!

The 6 Cs of SaaS

For "Software as a Service (SaaS) businesses, or really any recurring revenue business, I like Bessemer's 6 Cs of SaaS as a good summary of that business and how it is performing. Put these 6 metrics in place:

1. Committed Monthly Recurring Revenue (CMRR).
2. Cash Flow
3. CMRR Pipeline (CPipe). A SaaS version of our sales pipeline noted above.
4. Churn (Customers). We talked about this in chapter 2.
5. Customer Acquisition Cost (CAC). Mentioned above.
6. Customer Life Time Value (CLTV). Because a recurring business spreads the revenue over multiple years, the life-time value is similar to Average Contract Value mentioned above.

3-Step Sales Research Technique.

Some of your metrics will not be calculations but rather learnings you find through research. Here is a simple research test you should try when you first start with a company, and then annually thereafter:

1. Select 5 new customers won over the last 12 months.
2. For each, follow it through the CRM from the lead source, through the interactions, the sales stages, all the way to close.
3. Talk with the sales team to see what they felt worked.

What are your top learnings?

Now do the same analysis on 5 lost customers!

KICKING OFF THE YEAR

Let's assume you now have your marketing and sales strategy and plan defined. You are getting ready to lay out and communicate plans for the coming year. If you want to hit the annual plan, it starts in the first month of the first quarter!

As you think about rolling out your new ideas, and combining those with current programs and processes already in place, I want you to envision two roads coming from different locations merging together into two lanes going in the same direction. At the merging of the lanes, there is a slowing down, an awareness, and then an acceleration as the two lanes move on together toward their common destination. This is what Q1 should feel like in your business. One lane is your current business momentum, the current programs, the current focus, and the current pace of your business. The other lane is your new ideas, your new products, and your new initiatives. Being able to work these into your existing business is crucial.

I believe there are two actions you can take in that first month of the year to build momentum in your business and give you the best chance for an awesome annual performance.

Action #1. Focus on Q1 Sales Performance
Have you ever studied the 100-meter dash and why people win? Many sports science experts will tell you that the race is won or lost at the start and how effectively the runner gets out of the blocks.

Your business is the same way. For most businesses, and certainly for businesses with recurring revenue, Q1 is the most important quarter to hit. If you miss quote on Q1, it can be very difficult to catch up in the next 3 quarters. If that's the case, does your sales team have their annual and Q1 goals in January, including their new commission plan? Do they know how they will be compensated? If not, you need to move on this. Get the compensation plans and quota goals (by product) in place in January so the sales team can get moving and going after it!

Mike Tomlin, the Pittsburgh Steelers' coach, lost in the 2017 AFC Championship game. In the post-game interview, he said, "We will re-assess, it is never a continuation." Well that is true in football where they have seasons. But in business, it *is* a continuation. Your business performance never stops. It is full-go year-round! So, in January you do have to continue to drive your pipeline and your opportunities and keep your sales team focused on performance! It is not a time to sit back and relax and enjoy the fruits of last year. Relaxing means you will get caught playing catch up the whole year, which is not fun for the CEO or the associates!

Action #2. Conduct an Awesome Kickoff Meeting
If you have not had a kickoff meeting yet, schedule one for this coming January. It does not have to be a long, drawn-out event. You also do not have to be a big company to do a kickoff meeting. It could be the CEO and the marketing and sales team. If you can include other departments at least for part of the meeting, that

would be smart too because it is a teambuilding opportunity to get everyone working together toward the annual goals.

I recently helped one of my customers kickoff the year by planning and facilitating their annual kickoff meeting. We had a lot of interaction with the sales team and the execs about markets, the competition, and current activity. We reviewed our quota for the year in the core business and what we wanted to do specifically to achieve those goals and improve our performance. We also talked about the hurdles facing us, and the biggest challenges to the business. All of this leads to focusing on the areas that are most important.

> *"The kickoff meeting is more than just a meeting. It's a teambuilding, strategy-focusing, momentum-building experience."*

If you are planning a kickoff meeting, make sure to plan for these topics:

- Recognition of accomplishments from the past year
- Strategies for the coming year
- New products that will be launched this year and associated development plans
- Orders quota / targets by product
- Pipeline analysis (sales team)
- Have a "Call for Orders." This supports **Action #1** and hitting Q1 sales. It's also about keeping momentum going through the new year and into Q1.

Have a theme – where are you going?
Every New Year's Day while everyone was watching football games, I would personally walk around the office and leave a bookmark on every associate's desk with a message from me. The bookmarks would include our theme for the coming year. It was a symbol of where we were going – a commitment to a strategy for the coming year. It emphasized how important the associates were going to be in making it happen! Our associates seemed to love this.

What about the extra work?
Adding new initiatives is going to increase your workload, and you may feel maxed out already! The key is to figure out a way to be efficient and focus short-term on

Q1 results while at the same time planning for the future and positioning yourself in the market.

Have you ever done a spinning class? The idea of the instructor is to get you pedaling fast while you are standing upright, and then sit you down (where it will be harder), and have you maintain the same cycle speed. You can take the same approach. By leading your team through an awesome kickoff experience, one that is short but motivating to your people, you will get everyone into that faster business pace and a new momentum. You will be able to maintain that pace because you have clarified everything more clearly with your team. They will know what is important and what is not. There will be a synergy effect that the kickoff planning and events will have on the entire team focus and energy toward the goals!

> *"No resource is more important in an organization*
> *than a high-performance team."*
> —*Phil Bryson*

Did you see the New England Patriots take apart the Pittsburgh Steelers in the 2017 AFC championship football game? The key to the victory was in Quarter 1. New England came out of the gates and scored on their first possession, and then just kept building and adding on to their lead from there to the point that the Steelers just eventually threw their hands up and knew it was over. It shows that the start is vital, and that momentum is a powerful force!

Your annual kickoff meeting, the events that surround it, and your sales team's ability to hit their Q1 plan, is all about building momentum and excitement so that you can take your business all the way to the top in the coming year!

DIMENSION 3 WRAP UP – WINNING NEW CUSTOMERS

We started the chapter by talking about building your company strategy and moved into marketing, then sales, and we have covered a lot of ground. The bottom line is that if you build a great plan for your company and implement it effectively through a team effort, you will win new customers and see your sales growth increase and be on your way to solving the challenge of the 3rd dimension of The Growth Cube – *Winning New Customers*!

We have now built our **Marketing and Sales Strategy Roadmap** together! If you want a complete copy of the Roadmap, please download a copy from: www.thegrowthcube.com/resources

We have now learned 3 of the 6 dimensions of The Growth Cube, and we are starting to slowly unlock the growth potential of our company more clearly!

It starts with our commitment to creating a company with raving associates, who will build a customer base of raving fans. Those raving associates and raving fans are key to getting new customers to notice you, and to go with you.

We have given you tools so far that you can use to make this happen!

In Dimension 1 – *Creating Raving Associates* – you learned about the Inverted Pyramid philosophy and the CHEER process that provides the glue to keep your team inspired. We have laid out the Level 3 Certification Program that not only trains the sales team but everyone in your company, and positions you as a thought leader in your space.

In Dimension 2 – *Creating Raving Fans* – you learned about the 5-Step Customer Touchpoint Plan and how that can help you optimize the experience when your customer touches your company. We treated you to the 6-Stage Raving Fan Triangle program, which will guide you in building closer, long-term customer relationships. We have also outlined for you the 6 windows to growth with your current customers that, if done well, will put you on the way to doubling the size of your company!

When the customer loves your current product, they will look forward to your next product. This will pave the way for upsells and add-ons, but these are *earned* because of the resource you have become for your customer.

Now in Dimension 3 – *Winning New Customers* – you learned that by using a Point A/Point B approach and The Growth Cube 6, you can easily create a Growth Cube Report and strategic plan for your company, and then follow that with a marketing and sales plan built around the 5 Customer Touchpoints and the Big 4 Assets of Marketing. We gave you the marketing model framework that can help you build a program in your company to generate SQOs. We showed you the detailed steps for building your own Marketing and Sales Strategy Roadmap! Also, we mentioned that above all else, the most important marketing question a CEO should ask is: "When my customer experiences my product or service, do they love it?"

We have provided you with key marketing and sales analytics that will help you make sure you know that you are getting the results from your marketing and sales investment. We took you through how to organize and motivate your sales team – what I call the "art and the science of leading sales." And of course, we learned that if you can free up 23% of your sales reps' time, you can double your company sales.

Remember we have also learned that the sides of The Growth Cube are dependent on each other. If we fail at one of the dimensions, it can cause other dimensions to fall along with it. Do you agree with me now that:

Your success at creating raving fans is directly related to your success at creating raving associates.

To succeed as a business in the long-term, the pre-requisite for winning new customers is to have current customers who are raving fans.

What we have started to also unveil already, and we are going to cover now in much more detail in the next chapter is this:

Your products have to be awesome if you want to win new customers and keep the ones we have.

Successfully executing just the things we covered so far would be amazing for you. and I am confident would help you to hit some new and potentially record growth levels! However, we cannot stop there. To unlock the true growth potential of your company, being able to innovate and build new products – even build completely new startup businesses – is vital. Creating products that your customers love and your prospects will yearn for is exciting and can set you on the growth track you desired and dreamed about when you started as CEO!

So how do we make innovation happen in our company? Let's move on to the 4th dimension of The Growth Cube – *Launching New Products and Startups* – and find out!

CHAPTER 4 – LAUNCHING NEW PRODUCTS AND STARTUPS. The Cars on the Road™.

"Don't find customers for your products; find products for your customers."
—Seth Godin

As great as Microsoft was in their climb to the top of the PC software market, it put itself at great risk by not executing on new product opportunities like smartphones, tablets, e-books, and web TV. They stuck solely to their core business and did not execute on commercializing new technologies. As a result, their competitors have eaten away at their cash cow business.

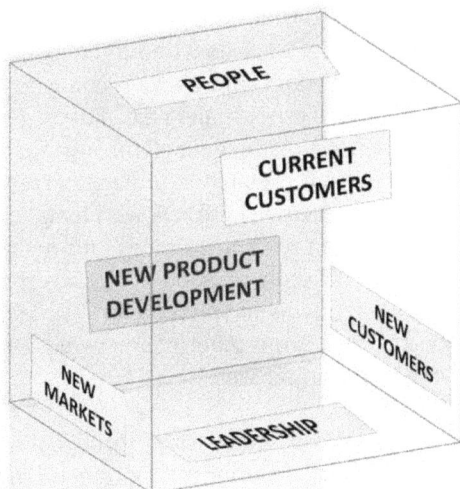

In your business, do you think that your competitors are feverishly working to get new products to your customers and move ahead of you? Yes, they are! Some of those competitors are bigger than you and have more resources than you. You have a responsibility as the CEO to stay ahead with innovation and speed and nimbleness. I am convinced that you *can* stay ahead if you and your team take time to focus on the vital Dimension 4 of The Growth Cube – New Product Development.

I want to help you develop a roadmap to innovation and win with new products by learning from the steps I have taken! In my four CEO roles prior to my startup businesses, we successfully launched **62** new products and **4** completely new business units! I have also started up 3 new businesses in the last 3 years. I am now coaching companies to help them succeed at these very important skills. I am going to share with you what I have learned about innovating – the good and the bad – and how we have specifically succeeded!

First, keep in mind that there are many routes to new product success that that you should evaluate for your company:

- Evolution of your current products
- Completely new products
- Products you gain through acquisitions
- Startup businesses

All of these are opportunities. Keep in mind, though, they are also very costly, so you must prioritize. There is major cost involved in developing just one new product – most likely at least hundreds of thousands of dollars. I see people who still develop these products without understanding if the customer even wants them! I just recently met with a CEO friend who asked for my help. He had developed a new software product and he could not get any customers to get excited about his product. He already spent all the money to develop this application, yet he did not do the upfront research to understand what the customer really needed. Now he cannot get customers to talk with him. As CEOs, we all vow to never let this happen, and then somehow it does. It's not a knowledge issue. It's a pressure issue. Pressure makes us respond differently than we know we should. Unfortunately, when we let this happen, it not only wastes money, but we take company resources away from other opportunities, thus adding an invisible opportunity cost to the company as well.

We have already emphasized throughout The Growth Cube that focusing on your customer is of the utmost importance. That applies here as well. To succeed with new products and innovation, it is critical that we understand our customer's products, markets, and strategic direction. Only then can we truly help them. Do you know specifically what your customer is trying to accomplish in their markets? This answer is crucial to the success of our new product investment. If you are finding that you are not aware or not part of strategy conversations with customers, then you really should challenge your staff. It's not just the sales team's fault. To achieve the results for your business, you really need your whole team to be innovating for your customer and bringing them new solutions that will make *their business* successful! If you make it important and add people to your team who share this customer-focused philosophy, your leadership team will learn what products and services it will take to make your customers raving fans. As a result, your company will be able to grow successfully!

150

*"Get so close to your Customers that you tell them what they
need well before they realize it themselves!"*
–Steve Jobs

If you are having issues today, and it really does tie to a few important metrics that can tell you, then you have to take a fresh look at your innovation and new product development efforts. From my experience, companies who are struggling with innovation are stumbling in 4 areas. These 4 major new product development hurdles are something your board and your investors expect you to address and overcome:

1. *Strategy disconnect*
2. *Weak innovation culture*
3. *Lack of development process discipline*
4. *Short on skills (design, development, product)*

I am going to share with you the 3 strategies you can implement to address these issues today:

1. Establish Your Product Strategy

In Chapter 3, we talked about the need to develop the overall company strategy before you implement the marketing and sales strategy. The same is true here. Take that same company strategy and use it this time to guide your product strategy!

First, remember the link between culture and strategy that we discussed in Chapter 1: if you want to affect your culture, start with your strategy. Let's apply this to our product strategy and our ability to get our teams fired up about our product direction. What problems are you helping your customers solve with your products? Is it exciting and meaningful to your product development team? Where is your customer's business headed? Do you understand it, and can you help them with awesome products and services that will position them for success?

Do you have a product line strategy defined yet? The overarching product strategy should cover all your product lines and should define the product solutions you currently provide and want to provide in the future. Assign a leader for each product – a product champion. Work your product champions and others on your team with the goal of defining your product strategy for each product line,

including financial growth plans with annual orders, revenue, and profit targets for each product line.

Once you define your product strategy, you will have a roadmap for developing the right products in the right niche. By the end of this chapter, you will be on your way to laying out your product roadmap!

2. Develop an Innovation Culture

As we sit here today, Apple continues to be a model of how to innovate new products. In recent years, the iPod, iPad, iPhone, and iWatch have all revolutionized their markets. Products like the iWatch are a prestige item. No other competitor had anything quite as intuitive for years, and even now, the iWatch far surpasses other copycat smartwatches. Although Apple may have peaked under Tim Cook now, there is no doubt they have been special to this point. According to a *Morgan Stanley Research* study, Apple has a 90% brand retention rate, significantly higher than its competitors. What is it that has made Apple so dominant in their industry?

To me, it is in large part because Apple has built a culture that includes an unmatched intrigue and interest in their customer and how they can develop cool products to help them.

> *"You need a very product-oriented culture. Lots of companies have great engineers and smart people. There needs to be some gravitational force that pulls it all together."*
> *–Steve Jobs*

Those of you in a smaller business may be thinking, "How can I do what Apple does?" Trust me when I say that you can.

It all starts with you and how you lead. You have to get personally involved in product development. You have to push for speed and get personally involved and hands-on in all of the key elements of new product success that we are covering in this chapter! Build a team atmosphere and get people involved with you and drive your execution process to get your products out the door effectively and fast!

If you feel you are a strong innovator today, what results are you getting? Can you improve?

In Chapter 2, we talked about the book by the former CEO of Intel called *Only the Paranoid Survive*. You have to be paranoid that someone is going to catch you. That someone is going to create something that your customers are going to love more than you. Never be satisfied. Your customers want you to think like this. I know because my customers have told me this! Don't let your team get complacent either. You should be strategizing with your team on how you can become even better! You should consistently reinforce and emphasize the importance of the product as a key aspect of your company growth. In fact, it may be THE most important aspect of your growth potential!

In a 2016 *Harvard Business Review* survey of 3,500 people from companies in the U.S., Canada, the UK, Germany, and India, they found that most employees say innovation is everybody's responsibility. However, the survey revealed that only 60% of employees say they are actually involved in their company innovation. The problem is that most employees believe that management does not inspire them to do great work – or give them the opportunity to do so! This cannot happen in your company.

I believe that innovation does affect everyone in the company, and that everyone in the company wants to be involved in the excitement and in the success of a major new product. Some CEOs may mistakenly leave innovation to the CTO or VP Product Management, but even a strong CTO can have a difficult time without support from the rest of the company. If we can all work together – led by the CEO, the CTO, the CMO – we can deliver exciting new products to the market and make our people feel like they are part of it!

As the leader, you need to inspire innovation through your own involvement and excitement, and by creating opportunities for your team to do "out of the box" thinking. At one of my companies, I worked with the CTO to hold monthly iteration reviews where we actually watched products being built before our eyes as developers stood up in front of all facets of the company and talked about their products and the progress they were making every 4 weeks.

I also like the idea of annual Hackathons – a competition among development teams to create something unique, different and new. But they only have 3 days to do it! Developers are freed up for 3 days to work on the project of their choosing. Their bosses have to handle their workload. A lot of great products

come out of this, and it is a lot of fun! I get personally involved throughout the competition and am one of the final round judges!

The point is to show your enthusiasm by visibly supporting the leaders (at any level) in your company who are excited and passionate about innovating with your customers.

You have to push innovation across every department. When I first joined one of my companies, the development updates were only iterated within the development department. How do you inspire innovation if it is being contained only in one department? We were launching products out of development and marketing was not aware. When the product finished, we had no plan to promote it! The finance team wasn't aware so they could not track the product performance separately. The implementation and support teams were not aware either, so when the customer finally ordered, we were scrambling trying to spread knowledge. This is why we open up communication during the planning and pre-launch by building awareness and communication across the company.

Overall, all of my companies have been known for launching awesome new products – it is one of our team's hallmarks for sure! Part of that is building a team that believes and has skills in new product development and startups. Part of it is also having the right CTOs and CMOs who display vision and drive. CTOs and CMOs (in a small company this could be the CEO) who know where they wanted to take our product line has made all the difference. They take time to understand our customers and want to become thought-leaders in our industry. You work through difficult moments together at times, but it's because you are both passionate, and because I champion what they and their team do, we find a way to make things happen successfully. Sometimes there is a disconnect between the CEO-driven business strategy and the products being developed in the company technical ranks. I have personally led monthly company-wide development meetings in all my companies. By staying involved, focusing on the customer, and developing relationships, you do not let this happen!

In the end, your customers want innovative products and services from your company. They need something that is going to help their business. You have to figure out a way to get this accomplished in a team-oriented manner. Remember, your goal is not to provide a product to your customer, but to help your customer win in their markets by utilizing your solutions. Start spending time, effort, and energy on these areas with your staff, and devoting your personal time as the

154

leader toward innovation. Your people will follow your lead and genuinely want to create products that help your customers!

So which products do we build then? Well, it starts with generating ideas from the people who know best.

Generating Ideas!
Once you have defined your overall product strategy, communicate it to your associates and ask for their ideas! I am not sure why more companies do not do this, but your associates would love it if you simply asked them for their ideas!

As part of our annual planning, we send a very short and easy electronic survey to all our associates, asking them for new product ideas, what they feel our company product priorities should be for the coming year, and what products we currently have that are not getting the attention they deserve. We ask them which products have the most potential, which products need more investment, and which should be scrapped. It is amazing to see the honest and helpful feedback your people will give you! By involving your team, you now have a solid group of associates who will help you implement the very best ideas. I find that they love to be involved in the process, and their feedback can be dialed back in to refine your product strategy!

3. Leading Operations. The Cars on the Road New Product Development Process
Let's say you are currently doing a great job generating enthusiasm around your new products. You have talked with your customers, partners, and associates about new product ideas, and they are excited to offer input. They are hopeful you will make their suggestion a reality. Now you are getting inundated with all the ideas! Many companies fail right here. They do not execute on the ideas! Not only do they miss business growth opportunities, but they demotivate the person with the original idea (the originator). We know this is not acceptable.

Imagine a very busy multi-lane highway with a lot of cars moving. Some cars are moving fast, some cars are moving slow. Sometimes there are no cars on the road, and sometimes it is so congested nothing moves. This highway represents your new product development. The cars are the ideas that you want to launch. How effectively and efficiently you can move these cars to their destination while bringing other new cars onto the highway will determine your success at launching new products!

We have the process to help you!

I am going to share with you my process that led to the launch of 30 major new products at one of my companies! It's called "The Cars on the Road." We created The Cars on the Road process to manage and launch new products more effectively. It has worked in real companies! It is tested and proven!

FEEDBACK FROM ONE OF GARY'S CUSTOMERS:

"...I continued to gain experience with Gary's company, its products, and employees, watching it change from a staid old provider, into a newly incarnated leader in their technology field. I observed as they developed and delivered new products and services, expanded into new business and increased their reach and reputation in the field. As I gained insight and familiarity with the other executives, managers and employees, and had many private discussions, it has been clear that the organization is well led..."

The process starts by screening your ideas. Ideas can be anything from add-ons to current products, to starting up completely new businesses – including startups. We screen ideas for many things, but the cornerstone concepts are: is there a large market opportunity and does it fit within our product strategy? We are probably not going to build robots for the home if we are a company that is in the business of servicing electric power plants.

As we take you through our process, I want you to remember one key concept: think speed. Google has said that the most important development skill they have is speed. And I agree!

The Business Opportunity Summary (BOS)

We created the Business Opportunity Summary (BOS) to swiftly organize the ideas coming at us. The BOS is one page in length and de-

Ideas > BOS (screen) > Develop best ideas

signed to be a simple and fast way to initially explain the idea and the potential opportunity. It is not supposed to be a business plan. We are looking for a high-level screen and whether we want to put any more planning resources into evaluating it beyond the one page.

Although the BOS is self-explanatory and straightforward, it is implementing the BOS *process* that you might find most challenging. You must be very disciplined and committed. Here are some points of emphasis for you to remember:

Respond within 24 Hours
When an idea is originated, the CEO assigns someone from the product and/or marketing team to take the lead. We respond back to the originator of the idea **within 24 hours** of receiving their idea. The message is, "We have received your idea, and thank you for your input." The originator will be impressed to get a contact within 24 hours! The originator feels heard, that their idea is going to be fully considered, and will be more encouraged to give us more ideas in the future!

Start Building the Product Launch Team Early
The originator must help us complete the BOS (shows commitment), and someone from marketing or product management helps them complete it by making sure new products synch with our product line strategy). Also, it means the originator becomes part of the launch team. It does not matter what position or level they are! You have to count on your team when it comes to the specific product ideas and acting on them.

Look at the sample BOS below. You will see that the information required is straightforward and it can be a simple automated form. The key is not the format – but getting it done! *The BOS needs to be completed within 30 days of idea generation – make sure your leaders commit to this goal.* We track this as a KPI (Key Performance Indicator). This sounds like a long time, but it will go by quickly! We are looking for speed here! Move it along. Make it happen! Think speed!

BUSINESS OPPORTUNITY SUMMARY (BOS)

Project:	**Name of New Idea**
Submitted on:	(date here)

Product Suggestion:
Fill in a short summary of the new product idea here.

Background Information:
Fill in a short background here on why the customers need this product and how it takes advantage of industry / market trends. Also, what is the fit with our current technology skill.

Competition:
Fill in a short list of competitors and differences between them and us, and the uniqueness of our idea.

Projections and Costs:

As best as you can, estimate the revenues, costs and ROI over the next 3 years.

Assumptions:

List assumptions used to arrive at these numbers.

Recommendation / Next Step:

__ Approved (become active Car on the Road)   Reason:
__ Not Approved *at this time* (moved to Unfunded)   Reason:
__ Not Approved (move to Dead)   Reason:

Product Manager	**Date**	**Originator**	**Date**

Marketing Manager	**Date**	**President / CEO**	**Date**

Prioritize Across 3 Product Success Factors

Your best product opportunities will be one where the customer need is high for your unique idea, where your company technology expertise fits, and where you can capitalize on the positive growth trends in an industry market sector.

If you focus only on your product or only on the customer need, and do not know the industry and market trends, you could spend a lot of money and miss the mark. If you focus too much on what the customer wants, the customer may not be an expert in your technology and may only understand it on a limited horizon.

For example, look at the convenient store (C-Store) industry. The C-Store has an interest in getting you inside the store through promotions outside, and once you get inside, the focus is to entice you through packages and promotions. The idea is to have you purchase items you traditionally would not have purchased. For example, many of these stores are offering fresh sandwiches that many of us would be interested in for breakfast or lunch. C-Store technology vendors that can provide analytics on customer demographics and buying behavior can help C-Store leaders determine which products they should be stocking and how to track if the inventory is moving. This is an example of capitalizing on all 3 product success factors!

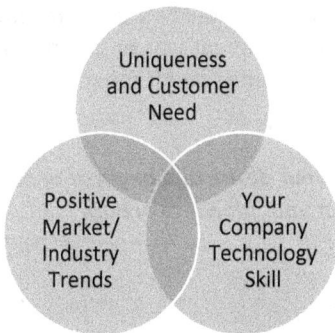

By evaluating all 3 product success factors together – the customer need for your unique idea, the fit of the idea with your technology skills as a company, and the market trend growth – you give your company the best chance for developing a road map that is going to lead to success!

The BOS process can also be used for startup businesses. We want to understand the same concepts initially.

Recommendations, Next Steps, and Sign Off

The input and learnings from your team review of the 3 product success factors will help you to complete the BOS. This is still early in the process, and your information is not totally complete, but this is a screen. Do the best you can in 30

days, and then make a recommendation on suggested strategy and the next steps. The ultimate questions are: should we spend any more time developing this idea? Should this become one of our cars on the road?

To make this commitment official, we ask for sign-offs from the originator, the product manager, and the marketing manager – whoever was assigned this role by the CEO. Not only does this hold them accountable, but it enables you to gain commitment and support for the idea if you decide to put the car on the road.

Finally, the president signs every BOS. If the president and other signatories do not sign-off, no development resources should be allocated to this idea. If you looked at your company, you may be surprised how many products are being developed that you are not even aware of! The sign-off should include a recommendation to continue moving forward with the development (car on the road) or to not approve any further time and resources at this time (car off the road).

> *"Create a definite plan for carrying out your desire and begin at once.*
> *Whether you are ready or not, put your plan into action."*
> *–Napoleon Hill*

Product Line Summary

Ideas that get "BOS'd" are either put on the road or taken off the road. Some cars may be great ideas, but if we do not have funding for them, we move them off the road. Take those cars that you want to put on the road and combine them with your current product direction, and you begin to develop a view that identifies plans, targets, and performance for each product line. Not only can you capture the current state of performance (if there is existing business), but we also capture also what can be done to improve the growth of each product line with new product development.

You can now build a Product Line Summary that looks like this:

BOS AND PRODUCT LINE SUMMARY
Prioritizing New Product Development

	Expected Revenue	Keys to Accomplishing	Investment required (high-level)	3 PRODUCT SUCCESS FACTORS		
				Customer Need - Grade	Industry Trends - Grade	Technology Fit - Grade
PRODUCT LINE A						
Current Product 1						
Current Product 2						
New Product 1 (BOS)						
New Product 2 (BOS)						
PRODUCT LINE B						

This information will help you get the budget you need and align your management team and board around the product direction and related investment and ROI.

You have now properly defined your product line priorities and identified the growth programs for your product line at a high-level. The priority programs have been selected based on the 3 product success factors, revenue growth, and ROI. I call the view: The Product Line Summary

What Cars Are On Your Road?
We have generated new product ideas, evaluated them rapidly through the one-page BOS process, and we know which new products we want to bring to market for each product line. These are the Cars on the Road!

Remember the commercial that asks, "What's in your wallet?" with Samuel L. Jackson. Ask your product manager, *"What cars are on your road?"* They should now be able to tell you!

Some of those cars are actively being planned and launched, while others will come later. It is the active cars that we really want to focus on with resources and pick up the momentum with!

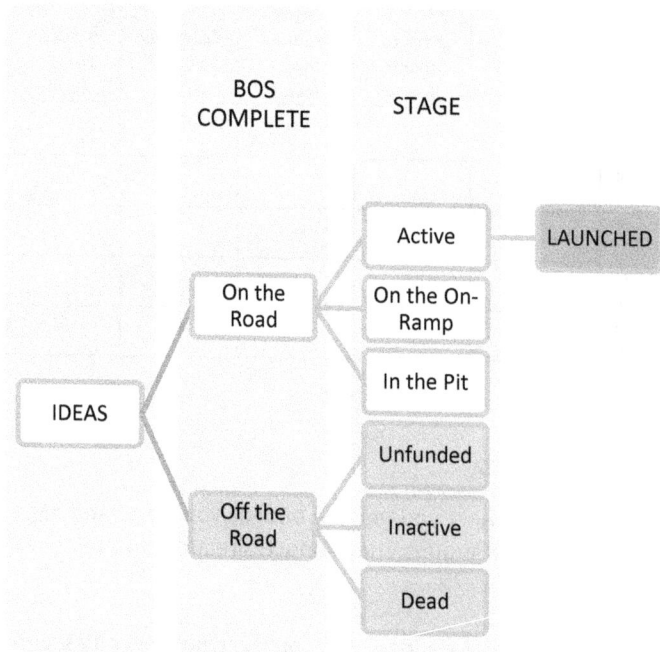

Active Cars – Get Them Launched!
Up to this point, we have basically done a lot of planning and screening. However, when it comes to actually launching that idea, it now becomes much more operational. We have everyone excited that we will launch these target products successfully. But will this happen? Will we execute? This is where many companies falter. But you will not!

The active cars on the road are assigned to a product manager and an operational leader to drive. What are they driving?

Our 10-Step Product Planning Process That Includes Defining:

1. Design document
2. Business case
3. Product development
4. Operational plan
5. Financial plan
6. Transition plan
7. Pricing
8. Billing
9. Contract documents
10. Sales launch

For Startups that clear the BOS stage, we use a modified 12-step Planning and Launch Process:

1. Market opportunity
2. Product idea, technology, and competitive advantage
3. Vision and value proposition
4. Business model
5. Technology stage and time to market
6. Financial stage
7. Commercialization strategy
8. Intellectual property position
9. Management team
10. Project plan
11. Budget
12. Funding opportunities

We operationally drive the completion of our process through what we call **"Speed Week."** Speed Week is a push that involves reviewing all active cars with their respective teams. Product team leaders are brought together to discuss progress, issues, and the next steps. The executive team is actively involved. Although this is a tremendous commitment in time, it also forces us to move things forward and make progress. We try to make it fun, but we also try to make it meaningful and useful to everyone. We use a "parking lot" to park subjects we would talk about some other time, but instead we call it a "retaining wall." Putting unrelated but sometimes important topics on the retaining wall enables us to stay focused on the subject at hand and keep moving the new product forward.

Speed Week is not meant to replace agile development practices within the development team but actually to reinforce and support it. Remember that I am writing this book from a CEO perspective, and how the CEO should be evaluating, leading, building, and growing their company. I totally support the agile development practices that are going on within those teams, and in fact have linked the leadership team into the iteration reviews. It is very unusual and very exciting to walk from a Speed Week meeting down the hall to the product development area and have the developers stand up and show us what they have actually done with the product in the last couple weeks. This is amazing, and you really get to know your technical team as well. They see that you value what they do – and you should! Everyone in the company is invited to these iteration reviews by the developers!

"We should manage the development process as vigorously and enthusiastically as we fight for the ideas we will work on!"

Cars on the On-Ramp
I hope you are seeing through this book how important it is to take a team approach in your company and communicate and involve everyone in what you are trying to accomplish. In regard to specifically launching new products, your team wants to be aware of what is coming down the road, plan for it, and help it be successful. You can create positive spirit and energy within your company by including them early! The leaders from every department can help you launch more effectively, and thus take ownership of the product once it is launched. For this reason, any cars that are approved and on the horizon, we put on the "On-Ramp." These cars are coming down the road next so everyone is aware they are coming!

Cars in the Pit
Sometimes we have issues with the active cars on the road. Something happens that is unexpected, and for some reason, we need to take that car into the pit for the time being. This is different than being taken off the road totally (if it is deemed unfunded, inactive, or dead), which can also happen. The "Cars in the Pit" should not be there long. It is a place for you to put a new product on hold for a *short amount of time*, to get a critical question answered, and then get it back onto the road.

If you want a complete copy of a sample **Cars on the Road™ Report**,
sorted by stage, you can find the download at:
www.thegrowthcube.com/resources

When your team completes this table, you will have a list of all the ideas, status of all the cars on the road, and even more details of those launched.

Once you have your table built, you can have it automatically create a high-level **Produce Road Map** showing your cars. This is part of defining your product strategy, discussed earlier in this chapter. Most product lines will have more than 1 car per year, but check out this simple Road Map to get the idea!

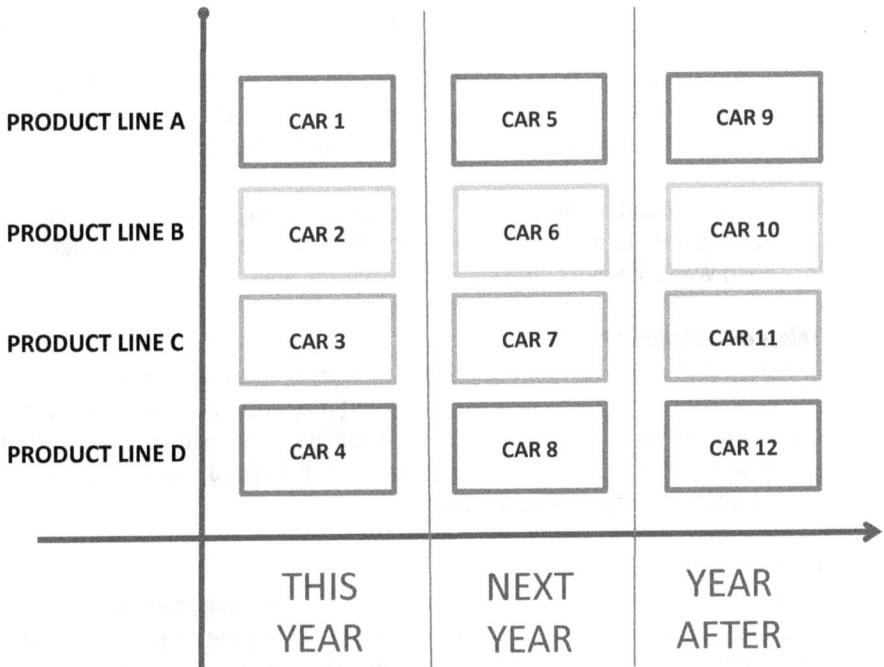

	THIS YEAR	NEXT YEAR	YEAR AFTER
PRODUCT LINE A	CAR 1	CAR 5	CAR 9
PRODUCT LINE B	CAR 2	CAR 6	CAR 10
PRODUCT LINE C	CAR 3	CAR 7	CAR 11
PRODUCT LINE D	CAR 4	CAR 8	CAR 12

Culture and the Cars on the Road
Now that we understand the Cars on the Road process more thoroughly, we can see some direct impacts here that are important for us to build into the innovation culture we discussed earlier in this chapter:

The Importance of Speed

We are covering a lot of ground in this chapter, and as the leader, you need to digest this, and in the end, get new products launched successfully into the market at a regular high-speed rhythm.

I ran into one of my former CFOs and we started talking about our times together, and he told me how he and our former controller were recently laughing (in a good way) about the emphasis we put on speed at our company. In fact, I even implemented a slogan that they still remember from years ago: *"Think Speed."* I wanted our team to have a sense of urgency in everything we did!

Years later, I read the importance of speed as it related to the company in *How Google Works*! Did you know that Google's belief is that the primary objective of any business is to increase the SPEED of product development and the quality of its output? The *primary objective*. Has Google been successful at innovation and new product development? Yes, and they emphasize speed!

We have incorporated the element of speed throughout our concepts, including 24-hour response to new ideas, completing the BOS within 30 days, implementing Speed Week meetings, and more!

This Is a Disciplined Process

Although at first glance it may seem that the cars on the road process is not serious enough to bring into your company, and may appear as taking new product development too lax, this is a very disciplined and focused new product launch process. The difference is that we make it fun and interesting, but it is also structured and execution oriented.

Involve Everyone in the Company

Make it a fun team effort for the whole company. All departments should be involved in generating ideas, evaluating BOS', and helping to plan and launch new products. When I first joined one of my companies, only the development team was involved in new product development. Products were coming out that other departments were not even aware existed. There were products released with no pricing and marketing systems in place at launch. We closed this hole by making the planning process a team effort!

The Goal: Awesome Products!

We already talked about one of our key learnings from The Growth Cube that you need to emphasize with your team:

Your products have to be awesome if you want to
win new customers and keep the ones you have.

We talked about Apple and how they have been leading in their product uniqueness and their brand reputation over the past 2 decades. Look at what they emphasize on their website. They **lead** with their products. It's the first thing they talk about and what they focus on. Why? Because they want to be a company that has awesome products! Without a doubt, it has succeeded so far. Apple hires talented, curious people, and they encourage them to think differently and create unique products!

Do you want awesome products? Then you need to build up your skills in design and development. How do you do that? Hire awesome people with skills, and make sure you have an ongoing training program so your people are always refreshing and learning new skills. If you do this, everyone in your company, all the way up to your board and your customers, will love that you invest here!

"Awesome products are made by awesome people!"

Hold Leaders in Your Company Accountable for Leading New Products to Market

We talked about the BOS process earlier in this chapter. You probably noticed that the BOS is a team effort with the head of development and/or product management head, and the head of marketing along with the originator. These product and marketing leaders should work hard to become experts in our products and the customer's industry, and they should work closely with customers and internal teams to evaluate and launch new ideas. The product manager for each product owns the forecast and should be bonused based on the financial performance of their product line. It's not about activity; it's about results and getting these products to our customers successfully!

The development team, if it is agile in development, can still track development productivity and performance. Do not let them tell you they cannot. We should

167

know the cost we expected in a development project compared to what actually happened. Stories and sprints can be used to calculate this. According to *Scrum Alliance*, Earned Value Management (EVM) is a popular method of measuring project performance, and an agile project manager/Scrum Master should know how to calculate this for better control on a project. It is calculated by comparing the planned amount of work with that actually completed in order to determine whether cost and schedule performance are proceeding per the plans. As the CEO, you should get involved and stay on top of this. In the end, you need to give your development team trust and the room to create, but do not let it become a gray cloud that you do not understand.

We need leadership to facilitate all of this. Product managers, design leaders, development directors all have different titles in different companies. In a small company this could all be the same person – the CEO. With a larger company, the CEO needs someone who is passionate to help on a daily basis in order to drive the cars on the road and help make sure you are launching awesome products!

What Is an Awesome Product?
Well, I talk about developing awesome products all the time. What does this actually mean? Here is my definition, and I will use Apple as an example under each point:

> *"An awesome product has a unique design, simply works, and has excellent customer service behind it."*

1. Cool, Unique Design.
Apple has real skill in design. Their *products are different* than everyone else's products. Their products are cool, sleek, and stylish. All the way to the white cables that still differentiate them to this day. How do you do this for your products? One of the areas I have found recent success is in design research. With a design research project, you actually visit the user of your product in person prior to designing the product. During this visit, the goal is gathering process and user insights and ideas, which are ultimately captured in a visualized process map. There are working sessions with your internal development and design teams to prioritize ideas. For a startup, this can help you define the Minimal Viable Product (MVP) and can also help to gain funding.

"The most important thing in a startup is that you make something! The goal is not investment capital. The goal is a great product!"
—Guy Kawasaki

2. Products that Simply Work

Speaking of something that works, I think you would agree with me – even if you are an Android user – that Apple develops *products that work*. Do you ever hear people complain about the quality of Apple products? Very rarely.

One of the reasons that products work is that those companies employ a strong quality and testing effort. Products that work have been tested and piloted before they are fully launched, where ideas learned can be incorporated, and small issues can be addressed before they become big issues. Although speed is important in the development process, we cannot sacrifice quality for speed!

"Products that work" is not just about fixing bugs. It's also about usability and getting traction. In a subscription software and service contract that can be canceled at any time, you have to get user traction. The same design research team that helped us develop the cool, unique design, can also help with your prototype once it is developed. You can evaluate it with users to capture feedback and to gain traction. We just did this with my startup company, and it works!

3. Extreme Customer Service

According to *Client Heartbeat*, 68% of customers leave a brand because they are dissatisfied with the service. Not the product. Think about all these ecommerce businesses that invest in a great technology product and do not back it with great customer service. There is no way to be profitable if you are losing customers under this model. If you do not retain your customers, you will never recoup the customer acquisition cost (CAC) that we discussed in the last chapter. If your business is built around a subscription model, and you do not keep the customer long enough to get the return on the original investment, then you have lost money on that customer. And because they don't like the service, you lose their business most of the time. This is something you can definitely fix if you focus on it. This shows you that investing time in your service business will pay off for you financially!

Apple has what I call *extreme customer service*. Being extreme means it is set apart from good and even great. It's more than that. Walk into an Apple Store and watch how you are treated and gauge your overall experience. None of their

competitors have this kind of service orientation – a service orientation powered by people that love the products themselves! Think about this for your business and imagine if you had your raving associates excited about your awesome products? See how this all ties together?!

You should look at service as a differentiator for your business! Especially if some of your products are commodities. Did you know that according to *Sage Business Index*, "55% of American business owners believe that customer service plays an increasingly important role in differentiation"? Get on the bandwagon!

I want to emphasize here that when I talk about products throughout this book, many of the concepts apply to service businesses as well. I have a very deep service background, and I coach service CEOs every day. I understand your issues. They are both different and similar to products. One of the areas where things are similar is in development. Development of service products should follow the same process we have outlined in this chapter. There are differences between service development and product development, but the lines between them are blurring as well. Take the software business, where Software as a Service (SaaS) combines a product with hosting and customer service in one package. For intangible services, packaging and productizing the service is very important. Also consider the concept of creating levels of service, which many companies do exceedingly well. The lowest level is of course the "freemium" level, which is free, but if you stay with that version, you typically have a lot of advertising which helps the company finance this free version! The goal is to move them to higher levels of service, a concept we covered with you in Chapter 2.

PILOTING AND GETTING TRACTION WITH YOUR NEW PRODUCT

So you have a new product or service developed but you do not have a pilot implemented yet. Now what? If you completed some design research in advance and talked to enough customers, you have some good indications what the market wants and how you want to validate during the pilot. Here is what you should do to get a pilot going and implemented successfully, and what you should aim for after the pilot to get traction:

Involve current customers:
- Your Customer Advisory Board can be a success catalyst and a valuable resource to build your customer base, but it must be done properly and thoroughly.
- Involved yourself in going out first hand to the market.
- Invest in customer service and keeping your current customers.
- Do a trade show for customers that features all your new products in a trade show format with developers of the product working the booths.
- Come to an agreement with your pilot customers as to what it means to be successful during the pilot. If you hit the goals, your customer should agree to a larger commitment.

As you get ready for market release, train your people on the product:
- Be able to demonstrate expertise early on
- Implement low-cost sales and marketing to drive early customer momentum.

As you are nearing completion of the pilot work on sales tools that:
- Reliably demonstrate ROI.
- Develop a steady flow of relevant content targeted to an expanded audience (IT, marketing, agencies) to demonstrate the breadth of their subject matter leadership.
- Show a validated, competitive, and clearly defined value propositions for each product.

NEW PRODUCT DEVELOPMENT ANALYTICS

At my last two companies, we spent 5% and 16% of revenues respectively on new product development. Of course, new product development means enhancements to existing products, or completely new products, wherever you are expending development resources to plan and launch something new. Most companies are between 2% and 10%. We could debate what this percentage should be for your company, but it is going to vary based on your company's current product portfolio versus competitors and versus what your customers are interested in. How big is the gap? Regardless, I do know this though: you do not want it to be 0%! $0 spent on new product development is a recipe to get ran over. And 2% seems light to me also. If you sit on a cash cow business and are only investing 2% of revenues each year into new product development, then you will be passed up eventually. You will likely spend even more trying to recover later.

To convince your board to invest 5-10% in new product development is probably doable. But rightly so, they will want to see results from that investment. ROI is paramount. With a product, is it leading to revenue? New product development is expensive because it means a lot of people in your company are spending time analyzing, planning, developing, and launching the new products you decide to target on your roadmap. When you break it down and look at the performance of your company's products and get the facts in front of you, some of your products are probably performing well and others are not getting the results you expect. You cannot afford to just throw money away on losing ideas, year after year. To get to the bottom of it, you should dig in and understand why products are failing. Is it market related, or perhaps competitor related?

What if the product you decide to develop completely matches the spec, but the customer never buys it? It is most likely because we did not do our research, and we did not get customer input. It was clearly not the right product.

Another key metric to focus on is the amount of revenues we are generating from products developed in the past 5 years. In one of my companies, we pushed this number to 35%, showing that not only did we launch a lot of products, but we were successful in getting financial results. With subscription based products, it will take you some time to build up the revenue since it is spread over the contract period. However, a healthy target is 33% – that is, target to have one third of your revenues being generated from new products. It is for this reason that I believe I left all of my past companies in great shape; they had new products that were recently launched and already significantly growing revenues. They also exhibited vibrant new product development effort that could launch even more awesome products after I was gone! Always leave the companies you depart in awesome shape and with growth momentum.

Your associates will appreciate the investment you make! The February 2016 *Harvard Business Review* survey we mentioned earlier suggests that fewer than half of those in the lower ranks who have the chance to think through an idea believe they have access to the necessary means to execute it. This means that many of your associates do not think you will invest the money, staff, and support to succeed with the ideas they are offering to you. You cannot let this happen to your innovation culture.

Finally, I will share this with you. If one product line is dragging you down and the others are growing, and your overall growth rate is negative, is that acceptable? One of the jokes among the executive team in a $20B company I know was that "our growth is declining due to mix." This is unacceptable in most cases, yet the executives laughed about it and accepted it. Then they would ask the team to lay people off! We should have strategies to grow EVERY product line. This is not going to cut it with me, and I hope it doesn't cut it with you either.

The bottom line is: we have to get results from our new product development efforts. This is not just for the financial benefits, but for what this means for the future of our company. If you have a great product or service, the customer will want more of everything else you produce! Because of that, you will grow faster than you are today! In fact, there is huge growth potential just within your existing customers base by providing new and better products and value-added services, let alone the broader market opportunity. It starts with building a culture that encourages and involves your people in new product development, and it is backed up by a process and resources that enables your team to build awesome products. If you can generate new product ideas and evaluate them rapidly through the one-page BOS process, and take the active cars on the road successfully to market, you can to take your business all the way to the top!

DIMENSION 4 WRAP UP – LAUNCHING NEW PRODUCTS AND STARTUPS

We started the chapter talking about building our product strategy, and then moved into the Cars on the Road Process. The bottom line is that if you build a great product plan for your company and execute on it successfully, through a team effort, you will launch successful new products that will help grow your business. You will be well on your way to overcoming the challenge of the 4th dimension of The Growth Cube – *Launching New Products*!

We have now built our **Product Strategy Game Plan** together! If you want a complete copy of the Product Strategy Game Plan, please download it from:
www.thegrowthcube.com/resources

We now have learned 4 of the 6 dimensions of The Growth Cube, and we are starting to see more clearly how, as the CEO, we can unlock the growth potential of our company!

It starts with our commitment to creating a company with raving associates, who will build a customer base of raving fans who love our products and services. Those raving associates and raving fans are the key to getting new customers to notice us as a major player in their industry and someone who can help them.

We have given you tools so far that you can use to make this happen!

In Dimension 1 – *Creating Raving Associates* – you learned about the Inverted Pyramid™ philosophy and the CHEER process that provides the glue to keep your team inspired. We have laid out the Level 3 Certification Program that not only trains the sales team but everyone in your company, and thus positions you as a thought leader in your space.

In Dimension 2 – *Creating Raving Fans* – you learned about the 5-Step Customer Touchpoint Plan and how that can help you optimize the experience when your customer touches your company. We treated you to the 6-Stage Raving Fan Triangle program, which will guide you in building closer, long-term customer relationships. We also outlined for you the 6 windows to growth with your current customers, which if done well, will put you on the way to doubling the size of your company! When the customer loves your current product, they will look forward to your next product. This will pave the way for upsells and add-ons, but these are *earned* because of the resource you have become for your customer.

In Dimension 3 – *Winning New Customers* – you learned that by using a Point A/Point B approach and The Growth Cube 6, you can easily create a Growth Cube Report and strategic plan for your company, and then you can follow that with a marketing and sales plan built around the 5 Customer Touchpoints and the Big 4 Assets of Marketing. We gave you marketing model framework that can help you build a program in your company to generate SQOs. We showed you the detailed steps for building your own Marketing and Sales Strategy Roadmap! We mentioned that above all else, the most important marketing question a CEO should ask is, "When my customer experiences my product or service, do they love it?"

We have also provided you with key marketing and sales analytics that will help you make sure you know that you are getting the results from your marketing and sales investment. We took you through how to organize and motivate your sales team – what I call the art and the science of leading sales. Plus, we learned that if you can free up 23% of your sales reps' time, you can double your company sales.

Now in Dimension 4 – *Launching New Products and Startups* – you learned that you should build a product strategy around a great team and a well-thought out product road map. We learned that we should "think speed," involve our associates, and lead the way as the CEO with our vision, enthusiasm, and on-the-ground involvement with customers and associates. We learned exactly what we mean when we say we want "awesome products." and we learned the most important goal of any startup company. We learned that we should manage the development process as vigorously and enthusiastically as we fight for the ideas we will work on. We call this process The Cars on the Road. *What cars are on your road?* We learned what percentage of revenues we should be investing as a company in new product development efforts.

Remember we have also learned that the sides of The Growth Cube are dependent on each other and if we fail at one of the dimensions, it can cause other dimensions to fall along with it. Do you agree with me now that:

Your success at creating raving fans is directly related to your success at creating raving associates.

To succeed as a business in the long-term, the pre-requisite for winning new customers, is to have current customers who are raving fans.

Your products have to be awesome if you want to win new customers and keep the ones we have.

Successfully executing just the first four dimensions of The Growth Cube would be thrilling. It would certainly have us blazing to new growth levels, with a very satisfied customer base, a steady stream of new customers, and products that are exciting to people. However, we know that other markets are out there that could utilize what we offer. To unlock the true growth potential of our business, we need to get to those markets and succeed. Succeeding in new geographies and new verticals is high-risk, but you can do it successfully if you think it through. It can really be exciting to your team if you can do it. This is the growth track you desired and dreamed about when you started as CEO!

So how do you penetrate completely new markets in a very smart way? Let's move on to the 5th dimension of The Growth Cube – *Expanding to New Markets* – and find out!

CHAPTER 5 – EXPANDING TO NEW MARKETS.

"Forget about your competitors, just focus on your customers."
–Jack Ma, Founder Alibaba

You may be getting overwhelmed by now with all the strategies and actions you are considering from the first 4 dimensions of The Growth Cube. As you enter this exciting and challenging chapter on new markets, you might be asking yourself, "Why should I read this chapter now? Why would I pursue new markets when we are still challenged in our core business?" That thought is natural and deserves discussion. If it is a matter of bandwidth and work-load, we can prioritize the strategies that will give us the most impact. If it is a serious core customer issue though, you will have to judge how critical your core business challenge is. Every company addresses satisfaction issues periodically, but if you have systemic and deep issues, you do have to focus there and fix your current customers first (remember the Raving Fan Triangle!). To succeed *in the long run,* we need our current customers to not only be happy, but to rave about us!

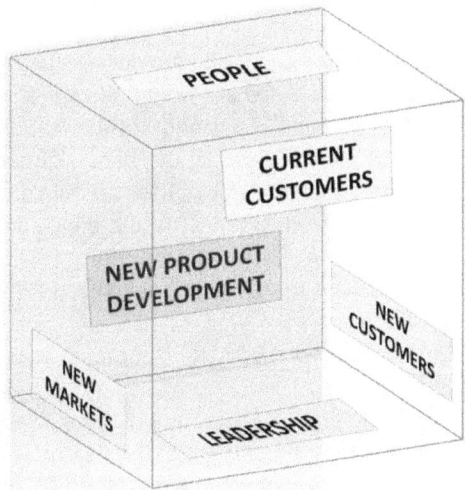

As we have revealed throughout this book, it is our current customers who are the key to unlocking the growth potential of our company, including this 5th dimension of our Growth Cube™ – Expanding to New Markets. This is not only understanding your current customers, their strategy, and their direction, but developing your relationship to the point where they include you in those discussions because they respect you and your team's talent and thought leadership. This will take time. It is a journey of which you will not make the destination overnight. However, as the

leader of a business, you cannot afford to wait too long. You have to make things happen rapidly. You have monthly and quarterly commitments and pressures to perform.

I continue to challenge you because I know that if you want to grow your company and truly unlock your potential, we need to evaluate all 6 dimensions and the associated opportunity. This is the whole point of The Growth Cube concept! Too many leaders only focus on 1 or 2 dimensions of their business at a time, and they may not have analyzed if those 1 or 2 areas are actually the most important.

If you are thinking, "Well, I am successful today, so I do not need to do anything different," then there are many examples of successful companies who did this and got passed up. You cannot let that happen. Vijay Govindarajan, a professor at Dartmouth's Tuck School of Business, sights companies like Motorola, Sony, Sears and Microsoft as examples of successful companies who became complacent and lost their market position. These are big companies with talented and smart people. As a leader of a smaller business, how do you avoid these traps and pitfalls? One of the ways to stay on top is to keep expanding to new adjacent markets.

Govindarajan says successful companies tend to fall into three traps:

1. *The physical trap*, in which big investments in old systems or equipment prevent the pursuit of fresher, more relevant investments.
2. *The psychological trap*, in which company leaders fixate on what made them successful and fail to notice when something new is displacing it.
3. *The strategic trap*, when a company focuses purely on the marketplace of today and fails to anticipate the future.

One of the recent examples of a successful company that fell into a trap was Yahoo. Yahoo was one of the pioneers of the internet, and they were once the most popular website in the U.S. However, it slowly started to decline and no one could stop the fall or shift the company. In July of 2016, Verizon announced its intent to acquire Yahoo's internet business for $4.8 billion. That sounds impressive, except the company was once worth over $100 billion!

Shortly after Marissa Meyer became CEO in 2012, she held her first public conference call to discuss the company's earnings. On that call, she said, "To succeed, we will have to predominantly be a mobile company." She set her goal, and plan, to shift and expand the business to a new market.

In February of 2016, nearly 4 years after that commitment, she admitted that they could not execute successfully on this mission and announced cutting 15% of its workforce and an interest to sell the company. Meyer had made some progress. Mobile revenue had grown to 23% of Yahoo's total revenue, but mainly due to acquisitions that did not deliver profitability. And Yahoo's competitors were moving faster and getting stronger. Facebook's mobile business was running at $18B / year and was 80% of its total business. How many of you have a Facebook app on your phone today? How many of you have a Yahoo app on your phone? Which one won? That's it. Most people feel the move to the mobile market was the correct strategy for Yahoo, and they simply failed in execution. The impact of this miss can be felt by Yahoo associates, their families, and their customers. That's why execution and results are so important.

> *"Strategy without tactics is the slowest route to victory.*
> *Tactics without strategy is the noise before defeat."*
> —*Sun Tzu*
> *The Art of War*

Why is it that market expansion seems to be difficult form of growth for CEOs? This is a question we unravel in this chapter. As we dig into new markets together, and we start generating ideas, we have to remember that it's not just about coming up with the idea or even completing a well-thought out plan. Those plans have to be successfully implemented before that idea produces profitability in your company. Let's first start by simply defining what we mean when we say, "We are going to expand to new markets!"

Expanding to New Markets

First, exactly what do we mean by a new market anyway? Is it a new type of customer; a new vertical? A new channel? Is it a new country or is it a new product? What is it? If we do not define it, how will we plan for it successfully and at a reasonable cost?

In reality, it can be any and all of these examples!

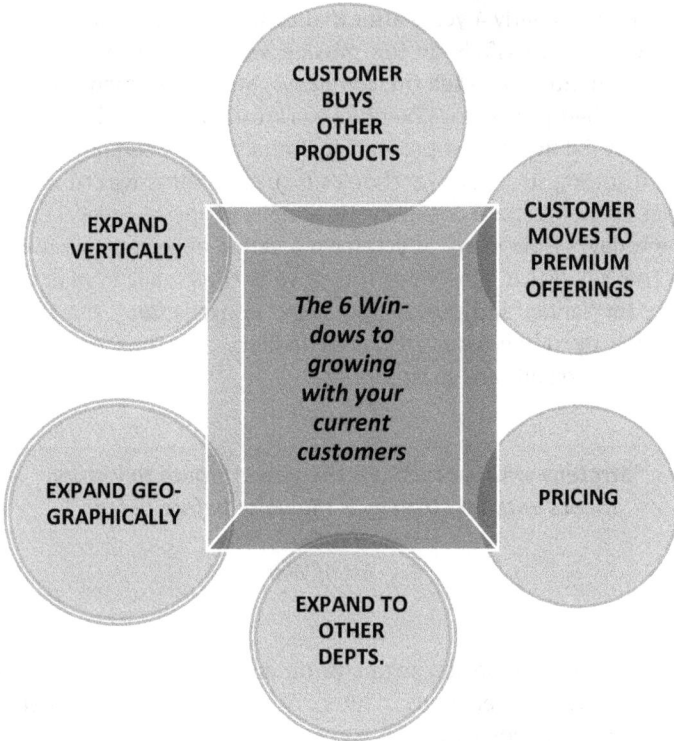

In Chapter 2, we said that your current customers are a natural and often over-looked window into new market growth opportunities. We showed you the diagram on this page to highlight all of the different ways you can grow just with your current customers. Well the 3 bubbles on the lower left-hand side are your new market opportunities! To me, the easiest way to get to these new markets is to start with your current customers and look for the products and services you are already providing to *non-traditional* departments, geographies, and verticals.

An example of *non-traditional* looks like this: you traditionally focus on three verti-cals, and yet you have one implementation in a fourth vertical that you do not traditionally target. Alternatively, you traditionally target the VP of Marketing in your marketing and sales efforts, and for some reason you have an implementation with the Director of HR. I want you to search and find these non-traditional contracts, partnerships, and relationships. Ask yourself, "Can we do this for other customers?"

Let's review the opportunities in these 3 target areas in more detail, and then show you how to attack it effectively.

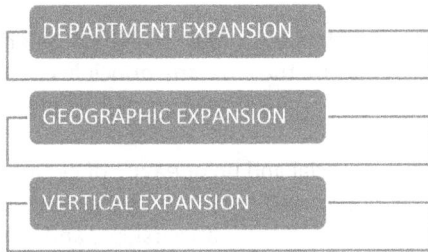

```
┌─ DEPARTMENT EXPANSION ─────────┐
└────────────────────────────────┘

┌─ GEOGRAPHIC EXPANSION ─────────┐
└────────────────────────────────┘

┌─ VERTICAL EXPANSION ───────────┐
└────────────────────────────────┘
```

DEPARTMENT EXPANSION

At this point, you have an installed base of raving fans that would love to give you input and be involved in your desire to expand within their company. You need to remember the Raving Fan Triangle though and make sure they – your core customer – are in good shape from a customer satisfaction standpoint. If so, you can get those customers to introduce you to other colleagues in their company who you might also be able to help. Raving fans will help you gain access to them a lot more efficiently than you could handle on your own.

You many need to strategically move upstream as a company to position yourself for the future – in which case you have to make this happen. While at one of my companies, we were dealing with the head of customer service, and as dynamics changed within the market; customer service was reorganized under the CMO across nearly all of our customer base. The bad news is, we did not know the CMO. We had to get there. The good news is that if we could get there, there were many other CMO-departments that we could provide products and services to expand our relationship! This is not easy to do, but you can see in this example that sometimes you have to move to other departments to continue growing strategically.

GEOGRAPHIC EXPANSION

One of the most natural evolutions of a company is geographic expansion, especially if you can move to other geographies and utilize the same product with minimal changes. In some small companies, it may be another state or city; In medium-sized companies, you may want to expand nationally or even globally. Do not underestimate this – it is not a slam dunk! You will have to take steps that will

help you be successful. If done correctly, this can be a great market expansion opportunity for you. Nearly everyone reading this book probably has an opportunity in their company to grow geographically. You just have not taken the step!

International Expansion

Some of you who are reading this book may not be considering moving into new countries, but even if that may be the case, the principles that I will share will help you succeed in the U.S., and really in any aspects of your life!

International expansion is a special and unique type of geographic growth, and it is usually the most difficult, costly, and risky of all geographic market expansions. I know because I have done acquisitions, partnerships, and run direct operations in the U.S. and abroad, and I have studied other companies who have done this as well. In three different roles, I have initiated successful strategies for global expansion. I led the globalization of the whole service business as President of a $20B global company, and I led a $20M company's successful expansion into Asia and Latin America through new partner programs. I have implemented international technical operations in Asia to build global follow-the-sun 24x7 support. I completely relocated a European HQ from England to Italy. I have experienced this first hand, and I want help you succeed as well!

The list of leading companies you would recognize that have faced and failed in international market expansion challenges is longer than you may think. Great management teams struggle to understand the competitive nuances of each market and do not adjust their growth strategies to match. So why is it that so many companies fail at international market expansion? The short answer: Bad leadership and lack of training of those leaders, terribly handled integrations, poor partner choices, or wrong entry strategies altogether. Sometimes it is simply just weak execution. Many very good companies simply miss the mark on international expansion fundamentals. Here are two examples:

Disney. Great company. However, the brand failed in its European expansion. Disney spent years in analysis and negotiations as well of billions of dollars planning for its Euro-Disney Grand Opening. Unfortunately, their failure to read differences between American and European cultures and spending habits contributed to a poor result.

Starbucks. Another great company. They started closing unprofitable international stores years ago, when the economy got tough. In Australia, they closed all their stores because they were failing. (The new owners were allowed to keep the brand, so if you go there and see it, remember I told you that part!)

TOP 6 TIPS FOR SUCCEEDING IN INTERNATIONAL BUSINESS

Based on many years leading international organizations through challenges on the ground in Europe, Asia, and Latin America, here are my top 6 tips for succeeding at international business!

1. Define Your Global Strategy

This sounds simple, but it is not. It is a challenge to implement a strategic plan across multiple time zones, locations, languages, cultures, practices, customs, and legal environments. A strategy that works in one location may require a different approach in another. Although you need to communicate your global strategy, it needs to be defined more in terms of a framework that can be flexible in each country instead of hard, fast rules that must be followed.

DEPARTMENT EXPANSION

GEOGRAPHIC EXPANSION

- **INTERNATIONAL SUCCESS**
  - **1. Define Global Strategy (Framework)**
  - 2. Be Patient, Build Relationships
  - 3. Go Yourself Into the Markets
  - 4. Build Global Culture in Team
  - 5. Each Country Is Its Own Market
  - 6. Engage with Local Partners

VERTICAL EXPANSION

As an American doing business on the ground in many different countries, I have experienced the difference in culture and how other countries view the U.S. HQ and its plan for success. Some things are not negotiable, like the fact that we have to grow revenues. I had a country manager once (not a front-line associate, so even more surprising!) challenge me in a team meeting about our global strategy to grow the business. He said. 'Gary, why is it important for us to grow?" That is something you might assume country managers in other major countries would want too, but that is an American principle and not every culture thinks like us! The bottom line early on is to gain as much consensus as possible around the global strategy and framework (especially at high levels), and recognize that different country leaders are going to view your ideas differently – even if they are great ideas in your base country!

Your international expansion strategy and the details to make it happen will vary based on: 1. whether you are trying to build a global team out of existing teams and locations; versus 2. if you are expanding your current business into brand new territories and do not have any experience or presence there now. You may be doing both.

If you do aim to build a global company, you are going to have to decide what you keep at HQ and what you allow each geography to control. In other words, what do you centralize and what do you decentralize? Not every function makes sense to centralize, but I believe the customer-facing functions like sales (direct or partner) are vital to have within that local territory since they will have the relationships and the cultural background to best allow you to succeed.

Some companies have decided to centralize functions and at the same time moved them off shore into Asia and other low-cost areas. Most commonly, this is done with functions like customer service, technical support, and development. This can be risky due to the cultural differences and the disconnect from other HQ functions. This can be also deflating if you close an operation, say in the U.S., to do it! This will demoralize your U.S. team. I know because I did it – very reluctantly and very slowly. (It went faster after I left). Why was I reluctant? Because I have actually seen our U.S customers actually hug our U.S. customer service team when they visited our headquarters. They literally hugged them! Is that a raving fan? Pretty close. In fact, at all of my companies our customer service people knew the names of our customer's kids! I am not kidding. Do we realize how close our people are with our customers? Why would we jeopardize a raving fan to save a few dollars when we are already very profitable today?

All of these decisions that I raised, and many more just like it, need to be defined and agreed about with your executive team so that everyone is on the same page. International business expansion can be very rewarding and fun, but it also can be very political and sensitive. Come to an agreement as a team on your strategy upfront if possible; you will have a better chance at succeeding in the long run in your role!

"A strategy by itself will not create change."

2. Be Patient. Build Relationships.

Jordan Spieth won his first major at the 2015 Masters Tournament with a score of 270 (–18), earning him $1.8 million. Spieth tied the 72-hole record set by Tiger Woods in 1997 and became the second youngest player to win the Masters, behind Woods. He was 22. They asked Spieth on Sunday morning, prior to his final round, what he needed to do to win. He said, "I'll just take patience."

Patience. Not great putting. Not a positive attitude. Not staying focused. Not even luck. He wanted patience. That just shows you the value of that quality. Like Spieth, we know that under pressure, people do unexpected things and make unexpected mistakes. Patience will help to you relax and do what you do best.

DEPARTMENT EXPANSION

GEOGRAPHIC EXPANSION

- **INTERNATIONAL SUCCESS**
  - 1. Define Global Strategy (Framework)
  - **2. Be Patient, Build Relationships**
  - 3. Go Yourself Into the Markets
  - 4. Build Global Culture in Team
  - 5. Each Country Is its own Market
  - 6. Engage with Local Partners

VERTICAL EXPANSION

The cultural differences of international business are striking, and you will feel them. It touches your feelings, your emotion. Just like you feel that way, all the people you meet in all the countries you visit feel that way about you too! There are cultural sensitivity and learnings that you must undergo if you are running an international operation, and especially if you are on the ground in that country.

It does not matter if you are partnering, acquiring, or going direct, you must develop relationships when you move into a new market. Yes, even today, we still see U.S. companies send American leaders over on a flight for 5 days and hope their international business will immediately change. They hope that the country operations across the world will see the light and follow the corporate strategy as soon as we send over a respected leader. In most cases, this is driven by unrealistic expectations from the corporate U.S. executive team that, with all due respect, may have very little on-the-ground international experience themselves.

I can remember many meetings being pressured by my U.S. headquarters team about, "why country xyz could not hit the same metrics that we did in the U.S." This is very difficult to accomplish. It can be done, but it takes time. In international expansion, you cannot expect to hit U.S. levels of growth and profitability in year 1.

It takes a good strategy, a good plan, the right team, buy-in from the team, a successful partner, innovative products, etc. If these are not in place, you have to build it. There is a lot of pressure on you and the country manager to manage a lot of things in their country. However, you will never get anything done that sticks if the country manager does not buy in. Build the relationship. I still talk with international associates from around the globe – the relationships go on long after you come back to the U.S.!

For that reason, stay the course and be patient. You will not get to U.S. metrics level of performance in the short run. Handle it in steps, stay with it, and be positive.

> *"Globalization means we have to re-examine some of our ideas, and look at ideas from other countries, from other cultures, and open ourselves to them. And that's not comfortable for the average person."*
> —Herbie Hancock

3. Get Into the Local Markets Yourself

So far in my career, I have traveled to many, many countries in Europe, Asia, and the Americas. I love meeting the people, experiencing the cultures, and doing business with them. I lived in Europe for 2 years. I relocated with my wife Vicky when my kids were 7 and 3. When our kids came back to the U.S. two years later, they were "global." They changed; they were more open to other

DEPARTMENT EXPANSION

GEOGRAPHIC EXPANSION

- **INTERNATIONAL SUCCESS**
  - 1. Define Global Strategy (Framework)
  - 2. Be Patient, Build Relationships
  - **3. Go Yourself Into the Markets**
  - 4. Build Global Culture in Team
  - 5. Each Country Is Its Own Market
  - 6. Engage with Local Partners

VERTICAL EXPANSION

cultures, tried other languages and other foods, were intrigued by meeting friends who came from other countries – schoolmates who were different. They were more open, and it expanded how they saw the world. Vicky and I felt this same impact. It was a challenging, exhilarating, and rewarding experience to be immersed in another country. It changes you because you are with the people on

the ground in their stores, their homes, their weddings, their backyard barbecues, their churches, their sporting events.

When you get accepted, get behind the scenes, and earn trust, you see the things I am telling you in this chapter. From a business standpoint, you will be amazed at the hurdles they face, and you may be able to help them!

When I moved to Europe, I instantly become more effective at my job. I was physically close, not suffering from jet lag, not trying to rush everything and get it done in one week. I tried to do the things I am telling you to do: building teams, respecting cultures and local leaders, understand the country challenges and opportunities, and having patience.

When I was running business in Europe, we had face-to-face meetings in each country. We learned about the local culture and the local food in the host country. By the way, I have done the same thing in Louisiana and New York City! The U.S. has many different cultures too. If you are interested in other people with different cultures and social norms, you are alright being a little uncomfortable outside of your typical culture, and if you love a challenge, you will want to do international business at some point in your career.

Not everyone has the opportunity to live abroad or manage an international business. We were lucky. However, the point either way is this: if you are responsible for another country, you need to go there, and you need to go there a lot. Do not let anyone fool you that the remote video technologies allow you to do things from the U.S. Some things can be handled remotely, but the view from the ground and the support you will get from your local teams because you came to see them in person is what you need to be successful! The same is true with the customers in those markets that you went and shook hands with. They know that your company has leaders who care about them locally. It helps you understand your people; it helps you become more knowledgeable about your customers. This is going make you a stronger global leader.

There is one last leadership point I want to share with you. Bad things can happen in any country. I must emphasize that your antennae has to be way up in international countries. No matter where you find yourself or where you are taken by the local teams, you have to be smart, show great judgment, and basically be ready for anything! I can tell you many stories over the years where my judgment was challenged. There are situations where the opportunity to do the wrong thing is right in front of you. Have you ever negotiated contracts in Mexico with tequila

shots being set in front of you right before the negotiation starts? I have. Have you ever been propositioned seven times zones away? I have. Do you ever find yourself going to an actual Chinese banquet? There is a technique to this that you must know – a respect you must show. Would you know what to do?

The point is this, you can enjoy the local cultures when you are traveling into local markets, but you should always maintain your composure, your values, and your work ethic at all times. You are the leader.

4. Build a Global Team and a Global Culture within that Team

You can't be global and respect other cultures if you do not make that important to your leadership team. First, build a team that supports this! Announce your **global leadership team** – someone needs to own the global initiative and the remote international countries need go-to people who can help them. So take it! The global leaders you assign must have superior people skills and be sensitive to cultural

DEPARTMENT EXPANSION

GEOGRAPHIC EXPANSION

- **INTERNATIONAL SUCCESS**
  - 1. Define Global Strategy (Framework)
  - 2. Be Patient, Build Relationships
  - 3. Go Yourself Into the Markets
  - **4. Build Global Culture in Team**
  - 5. Each Country Is Its own Market
  - 6. Engage with Local Partners

VERTICAL EXPANSION

differences. Allowing the country to maintain their local flavor while adopting some of the global programs is an art form. It is for these reasons that I always look for great relationship-builders when I hire or recommend someone for international or global assignments.

Have your global team take responsibility for establishing **global metrics** for the business and reporting on them monthly. This is going to become a dashboard that shows progress by month and by country. You want to make sure that all this work you are doing is resulting in ROI, and simultaneously make sure that things are being executed effectively. Start having **global meetings** and communications with the team. Some of these meetings should be face to face and some should be webinars. You should establish global best practice discussions. There may be someone in Singapore doing something very unique and having success that you should share with other countries. It is not always the U.S. that is doing things right! Also, make sure to change your meeting times – so that it is not Europe, for example, that is up late, and that the after-hours involvement is shared.

Finally, lead the way yourself in building the *global culture* in your team. One example of something I did was learning a 2nd language. What you find many times is that the local country teams, especially the Europeans, speak 2, 3, or even 4 languages. The U.S. HQ team speaks one – American English. I told my HQ team that, if we want to be global, we have to speak more than just American English. So the leaders at HQ committed to learn a 2nd language. We had people come in during our lunch hour and train us! I led the way. I became survival level-trained in Spanish, and got to the point that I could communicate in Spanish on the ground in Spain and Italy (Italians seemed to like when I spoke Spanish rather than English). The local teams in those countries loved that we did this!

5. Look at Each Country as a Separate Market. Recognize that the Country Manager is King!

No matter what anyone tells you, if you remember one thing about international expansion it's this: the country manager is king. If you try to run over them, or run around them, you will probably do that at your own peril. Work with them, and you will find the path to success!

DEPARTMENT EXPANSION

GEOGRAPHIC EXPANSION

- **INTERNATIONAL SUCCESS**
  - 1. Define Global Strategy (Framework)
  - 2. Be Patient, Build Relationships
  - 3. Go Yourself Into the Markets
  - 4. Build Global Culture in Team
  - **5. Each Country Is Its Own Market**
  - 6. Engage with Local Partners

VERTICAL EXPANSION

U.S. corporate strategy means very little to the German country manager for example. They are running their "patch." They do the hiring, they do the HR, they negotiate the contracts, they put together their financial plans, and they pay the bills. They do it all. Country managers run their country like a kingdom, and most of them do not want a U.S. program slammed down their throat. Please do not do that. They do not want to "synergize." That is a U.S. corporate term that country managers do not typically support if it affects their team in any negative way. What I am talking about is your attitude and your approach. It is something so easy to change and adjust to, yet many mistakes are made here.

When you put your marketing and financial plans together, you should view every country as its own market. They are all different, with their own competitors, own partners, and own challenges. Put your plan together with the country manager and include their partners. Make it a team effort, and help them get the resources

THE GROWTH CUBE^{TM}

to succeed. If you ever get the opportunity to hire a country manager, get involved in the interview process and make sure you hire the right person!

> *"Every Country needs a Minister of the Future."*
> —Mark Benioff

6. Engage Local Partners

Local partners can be so valuable to you in international markets, especially if you do not have an existing operation and need to push penetration quickly. The local partner already has relationships on the ground that will take you years to develop. The partners understand the local culture and speak the language. They know the competitors, and they may have the technical skills you need. Your product could compliment and fit within their existing portfolio if you pick the right partner.

DEPARTMENT EXPANSION

GEOGRAPHIC EXPANSION

- **INTERNATIONAL SUCCESS**
  - 1. Define Global Strategy (Framework)
  - 2. Be Patient, Build Relationships
  - 3. Go Yourself Into the Markets
  - 4. Build Global Culture in Team
  - 5. Each Country Is Its Own Market
  - **6. Engage with Local Partners**

VERTICAL EXPANSION

If you have a country manager, work with them on selecting a partner to help their business. The country manager has to eventually manage the local partner and must take ownership of achieving their quota. They may already have a relationship with the partner you want!

The key, and were many companies fail, is choosing the right partner for you and your goals. There are many types of partners – sales partners, technology partners, operational partners, and subcontractors. What do you need? The partner scorecard that we will cover with you shortly is an invaluable tool in helping you make a smart decision. If we find and sign an excellent partner in your target country who gets results, you will be on your way to success as a leader!

CASE STUDY.
We acquired a competitor in Europe that enabled us to gain a channel to the EMEA markets, gain products we did not have, and in the process eliminated a competitor. Here is a case study of what I experienced, and what I learned:

**CASE STUDY –
GARY'S BIGGEST INTERNATIONAL CHALLENGE …
AND BIGGEST ACCOMPLISHMENT**

After being selected to be a member of the due diligence team to acquire our largest European competitor, we closed the deal. I was then asked to go to Europe to integrate and rationalize the technology services business. As part of this, I relocated for 2 years with my family to Europe to lead the combined $50 million P&L spanning 12 direct-country service operations and 47 distributor countries across EMEA.

What made this a complex challenge:
- My assignment was to shut down the acquiring company headquarters (which included many talented colleagues I had worked with in prior years) and relocate/assemble the new management team in another country (the acquired company HQ). This was considerably challenging and interesting in that our prior Euro team felt they should be the new HQ – after all "we acquired them."
- I was tasked with separating the services business from the product business both financially and operationally. Prior, it was a combined organization and P&L under one leader.
- We had to make a decision on what functions needed centralized and what should stay decentralized in country operations.
- This was a very politically charged move. Not only was it a merger of competitors, but our U.S. HQ wanted immediate results so that they could achieve acquisition synergy targets. The acquired company CEO did not want to change anything. The country managers did not want change either!

The results:
- I accomplished this assignment in 2 years and did everything that we had targeted.
- In addition, amidst all this change, we improved the business financially. During my tenure as president, we achieved 17%/yr. revenue growth and 35%/yr. operating margin growth (both had been single-digits prior).

How did I lead the organization to overcome this challenge?

- I took the reins and led our team and our division!
- We worked hard to gain the respect and support from other Euro business leaders. We were not successful in all cases.
- We broke down each goal into an execution plan and assigned leader(s).
- We worked closely with country managers to listen to them and make them part of the decision-making process.
- We put the new leadership team together as quickly as possible as they had the most interest and energy to get us into position for future success.

What could I have done differently?

- I should have pursued more time with our group President and the acquired company CEO prior to moving to Europe, to agree on our goals together. Although we accomplished the goals I had been assigned, my assignment was not supported by everyone involved, and I could have worked harder in advance to try to get this agreed properly.

What did I learn about myself?

- I am a strong relationship builder and team builder. I implemented what I had learned in years of prior international work: you must build a relationship in international operations first, gain respect, and be respectful, and then you can be effective and create change that will last.
- I have an awesome wife and children! My wife has always told me, "I will follow you wherever you go," and she did despite the fact that she had a successful career and ambitions herself! This was a challenging and exciting time for our family – and our kids became global in the process, open and interested in other cultures and the diversity the world presents to us all!

VERTICAL EXPANSION

Your company most likely has deep expertise and thought leadership in at least one vertical today. Expanding to a new vertical is a risky move if you do not hire or acquire expertise in that vertical. However, if you can do that, you can tap into a new group of customers to offer your products and services. Being in that vertical will also help to diversify your business overall, which can be healthy for your company.

DEPARTMENT EXPANSION

GEOGRAPHIC EXPANSION

- **INTERNATIONAL SUCCESS**
  - 1. Define Global Strategy (Framework)
  - 2. Be Patient, Build Relationships
  - 3. Go Yourself Into the Markets
  - 4. Build Global Culture in Team
  - 5. Each Country Is Its Own Market
  - 6. Engage with Local Partners

VERTICAL EXPANSION

Another way to look at vertical expansion is to take some of your horizontal products – products that are not vertically specific and can be offered horizontally (to any vertical). Follow those products into the new verticals and the new relationships that you generate.

The problem with a vertical expansion is that you, in most cases, will not be able to leverage your existing customers. When we talk about this later, we will introduce you to market entry strategies like acquisitions and partnerships, which will help you to capitalize on the relationships of the companies you decide to partner with.

MARKET EXPANSION – 4 STEPS TO SUCCESS!

We now know that when we talk about a "new market," we are referring specifically to expanding into new departments within our current customers and expanding into new geographies – including international markets, or expansion into new vertical markets.

The first step we are going to take is to review our customer base and see what we find in terms of partners we are already doing business with and customer relationships that are non-traditional – meaning we are in a department, a vertical, or an unusual geography. We are going to review why that non-traditional situation exists, and if there is an opportunity to capitalize on it with other customers. We are going to search and find these non-traditional contracts, partnerships, and relationships and ask, "Can we do this for other customers?"

THE GROWTH CUBE™
Unlocking the Growth Potential of Your Company

Are you ready to move forward with an action plan? Take these 4 steps to succeed with your new market expansion plans!

Step 1. Customer Base Analysis

I like to start evaluating your potential market expansion with a customer base analysis. This will

| STEP 1 - Customer Base Analysis | STEP 2 - Market Expansion Strategy | STEP 3 - Research and Plan Target Markets | STEP 4 - Execute the Expansion |

uncover golden nugget opportunities you may not have thought about before! Go through all your current/recent customer contracts and projects and categorize them into Renewals, Add-ons to Existing customers, and New Customers. Also, enter into your analysis the vertical industry, the size, and the geography, the products they purchased, and which department bought those products. Based on my experience, some of those customers are going to be partners or potential partners. Strip them out separately. Analyze this: why are these potential partners working with you? What observations do you have about the nature of the partner relationships that we have going today, and why they are beneficial?

Are You in Non-Traditional Departments?

As you go through your customer analysis, pay special attention to the departments that you are in and the traditional departments that you target. Are there any implementations that land in a non-traditional department with a different decision-maker? Although this may reveal a potential growth path, the opportunity to move to other departments within the same company is not as easy as it sounds. Typically, from my experience, it takes a new or modified product, nut at least there is a relationship there to build from. That's what you must leverage.

At one of my companies, we had a system installed in the customer service department in a major restaurant chain, which was our traditional department to be doing business. However, this customer asked us to help them adopt the product to their HR department to use with internal employees to provide them better service. This opened up a new opportunity for us to take this new use of our product and offer it to other customer's HR departments! You may have been pushed by your customer to do some different applications of your product, yet you did not take it and "productize" this application to other customers. This is a missed opportunity, but you can probably still do it! What can we do to expand to those departments in other customers? What if you did this for all your customers? What is the size of this opportunity? The key is to identify those active customers that are different, where you have expanded out to another department, most likely with a modified version of your product. What is the potential growth for your company if other similar customers did the same thing?

Are You in Non-Traditional Geographies?

If you are only involved in a portion of the U.S. and want to expand nationwide, or if you have the U.S. and want to expand globally, this should present a nice growth opportunity. You have probably traditionally pursued certain targeted geographies more aggressively than others. But where do you go next? I have an answer that is so simple it will surprise you: start with where you have already landed. In your customer base file, you may have noted that you are in geographies where you have a small presence but there is high-potential. If you only have 1 or 2 implementations, why not leverage those and expand in that local area? It is always more difficult to get the first sale in any new market because you may not have the reputation or product developed yet, so if you have already have done this, you now have the opportunity to work on leveraging a referenceable customer and a product that's already working in that non-traditional area! What if you took some time to evaluate and quantify the opportunity in that geography?

Of course, in addition to existing geographies, you can also start to identify geographies where you have not landed yet and feel like there may be potential for you. Work with your team on what the potential could be in these completely new territories, and take time to understand the related investment. What will the ROI be in 3 years if you invest there?

I keep talking about quantifying and calculating for two reasons:

1. You need to develop a ROI for expansion opportunities so you understand the potential verse other growth programs, and without it you probably will not get funded anyway.

2. If you develop the metrics around your ideas, you will have a much better chance at successfully executing your ideas because you have thought more thoroughly about them!

Are You in Non-Traditional Verticals?

A vertical industry analysis is very important. You may find you fall into one of two general buckets: your product is focused on one or two verticals today; or your product is horizontal and cuts across many verticals. If you are the company that is in one or two verticals today, what verticals do you focus on and where have

you succeeded? Why are you succeeding? I Is it because you have people in your company with a reputation for expertise and thought leadership in that vertical? If that is true, you have significant growth potential – continue to drive this home and never let it go. If you research some of your bigger competitors, you may notice that they are in several other verticals that you are not in. Analyze the opportunity for you to expand the business into some of those same verticals. Work with your marketing and product management leaders about other potential verticals that should be targeted, especially those in adjacent markets. Do not try to be everything to everybody. I recommend you start with those adjacent verticals that are close to your thought leadership strengths. What is this opportunity within those verticals? Quantify it.

I conducted a project for a customer as part of my business coaching. The goal was to develop the strategy of the company in terms of market and vertical expansion. I took two approaches to help them grow into new verticals:

1. I researched other competitors in our current vertical and databased what other verticals they were in, taking specific note of those similar or slightly larger in size and successful. This competition is always someone that represents what we want to become. I identified those verticals that were close to my client's expertise.

2. In parallel, I researched markets that were adjacent to our current markets. We certainly want to be thought leaders in any market we pursue, and by pursuing markets adjacent to our current markets, the leap to thought leadership in those new markets should be attainable. I identified those verticals that were adjacent to us.

Finally, if you are a company that has a horizontal product and no specific vertical focus, that is both a curse and an opportunity. The opportunity is that you can go out to all verticals and your market potential can be very large. Your curse is this: what are you great at, specifically? You have to be an expert in something. I always say to my clients, "What are you the thought leader of?" For a smaller business, it makes much better strategic and financial sense to work on a focused vertical of expertise in a focused geography. Offer something that no one else has!

"Without change, there is no innovation, creativity or incentive for improvement."
—William Pollard

Step 2. Market Expansion Strategy

If you recall in Chapter 3, we developed a company strategy. From that, we have developed: a market-

STEP 1 - Customer Base Analysis ⇒ STEP 2 - Market Expansion Strategy ⇒ STEP 3 - Research and Plan Target Markets ⇒ STEP 4 - Execute the Expansion

ing and sales strategy (Chapter 3), and a product development strategy (Chapter 4). Now in Chapter 5, we again leverage that very valuable company strategy as a basis for developing our market expansion strategy.

The new target markets you have identified so far are most likely markets where you have traction today, or they are a natural progression from where you are currently. These adjacent vertical and geographic target markets offer a potential new growth path for your business that can be very exciting for your team. Take all the information gathered from the analysis you did in your customer base analysis (Step 1), and have a brainstorming session with key members of your team about the markets we are in and the potential target markets you have identified. It's important to include your team if you have not already. You need their involvement and buy-in, and you will benefit from their expertise. You know that a team is much stronger than one person, right? Start to identify the pros and cons of each market expansion, both from a strategic and market opportunity standpoint, and also from a cost and investment standpoint. As you lay this out, you will uncover that expanding to new markets is an investment – mainly in sales, marketing, and new product development. Also, there could be significant investment in time to set up partnerships and potentially acquire companies.

Although the rewards can be significant for new market expansion and we should quantify those, we also need to balance that with the costs for new market entry. The secret sauce is this (and if you read this deep into the book you got it!): the market expansion approach I am sharing with you substantially reduces your risk and increases your chance of success if it *leverages current customer relationships and offerings you already have in place today, extended to markets that are adjacent*

Now that we have worked with our team to further clarify, expand upon and solidify the target markets we are most interested in. Let's research the targets we have identified in more detail.

Step 3. Research and Plan Target Markets

Step 2, although very important, will be very fast and will flow quickly into this step. You have taken time to identify and quan-

| STEP 1 - Customer Base Analysis | STEP 2 - Market Expansion Strategy | STEP 3 - Research and Plan Target Markets | STEP 4 - Execute the Expansion |

tify opportunities for several new markets that you want to pursue. Now is the time to do further research on those segments and develop a plan to attack and win. Step 3 will take some time and effort to complete.

"There's nothing wrong with market research as long as you remember that marketing is a game of the future. Most market research is a report of the past."
—*Ries and Trout*

To gain knowledge, you should begin to talk with customers and partners. Meet with them. Discuss your target markets with your Customer Advisory Board. Learn as much as you can – for example: will each target market require a new product, and if so, what are the specifications? You may be getting pushed by current customers who want you to come out with a new product or expand to a new geography where they have other locations. These steps with your current customers happen because they see you as someone who can help them solve a problem. You know about it because they are involving you in their strategy – Step 4 of the Raving Fan Triangle we discussed in Chapter 2!

The partners you talk to should have some expertise in the markets you are targeting. Again, meet with them. Can this benefit them in some way? Ask them to talk with you about ways you can potentially grow your businesses together; see where the conversation goes. This may uncover new ideas and new opportunities.

In terms of the plan itself, for each target market, we should have a discussion and define how we will penetrate that market and specifically the market entry strategy. Should you go direct, partner, acquire, or some combination? Who are the competitors in the new markets you are pursuing, and how will you beat them? We should refine our value advantage. Financially, we should define a P&L (Profit and Loss) for this pursuit, including estimated costs to penetrate and develop the necessary products that the new market most will likely require. What is the Return on the Investment (ROI)? Which target market opportunity has the highest ROI? Should we pursue that target market first?

Finally, you need to get your market expansion plan approved by your board. The conclusions from your business planning, including investment and revenue generated, defining the go-forward team, strategies and financial plans, should be documented, prepared, and shared with the board input and approval. If you do what I have recommended, you will be ready! They will love that you are being aggressive and creative in building a more successful company.

Step 4. Execute the Market Expansion

Here is a compelling riddle from Feldman and Spratt:

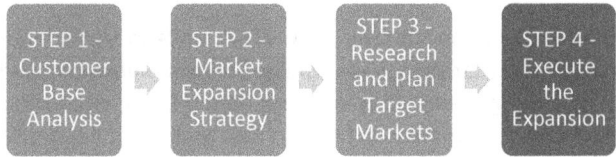

STEP 1 - Customer Base Analysis	⇨	STEP 2 - Market Expansion Strategy	⇨	STEP 3 - Research and Plan Target Markets	⇨	STEP 4 - Execute the Expansion

Question:
There are 5 frogs on a log.

4 of them decide to jump off.
How many are left?

Answer:
Still 5.
There is a difference between deciding and doing.

It is amazing how many companies I see handle all the planning work we have just outlined, and yet they do not jump in the water and do it! That is why I specifically define Step 4 – to execute the expansion. You did all the work. You have analyzed the best opportunities, defined the target markets, and developed your strategies and financial justifications. You have involved your team, your customers, your partners, and your board. What more do you have to do? The plan is ready, so why are you holding back? I see it happen all the time, and that's why I am stopping here to talk with you. You are doing the right thing. You have the bandwidth to make it happen. So let's go *execute the expansion.*

We have talked about the importance of execution throughout this book. Many companies have great ideas. Those ideas span across all 6 dimensions of The Growth Cube, but many of those ideas are not successfully implemented. Not only

does this cause plans to be missed or left unfulfilled, but it also impacts the enthusiasm of your people, and ultimately, it may affect their careers. That's why execution is so important! We have helped you in The Growth Cube with the ideas, the steps, and the tools and techniques to make your growth dreams come true. I truly want you to succeed!

Market Entry

Your options for entering your target market are only 3 (or a combination of the 3):

1. **GO DIRECT**
2. **PARTNER**
3. **ACQUIRE**

Another common mistake I see CEOs make in this situation is not executing the market entry strategy successfully. The market opportunity is there. The market entry strategy selected is fine, nut then it is executed poorly and the board determines that the market expansion idea was not a good one. More often than not, the reason it failed was due to poor *execution*. It's not because it was a poor idea.

1. Market Entry – GO DIRECT

This appears on the surface to be the least costly, but it also is the slowest route to success because you most likely do not have the relationships and reputation in that target market. Your partners or acquisition target already has this reputation. It will take you years to get there, assuming you can survive that long. The bottom line is: if going direct means hiring or placing someone in a new market who does not have the expertise or connections to the local market – don't do it! Your initial entry move has to work or it could fail, be very costly, and hurt your credibility with your board. I am sure you have seen companies spend a lot of money trying to roll out this kind of initiative only to shut it down 12 months later with no results. Remember: it is not your *current* core market we are trying to penetrate; it is a *new* market. If you are going direct in a new market, hire someone who has the local connections and expertise in the new target market.

2. Market Entry – PARTNER

Another strategy to enter a new market is to find a credible partner who already has the market expertise, customer reputation, and relationships. This can get you the results much quicker, although you will give up some margin points to get it. How do we make sure we get the right partner? There lies the challenge. Many companies have failed at market expansion because they align with the wrong partner.

At one of my companies, we wanted to expand the business aggressively into new markets by partnering with local players in targeted international markets. Within 2 years, we signed up 9 partners and started generating revenue in Latin American and Asia markets where we had absolutely no presence prior. We had no direct associates in Latin America and made it happen through partnering by bringing a deal to the table for them. In Asia, we added a direct associate to lead the Asia territory, and then we added partners in each country. This was significant and successful, and we could not have done this successfully without a system of managing the expansion. Part of the success of our system was our Partner Scorecard. This is a method to effectively screen partners and make sure we were bringing on partners that match the critical success factors we decide are most important to success.

The Partner Scorecard
The Partner Scorecard is a tool that helps you to objectively look at the pros and cons of each partner you are considering, weighted against the Critical Success Factors (CSFs) that you and your management team agree are important in advance.

At the bottom of the scorecard, you can also add your team's progress against the partner sales process, including dates you have accomplished each of the milestones, agreement with the partner on quota, and how that will be achieved – prior to signing the contract.

To help you envision this, please download a sample **Partner Scorecard** from our website resource center: www.thegrowthcube.com/resources

In the example that you download, you will see 8 CSFs with a potential score of 5 points each. This means that the top score a partner can achieve is 40 points. We will not go forward with any partner who has any 1 or 2 ratings, and even a 3 is concerning. The partner and your partner leader must submit a plan for improving any low scores.

A partner can give you access to a new customer base, new products, new verticals, and new geographies. They can help you dramatically increase the growth of your company. It is a fantastic way to expand into new markets, but we must keep in mind that this takes significant time and effort to put in place. You should develop a formal partner onboarding program, as that partner will either be reselling or selling (for commission) your products and services and will need ramped up, training, and support. all before they close their first deal! We call this partner

enablement, and we actually certify the partner. You and your partner should put together a business plan for enablement and achieving the first-year quota prior to closing the deal. We need their input, buy-in, and commitment to the goals. The process of developing this plan will bring you closer together.

"Our success over the years at Microsoft has been based on partnerships."
—Bill Gates
Co-founder Microsoft

3. Market Entry – ACQUISITION

I have now driven or been intimately involved in consummating 15 acquisitions across multiple countries, including the planning, due diligence, and integration involved with each. I have evaluated hundreds of acquisition ideas, and have screened many that just did not fit or make it through the process for various reasons. I continue to work through the required due diligence and acquisition strategy as part of my coaching today. If executed successfully, an acquisition can be much faster (over the longer term) and much more effective than other types of market entry.

Because of the level of time, effort, and risk involved in acquiring a company, there has to be a smart reason to acquire a company in your target market. What does this company have that is valuable to our company? Does the target company have products / intellectual property (IP) that we need? Do they have presence and people who are respected in our industry? Do they have a customer and contract base in place already? These are very solid reasons to consider acquisition.

Having those reasons vetted and reaching the point where you all sign on the dotted line is a long and winding road. I have had some acquisitions fall apart near the end because of the egos of the leaders involved in signing. I have had deals fall through at the end due to a silent family member not approving it "just because." It's not just small companies. A chairman at a Fortune 100 company told me only 1 in 100 acquisition ideas make it through the internal process and actually get signed.

Acquisitions will also take you and your team's focus away from the core business, which we can all agree is risky. Reducing the risk starts with asking yourself, "Does this acquisition fit within our strategy?" That is why outlining your strategy is so important. If you have a strategy to move into a new market, moving into that market via acquisition is one way to get it done. Utilizing the Partner Scorecard can also help you with this endeavor.

At one of my companies, we found great success acquiring companies in an adjacent market. The results were the same decision maker our sales team was accustomed to working with but a new and different set of skills and products that we did not have. We researched the market and found highly-skilled regional and local players that would be great targets for acquisition, so we went out and did just that. It took a year to get approved, and many times I thought the program was going to get killed internally. However, as the leader of the idea and the driver of the project, I did not give up. For us to go out and build what these companies already had would take a long time, and these companies were entrenched in the customer base. The good news is that we took one acquisition and parlayed that into eventually acquiring more and more regional companies. This business, started from scratch, was just an idea in a planning document and eventually turned into a profitable $250M business for the company! Today this is a major accomplishment in my career, and it has generated significant financial returns to the stockholders. Whoever leads your next acquisition idea has to do the same thing. Someone in your company has to have the passion and drive to get the deal signed. In a small business, that might even be you!

I have also come at this from the investor side of the table. At one of my companies, I successfully led an exit of a private technology company sale to private equity. This included use of an investment banker. My CTO and I were quoted by the owner as, "The best he had ever seen," at the effort. This is very humbling and appreciated. I have since been coaching small business CEOs on how to increase their company value and how to get positioned with investors. One recent project included evaluating expansion of a standalone business unit by partnering, including use of the partner scorecard. I presented 4 options for their business, along with the revenue, profit, cash impact, and expected company valuation expected under each option. As part of my experience doing these kinds of projects, I have developed some unique tools, including *12 Weeks to Investment; 12 Challenges to Increasing Value* and the *4 Drivers to Highest Valuations*. These are excellent tools for both established companies and startups!

Final Thoughts on Market Expansion
There is no hard, set rule on which way to go between direct, partner, or acquire. It depends on the specific goals and specific market circumstances. Once you decide, go for it and stay focused. This table may help you to think through the different options:

Dept. Expansion
- Different decision maker
- Go direct
- Leverage existing products but will need to modify
- Or acquire a partner that has a customer base

Geographic
Expansion - U.S.
(base country)
- Go direct in U.S. Hire smart though
- Leverage existing products
- Acquiring competitors is much faster than taking it from them

Geographic
Expansion -
International
- Partner to get channels to customers and cultural integration
- Will need technology investmnet
- Acquire to get customer base and tech personell to get quickly into a new country

Vertical
Expansion
- Can go direct if you have a solid start with current customers
- Partners can help with sales channel and with new product specs

Sitting back is not an option you can afford. You want to be disruptive and see accelerated growth, so you have to be aggressive by identifying and pursuing opportunities to expand into new markets. Whether it is your goal to acquire, partner, or go direct, there are opportunities for you to expand into new departments, new verticals, and new geographies. Some of those new geographies may be in other countries.

Will the steps you are taking increase the growth of your company, the profitability of your company, and ultimately the value of your business?!

*"You will never reach your destination if you stop and
throw stones at every dog that barks."*
—*Winston Churchill*

DIMENSION 5 WRAP UP – EXPANDING TO NEW MARKETS

Remember you did not learn about The Growth Cube because you wanted to continue incremental 5% growth. The Growth Cube is about being disruptive and changing the game across 6 dimensions of growth. And 1 of those dimensions is about entering new markets and succeeding, and doing so efficiently without wasting a lot of money with no results to show for it.

We have now learned 5 of the 6 dimensions of The Growth Cube and we are starting to see more clearly how, as the CEO, we can unlock the growth potential of our company! It starts with our commitment to creating a company with raving associates who have the passion to build a customer base of raving fans. Those raving fans will then help us win new customers, launch new products, and expand to new markets. This is because they care, and because they value what we do!

We have now built our **Market Expansion Game Plan** together! If you want a complete copy of the Game Plan, you can download it from:
www.thegrowthcube.com/resources

We have given you many tools and techniques to help you make it happen in your company, many of which are very unique. There is nothing out there like this because it is nearly all original content and programs I have created, tested and proven while implementing them successfully in my own companies.

In Dimension 1 – *Creating Raving Associates* – you learned about the Inverted Pyramid philosophy and the CHEER process that provides the glue to keep your team inspired. We have laid out the Level 3 Certification Program that not only trains the sales team but everyone in your company, and thus, positions you as a thought leader in your space.

In Dimension 2 – *Creating Raving Fans* – you learned about the 5-Step Customer Touchpoint Plan and how that can help you optimize the experience when your customer touches your company. We treated you to the 6-Stage Raving Fan Triangle program, which will guide you in building closer, long-term customer relationships. We also outlined for you the 6 Windows to Growth with your current customers that, if done well, will put you on the way to doubling the size of your company! When the customer loves your current product, they will look forward to your next product. This will pave the way for upsells and add-ons, but these are *earned* because of the resource you have become for your customer.

THE GROWTH CUBE™
Unlocking the Growth Potential of Your Company

In Dimension 3 – **Winning New Customers** – you learned that by using a Point A/Point B approach and The Growth Cube 6, you can easily create a Growth Cube Report and strategic plan for your company, and then follow that with a marketing and sales plan built around the 5 Customer Touchpoints and the Big 4 Assets of Marketing. We gave you marketing model framework that can help you build a program in your company to generate SQOs. We showed you the detailed steps for building your own Marketing and Sales Strategy Roadmap! We mentioned that above all else, the most important marketing question a CEO should ask is, "When my customer experiences my product or service, do they love it?" We also shared the key marketing and sales analytics that will help you get the results from your investment. We took you through how to organize and motivate your sales team – what I call the art and the science of leading sales. Plus, we learned that if you can free up 23% of your sales reps' time, you can double your company sales.

In Dimension 4 – **Launching New Products and Startups** – you learned that you should build a product strategy around a great team and a well-thought out product road map. We learned that we should "Think Speed," involve our associates, and lead the way as the CEO with our vision, enthusiasm, and on-the-ground involvement with customers and associates. We learned exactly what we mean when we say we want "awesome products," and we learned the most important goal of any startup company. We learned that we should manage the development process as vigorously and enthusiastically as we fight for the ideas we will work on. We call this process, "The Cars on the Road." *What cars are on your road?* We learned what percentage of revenues we should be investing as a company in new product development efforts, and other key product development metrics.

In Dimension 5 – **Expanding to New Markets** – you just learned that you build your market expansion strategy with input from your associates, customers, and partners. We learned that 3 of the 6 Windows to Growth we discussed in Chapter 2 are related to market expansion, and that once again your current customer can lead you to new opportunities! We learned how to do a customer base analysis and identify the non-traditional departments, geographies, and verticals, and to ask yourself, "Can we do this for other customers?" We gave you our 6 keys to international business success, and shared with you the pros and cons of 3 different market entry strategies. We learned how to utilize a Partner Scorecard to assess potential partners against established critical success factors (CSFs). Additionally, you learned that the market expansion strategy we shared in this chapter is unique and proven to work. It reduces your risk in expanding to a new market

208

because *it leverages current customer relationships and offerings you already have in place today*, extended to target markets that are *adjacent to what we do today*.

Remember we have also learned that the sides of The Growth Cube are dependent on each other, and if we fail at one of the dimensions, it can cause other dimensions to fall along with it.

1. Your success at creating raving fans is directly related to your success at creating raving associates.

2. Your products need to be awesome if you want to win new customers and keep the ones you have.

3. To succeed as a business in the long-term, the prerequisite for winning new customers, launching new products, and expanding to new markets is to have current customers who are raving fans.

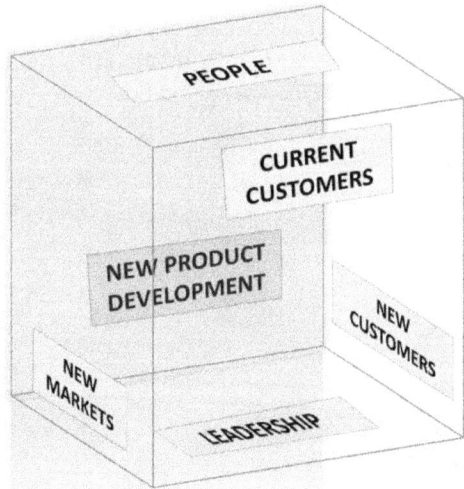

And two important ingredients to solving The Growth Cube are starting to emerge:

1. It's your current customer that is the key to your success in business. This is the secret sauce.

2. If you bring in unique approaches, tools, and techniques that can make the "business of doing business" fun, rewarding, and challenging for your associates, they will help you push your company to new heights!

If you were to capture everything we said and everything we taught you to this point, and implemented it, you would find blazing success with a raving fan customer base, a stream of new customers, innovative products that are exciting your people, and moves into new markets that are opening even more doors to growth. Of course, we know that we can blow it all as a leader if we do not lead properly or do not push the right metrics and financial levers. To unlock the true growth potential of our business takes all 6 dimensions supporting each other!

So exactly how do you lead, and what should you focus on to stay at the top and succeed as the CEO? Let's move on to the 6th dimension of The Growth Cube – *Leadership and Financial* – and find out!

CHAPTER 6 – LEADERSHIP AND FINANCIAL. The Foundation.

*"Courage is rightly considered the foremost of virtues,
for upon it, all others depend."*
—Winston Churchill

THE BIGGEST MISTAKES I EVER MADE!

If you had to dig deep into your heart and deep into your history to the place you have your mistakes hiding, to the place you put things when you do not want to remember, what would you tell me were the biggest leadership mistakes you ever made?

Do you want to know mine? I am going to tell you, but I want to first tell you a little story.

I participated on a panel at an industry conference of global service leaders a few years ago. After 30 minutes of responding to various questions from my good friend and moderator, Dennis Gershowitz, we panelists received the question we have all heard many times before. "What is leadership?"

I was ready. Why? Because I have studied the topic of leadership, I had thought about what it meant to me, and I yearned to be a better leader. So when the question came to me, I knew my answer. All of the other panelists – high technology service executives – answered fantastically. Right out of the text book. Then Dennis turned to me, "Gary, how about you? What is the definition of leadership to you?"

I said, "Dennis, I have thought a lot about this. I have lived this, the ups and the downs, and I am convinced that the most important quality of leadership is…"

The crowd leaned in and was silent, awaiting the possibility of something different, but expecting more of the same. And then I told them:

"Courage. The most important quality of leadership is courage!"

All the panelist's heads simultaneously snapped toward me in surprise and wonder, but I could also tell that they felt the same way too. They knew in their hearts that it was true. Courage *is* the virtue we all pursue as leaders; we know we need it. We all face pivotal moments, but with courage we can make the game-changing, gutsy decisions that can ignite a turnaround or a new growth spurt within the company.

There are a lot of ideas and tools packed into the first 5 dimensions of The Growth Cube, but arguably the most important of all — the foundation of The Growth Cube — involves how you lead. Without talented leadership, a company has no chance in the long run. This is what makes the CEO and the executive leaders so important to the company. Leadership, and the financial and analytics we drive, are the foundation of the company, and they are the foundation of The Growth Cube. It makes everything else possible.

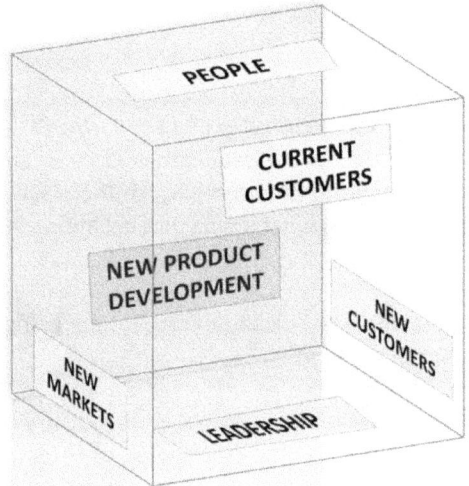

After the panel discussion was over, I was exiting the stage and a young woman in her 20s stopped me and said, "Mr. Ross, I want you to know you inspired me. I find your leadership style so refreshing!" I was honored and surprised. I tried to lay my passion and my heart out there for everyone, and I was not sure how everyone was going to take it. That was the beginning for me. This is when I started to realize that if I would just be myself as a leader, show my teams my passion, let them see my true self, and overcome the fear of doing this, that it could inspire people.

"The most important quality of a great leader is courage."

I have been so excited to get to this chapter because I love studying great leaders, hanging around great leaders, and watching great leaders and how they inspire people to do unbelievable things. I have always aspired to be one of those leaders myself. I am not there yet. I know that my leadership approach is unique and different, and I know that it works because I have walked in your shoes and tested the concepts as a CEO in 5 different organizations. By testing, that means sometimes things did not work.

As I think deeply about all the successes and the missteps throughout my times leading companies, my quest is to get to the root of what I think might help you move your professional and personal success forward, to give you the essence of what it takes to unlock what may be holding your company back, and possibly holding you back as a leader.

Have I ever been fired? Well, I would rather term one departure as "mutual," but that's nothing to be proud of. I mean, that's really not what I want. I am disappointed for a relationship to end in a mutual decision to separate. That's not me. However, what I pushed myself to do was to think about moments when I did make mistakes in order to give you some examples, and better yet, some tips to help you succeed in the future!

If you ever have been fired, don't take it too hard. You are not alone. You have to get back up and move! Some great leaders have been fired and did just that. Steve Jobs was fired from Apple, the company he co-founded! During his time away from Apple, Jobs co-founded computer company NeXT (later acquired by Apple) and launched Pixar Animation Studios. When he returned to Apple nearly a decade later, he was unbelievably successful, as we all know, in leading the launch of the iPod, iPhone, and iPad.

> *"I didn't see it then, but it turned out that getting fired from Apple was the best thing that could have ever happened to me. The heaviness of being successful was replaced by the lightness of being a beginner again, less sure about everything. It freed me to enter one of the most creative periods of my life."*
> —Steve Jobs

Walt Disney was fired from one of his first animation jobs at the Kansas City Star newspaper because his editor felt he, "Lacked imagination and had no good ideas." Disney's company later set the bar for imagination and ideas in film! As a

film producer, Disney holds the record for most Academy Awards ever earned by one individual – he won 22 Oscars.

> *"All our dreams can come true, if we have the courage to pursue them."*
> —*Walt Disney*

We have all made mistakes in our careers. The good news is that we can recover from them if we open our heart and are willing to adapt and evolve as a leader.

If I asked you about the biggest mistakes you ever made, would you say that they were people-related?
So were mine.

The biggest leadership mistakes I have made can be very simply broken down into 2 categories:

1. *Hiring people I should not have hired.*

2. *Firing people I should not have fired.*

1. Hiring people I should not have hired.
I have built some unbelievably successful teams. In the process, I've hired some top performers at all levels. These individuals have gone on and are accomplishing incredible things for themselves today. I am very proud of this. However, you do not lead and build five companies over a couple decades and not have some people issues.

One example is the key VP I hired at the insistence of my corporate office. This turned into a total disaster. When a VP is performing poorly, they can destroy so many people, processes, and cultural initiatives that have taken so long to build. They influence so many people. What bothers me about this is that I knew this VP was not going to fit. Yet the person was highly recommended by corporate (from success in a completely different role), and was pushed and forced on me as their "next step." Bad move. Took me 1 ½ years to run the person out, and by the time that happened, there was a wake of trash left behind to be cleaned up. I am sure many of you can relate to this story:

216

I wanted to get to know the VP candidate so before bringing the person on board, my wife and I met the VP and their spouse for dinner. After the dinner, my wife turned to me in the car and said, "Are you going to hire that idiot?"

She was right. And if she had that impression in 2 hours, what would the team think after days and weeks of involvement!? I hired him anyway. Bad move.

When you are the CEO/President, you have to take responsibility for hiring, even if the candidate is highly recommended. In the end, there is nothing worse than having to fire someone who YOU have hired. Think about that. That is the ultimate mistake. This spurred me to develop the Critical Success Factor (CSF) hiring process that I used later at my other companies, which we covered for you in Chapter 1. This is an objective, logical, and focused way to hire the best talent for the need that you have! I should have built *my* team based on the skills we *needed*. I should not have let people above me influence and control a decision I was not comfortable with myself.

2. Firing people I should not have fired
Now that you have read most of the book (thank you so much, I am honored!), you can see that I have had a lot of success. That is true. I have had so many awesome teams that performed at such high levels! Most of my teams I get to know personally, including our spouses and our families. We become close. This is because I build this theme that we are fighting against the world, and that bonds us! When I look back, I also realize that I am heartbroken over some lost friends. They were lost over us letting them go. Not just my staff; it's hardworking front-line associates who we let go to make the month or make the quarter. My heart breaks when I think of these people that I have let go over the years. Why did I do it?

In my first President role, I was trained in a professional management system in a large public company. The training suggested that you do what you have to do to make your profit targets for the quarter. That was the ultimate metric: quarterly profit improvement. I did it. I did it well. I was promoted for doing it. It's business, and I carried it forward to my other company leadership roles.

But you know what I learned? That is not me. That is not how "I roll." I am a team builder, a people builder. I build people up. I give people enthusiasm and

optimism and hope. That's my gift. I was the President and CEO of the company – is there no power that I had to help this situation other than firing someone? They are people. They have families, and they have feelings. They are NOT just a number. To all of these associates, I apologize. I learned something, unfortunately too late. People will rise to the occasion if you have confidence in them and give them a chance! I did not sacrifice myself for my team. That would not happen today.

> *"Do you have enemies? Good. That means you've stood up for something, sometime in your life."*
> —*Winston Churchill*

A specific story I can tell you was the time my boss came to me and told me I needed to lay off people in our division. I asked, "Why do I have to do that? We are growing our division revenues and profits and are ahead of plan. This would not make any sense to my people. I could not even explain it to them!"

He said, "You need to do it because you are part of the corporate team, and there are other divisions way off their plan. We need you to cut in order to help the parent company hit our quarter. I fought it because I thought if we could do even better, we could increase profit dollars and help the corporation. But in the end, I did what I was told and eventually squeezed some cuts out from not replacing departures. This disappointed my team, and it actually ended up adding more workload and more pressure on a team that was performing well! That did not make sense to anyone.

In these cases, I should have figured out a way to be creative, to work harder, to solve the problem so that I did not have to pull people I loved into a room and let them go. Yes, I loved them. And I hurt them, and put them in a tough situation. I am the CEO/President of the company. Surely I should be able to figure out something to save them, right!?

The good news for CEOs is that, according to *Boston Consulting Group*, boards are not looking for CEOs who are cost cutters any more – they want growth CEOs! In the past, boards looked for leaders who were strategic and good with cost efficiency, but now they need CEOs who are gifted at setting ambitious goals and motivating people.

*"In regard to selecting CEOs, it's always easier to trim and optimize
and cut costs than to figure out something new. What firms need
from their CEOs now is growth."*
—Boston Consulting Group, March 2017

What can you learn from my mistakes? What can I offer you as advice to help your career and your leadership decision-making?

Here are my *4 Tips for Preventing Major Leadership Mistakes*:

1. Evaluate *YOU!*
I recently read an article that outlined the "8 Qualities That Make Unforgettable Bosses." It intrigued me. I want to be a great boss, and I want to continue to be better. So I did an exercise:

1. I graded myself on a scale of 1-10 on each of the 8 qualities from that article, for each of my past President/CEO roles.

2. I then looked at my results in all those roles: Financial. Key Metrics. Project success. Growth culture success. In which roles did I have the best results? I figured this out.

3. I then cross-mapped the roles where I had the most success, with the high and low ratings on the 8 qualities, and summarized my observations and learnings.

Do you know what I discovered above all else? *When I lead with passion and share my feelings and my heart, my teams perform best!*

Your people want you to be passionate about what you are working towards. They want you to open up, and they will gladly help you if you let them! They will respond to you; they want to be part of it. Associates, customers, and the board can all appreciate this passion. They will all love when you are passionate about what you are doing.

Tell me something. Are you passionate today? Show this to your team. Put yourself out there. Based on my learnings, you will perform at higher levels if you are leading a team this way.

You should also consider an executive coach to help you improve even more. I have used a coach myself throughout my career. A 2016 study by *Concord Leadership Group* found that CEOs say that being coached helps them grow in confidence by giving them an informed sounding board when they need to talk through situations and create strategies. More importantly, staff in organizations with CEOs getting executive coaching have noted how much calmer, more confident, and more effective their leader is. Studies also show the ROI on executive coaching is more than 300%.

Whether you are having good times or difficult times in your career, you should look in the mirror. Don't point at others, even if they are in the wrong. You cannot control that. Search for ways you can be better. I like suggesting leaders to conduct a SWOT (Strengths, Weaknesses, Opportunities, Threats) analysis on themselves. And then have their direct reports complete the same report on the leader. Compare them! Be willing to admit that you can learn and improve yourself! I have always thought I could get better, including today. Keep pushing yourself to "beat yesterday."

And keep in mind it's not just about you. It's about you developing the associates in your company too. That's why I call my quarterly reviews HDOs. It stands for "Hopes, Dreams, and Objectives." I want them to tell me their hopes and dreams so that I can help them achieve them! And just the title alone sets the tone that you are going to be a different leader. One who cares and supports your people. I want our interactions to be inspirational. And the funny thing is that my Directors and VPs started using the same process with their teams without me even requesting it. They just started doing it – which was awesome!

Your team is watching you. They want you to inspire them! Yes, that team that YOU put together. They have run through the wall for you so that the company can succeed! That team is watching you and taking their cues from you. Accept this responsibility and be courageous!

"As I look back at the various teams I have been honored to lead,
I found a common thread: That when I lead with passion and
share my feelings and my heart, my teams perform best!"

2. Listen to Your Family's Advice.
No one knows you as well as your family. They are close to you, your past, your dreams, your strengths, your weaknesses, your values, your aspirations, and they can help you with advice. My wife Vicky is unbelievable in her heart for people and how she builds relationships, her dedication and determination. I met Vicky when she was 21. We started going together and have never broken up. She has followed me literally around the globe while trying to keep her own career together, and she did! We have raised two successful, fun, and warm-hearted children who we are so, so proud of. Our family is a team. We love each other, and we want the best for each other and our friends. When you are down, your family can pick you up. When you are up, they are there to celebrate. I have had this support throughout my career.

You might be thinking, "Gary, having a family has nothing to do with being a great CEO!" But that is what makes The Growth Cube so unique. This is my own view after successfully walking in your shoes as CEO. I am giving you my perspective. I know this is delicate ground, but I do believe that "family" can impact a CEO's success. Building a strong family can make a CEO stronger because you have this "team" that lives with you. They know you, and they are honest with you unlike any others could be. The family unit can make you stronger, deeper, more balanced, and more sensitive to family issues at work. There are so many benefits!

In your quest to lead in life, the most important team that you can build in life is your family. Your family can be a motivating and contributing force to anything you decide to take on!

3. Take Control of Your Responsibility.
The moment you relinquish control of your unit to someone above you, this is the beginning of the end for you. You have to take control of what you are responsible for. I know to some extent your boss impacts this, but in the end it really has nothing to do with your boss. It has to do with you and if you can manage through this challenge!

I remember one story where my boss came over to my office and wanted to start having meetings about the terms and conditions of our contracts. He wanted to go through all the terms with me and my CFO and update them one by one. Why? We had no contract issues, but he insisted. So, he was coming over to our office every other day, and we would be in 3 hour meetings each time. We were wondering what was going on. Why are we wasting our time on this!? This went on for several months, and sometimes I had other commitments with customers and

associates, so some days I was not in attendance. Finally, he got the terms and conditions the way he wanted them, and we thought it was over... until one day in our monthly board meeting. With his boss in the room, his peers in the room, and all my peers in the room from all the other divisions, the backstabber turned to me and said, "Gary, we are going to cover those terms and conditions with everyone."

I said, "Yes, okay, let's get the presentation up for you."

Then he threw the big right hook, 'Gary, why don't you present it?"

I said, "What do you mean?"

He insisted, "You present it."

So I did! And it was not good. I was setup. It was political – I found out later he hated my former boss and everyone who supported my former boss. Welcome to the shark tank within.

What could I possibly teach you from this and still be positive!?

I have been able to successfully progress my career from manager to director to VP to president and then to CEO. Along the way, I have had the learning experience of both great bosses and bosses that weren't so great. I can tell you this: if you get a boss that you are in synch with, hold onto it and relish it. It is special. You know what I mean by synch, don't you? It is that feeling that you can be totally you, totally honest, and that you have each other's trust, respect, and support. There is nothing like that feeling. No matter what the relationship is with your boss, as a leader, you have to take control of your responsibility and exhibit that to your boss and the organization. Take charge. You were hired and put into a leadership position for a reason. Do what you were hired to do! That does not mean you do not listen, but you also cannot be a wallflower to your bosses. One technique I will share with you that has worked for me when I have an aggressive boss is this:

Next time you walk into your boss's office, I want you to imagine him or her working for you. This is difficult to do, I know, especially if you have an aggressive boss who takes control themselves. But please just try to do it. Envision that you are the boss and they work for you, and cover the same topics you always cover. In the least, if you succeed, you will make it an equal dialogue, and if you are doing more of the talking and even taking control yourself, you will be doing very well, and your boss will like it. Trust me. Try it! It is a mindset – and it will give you more confidence, and ironically give your boss more confidence in you.

4. Stand for Something Personally – BEYOND CEO

I am going to shift gears here, and I would like you to think deeply about this. Who are you? I mean, who are you beyond your title? What do you stand for personally? What is important to you? What are your strengths? What is your gift?

I know sometimes we want to separate our personal and professional lives, and there can be good reasons for this. However, you should not be two different people. You are the same person. The lines between work and personal lives continue to blur with improved ways to communicate, social networking, and remote workers.

Is it possible to have faith and show that as the CEO?

I have always been trained that you should separate your faith from your work, and I have been very careful throughout my career about openly talking about my faith. As my faith grew stronger, I struggled with this – being one way at home, and holding my values back at work. How should I properly let that show at work?

I believe that if your people get to know the real you, to see and feel your heart, that overall they will love your authenticity and you showing your human side to them!

I do not go out of my way to talk about my religious commitment at work or even socially. But it comes out. It is part of me. I am not afraid to talk about being faithful, following God, or giving advice to others. I buy religious cards for people. I talk about my involvement in my church. And despite my human mistakes and weaknesses, I try to set a positive example; a road to follow. I try to be someone that younger people can look up to and say, "I can see that God is working through Gary and I want some of that!"

Finally, for those of you reading this book who have a lot of experience and may still be searching for something more, remember that leadership and the ability to lead and create successful change have nothing to do with age. It's about your energy level, your dreams, and your passion! That's why people follow you. Look at what Bernie Sanders ignited in young people during the 2016 presidential election. His message and his passion caused young people to vigorously rally around him. Think about that. He was a 75-year old man! And that's my point. His age did not matter. It was his energy, his message, and his passion! Donald Trump did a similar thing on the Republican side, igniting a middle class to go out and vote for him because they thought he represented them and would fight for them. He was

70 years old. Many of us let age influence us. We talk about it. We worry about it. If we simply focus on keeping ourselves in top physical, mental, and spiritual shape, keep learning and staying sharp on the latest technologies, and stay engaged in our community, we can take ourselves all the way to the top!

> *"You will never do anything in this world without courage.*
> *It is the greatest quality of the mind next to honor."*
> —*Aristotle*

Courage

Before I talk with you about courage, I want to talk with you about fear.

Everyone has fears. This is important for leaders because fear stops leaders from reaching their full potential. These fears could be worry about achieving aggressive goals, how you are going to cut costs, how you are going to handle the board, a competitor that is making aggressive moves, or a fear that maybe you are not "CEO material."

I am going to share something personal with you. I have faced and beaten prostate cancer! Now there is fear staring you in the face. Many people fear cancer – but when you dig deeper, what they truly fear is dying. Have you faced this kind of battle in your life; this kind of fear? I was so determined to win that I ran a marathon in the middle of radiation treatment. At the same time, I never missed an hour of work. In fact, I kept my work hours up at 70 hours a week the whole way. I did not choose to fight cancer – God chose that battle for me because he wanted me to take my game to the next level. And you know what? God knows what's best for us. It made me a better man. A stronger man! It is one of the most significant and positive events in my life to this point. And it has inspired me to take the fight and the passion to help others with cancer - I call this passion "Gary's Race," and it did not end when I beat cancer. It includes fighting for children with cancer at Children's Hospital who I now run for every year in the Columbus Marathon as one of the leaders in the Children's Champion program! I do this to inspire them, and in return they inspire me. I have taken my talks on the road. I have a talk on "How to Overcome Major Life Challenges" – where my message is simple: *you can overcome any challenge in life if you strengthen yourself physically, mentally, and spiritually.*

God is using me to inspire others facing challenges.

224

I have faced fears, and I have been afraid. I have seen my associates fight similar challenges. Those fears may relate to your work, or they may be something personal. They can all certainly affect work performance.

We all have the potential to beat our fears. Like many challenges, it can be dealt with, but we have to focus on it. We just need a goal or a cause that means enough to us. With that, we can overcome the fear! Mark Twain said, "Courage is not the lack of fear. It is acting in spite of it."

I am confident you will face moments this month or this quarter or this year, where your courage is called upon. It may be in a customer situation, in an associate meeting, in a presentation, in a one-on-one talk with a struggling associate, or in facing a mistake. These events may seem so small when we look back 10 years from now, but at the time they are happening, they can seem daunting. You can succeed in these inflection point moments in your career as long as you continue to strive to improve, are passionate about what you are doing, remain true to yourself, and are willing to work harder than any of your competitor CEOs!

So what does Gary Ross stand for?

I hope I stand for courage. A leader of people. Leadership is courage. It is the number one value we as leaders should pursue. The courage to set daunting goals and to go after them. The courage to face major challenges and overcome them, whether in the board room, with our associates, or in our personal life. Despite the fears that we acknowledge are there, it is our ability to have the courage to drive forward, get excited, and get others excited and inspired as well!

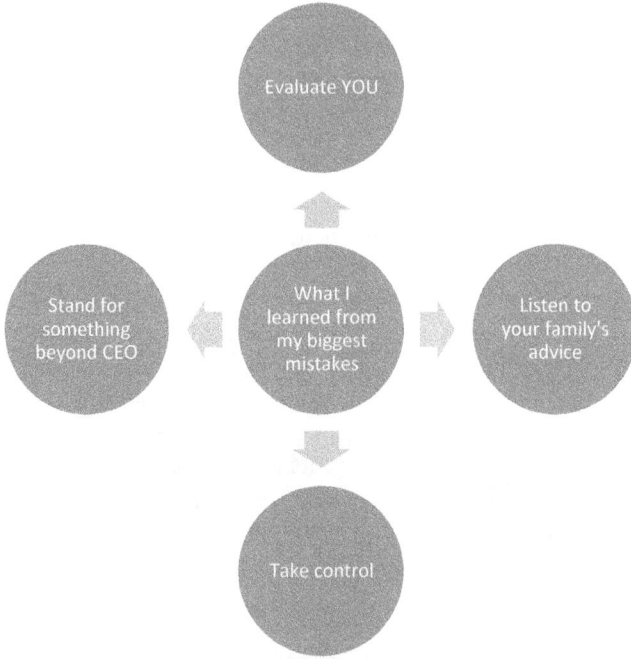

"We rejoice in our sufferings knowing that suffering produces endurance,
endurance produces character, character produces hope,
and hope does not disappoint us."
—Romans 5:3-5

The Epicenter and Its Pressure

As we delve into the important 6th dimension of The Growth Cube, the main question is this: how do we "run" the company? "Running the company" refers specifically to what we do every day when we go into the office and sit in the big chair as the CEO. How we move, what we say, how we treat people, what metrics we focus on, the decisions we make, and who makes them. Every minute of every day, what do you do? I believe that everything you do as the leader, at every moment, impacts your associates, your customers, and your stakeholders, whether that's positively or negatively.

As the CEO and operational leader of your company or unit, you are the closest to the business. You know the customers, and they are pressing you to innovate and

226

develop new products that will help them compete, and they are pressuring you to be more responsive in your customer support. You also know your associates and what they want. You have to recruit and keep top-notch associates, and overall, you must keep the troops fired up and motivated no matter what is happening to the business financially.

The funny thing is that you often feel alone in your effort to succeed as CEO. Even though you have many people around you, and there are many interactions with people throughout the day, there's just no avoiding it. As you work to determine your strategies, your culture, your organization, your products – very important things – you are sometimes surprisingly facing resistance and pressure from people that you thought were on your bus, who were supporting you, but now appear to be doing just the opposite of that.

Do you know why you feel this way? I believe there are 3 compelling desires at play when you are running your company: These forces are powerful and impactful, and if you fail at any one of them, you will no longer be the CEO. These 3 forces are the sometimes-competing desires of: your associates, your customers, and your board.

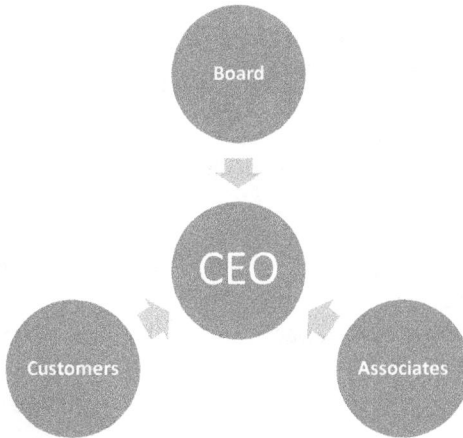

The challenge of managing these 3 forces is that the success of one force may be at the total expense of the other. For example, the board may want you to improve profitability, yet your associates may want more pay, while your customer may want a lower price. How do you make all 3 of these happen simultaneously? Therein lies the challenge and the fun of being the CEO! There is pressure... a lot

of pressure. This is coming at you from many directions. Welcome to the epicenter!

It's not a matter of if you'll encounter pressure as a CEO, but when. As you move into a leadership role and are taking on more people to your team, and interfacing more with customers and boards, the pressure will come. Some handle it better than others, but it can be overwhelming to those who are not used to it. Will you still make great decisions and take the best actions? This is where many mistakes are made – when the pressure and conflict are coming at you from all 3 groups! This may make you feel like you are alone, and it's why many people say it is, "lonely at the top." Rarely can you please all 3 groups. Your success at managing these three forces will mark your grade as the CEO, and sometimes you feel like you are not pleasing any of them. I call this talent: *Managing the Epicenter*. Managing the epicenter is about developing all your skills, so that you can deal effectively with the needs and desires of the board, the customers, AND the associates.

Regardless of the situation inside your company, any executive is going to feel pressure to perform and exceed expectations. With time and experience, you get used to this feeling. I promise you. You will adapt to it. No, it will not go away. In a sick kind of way, you will yearn for it and smile at it. You will become courageous and challenge this feeling. Have confidence that you will make it through the challenges. Learn to trust that what you are feeling is a natural part of this job.

Just because you may feel like you have it all figured out one month, the next month may be totally different. There are ups and downs, and there is pressure to perform at higher and higher levels each year. You will sometimes question yourself and pray that you are doing the right things, that your decisions will lead to results and success for your people. There may be no one to ask who understands the intricacies or the background to make the call but you. It is all up to you. It's why you lead. It's why a running back is a running back. They want to run, and score! It's why a great basketball shooter wants the ball in the last seconds. They want to take on the pressure and want the challenge of making the last shot.

You must learn to embrace this pressure when you are CEO. I want to inspire you to be positive and to approach this as a challenge you can win.

> *"If your actions inspire others to dream more,*
> *learn more, do more, and become more... You are a leader."*
> —John Quincy Adams

MANAGING THE EPICENTER – LEADING YOUR CUSTOMERS

Customers play a huge role in your success as a CEO. Nothing else we have talked about matters if you do not get customers to choose you and stay with you.

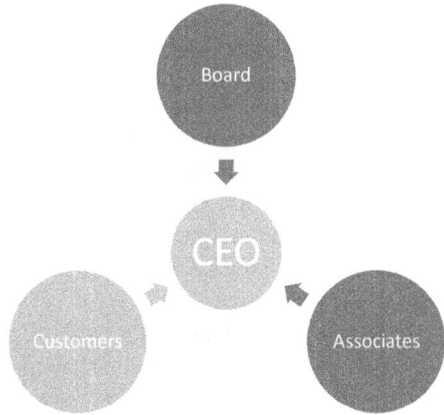

We talked a lot about customers in Chapter 2, and I encourage you to please refer back to that chapter for more details. The focus of this chapter is about managing the epicenter pressure from customers, which can be especially strong if you are not performing well because you have products and services that are not meeting their expectations. The customer is usually pushing us because we are not performing in some area.

Here are 4 ideas to better help you manage the pressure at the epicenter with customers!

1. You Should Get Personally Involved with the Customers!
It starts with the CEO. You set the tone for the importance and type of relationship. Your relationship with your customer is not about you being a supplier. You and your company need to move from supplier to someone who helps your customer compete. Your team should compete right alongside your customer and help them win by using your products and services. Stay intimately connected to your customers yourself. Stay on top of your products and services and how you are performing (remember the "fault line" we discussed earlier in the book), and have a relentless focus on that customer's success utilizing your solutions.

2. Get the Customer Involved with Your Associates!
The customer should never be delegated to sales or support. You and your leadership team should have active and consistent discussions with the customers. This applies to every department! Likewise, there should be KPIs in all the departments – on the walls – related to customer performance. Just start putting them on the walls. I am not kidding. I actually did this early in my career. I did not ask. I started taking customer success stories and customer metrics and put them

on the walls throughout our office. They never came down. It ended up becoming the company "Wall of Fame!" Build a culture of passion for the customer, lead the way yourself, and understand your own internal metrics in terms of your performance. Be the voice of the customer in your office every day!

You are going to have to create activities, programs, and opportunities for the customers to mix it up with your people. Tell your customers what you want to accomplish. Ask them for their ideas and input. You can trust your customers. They will come through for you. Bring them into your company, and give them a close-up view of your company, your people, and yes, even the issues you are tackling. I find that if you are honest with them and ask for them to be part of the team, this outweighs any concerns you may have. It is actually just the opposite. I If you trust them and share your leadership challenges with them, they will open up to you and trust you with their leadership challenges!

As an example, I have a tradition of bringing a customer into our annual internal kickoff meeting every year. This is our internal meeting where we fire everyone up about what we want to do in the coming year! The customer is always a surprise keynote speaker – only I know who is coming in advance. This is motivational and makes your meeting much more exciting, and much more focused on what we should be talking about – the customer! Customers love being part of it and helping us. I am not kidding when I tell you that one of the years, our customer actually opened up so passionately about her view of our company, why she thought we lost our way, and how we were now getting it back, that she literally had some of our associates crying. I am not kidding you. Our people cared. Our customer cared. It was unbelievable – a moment I will always remember and I doubt ever duplicate.

3. Form an Impactful Customer Advisory Board (CAB)
One of the best weapons you can utilize in leading your company to manage the epicenter pressure is to have customers close to you and advising you. That's why I have personally formed, led, and chaired the Customer Advisory Boards (CAB) at all my companies.

The CAB is an active part of my leadership team. I always show them on my organization chart as one of my direct reports. I do this because I want them involved. I want their ideas, and I want to give back to them and help them. I invite them to my staff meetings. What do we cover when they are there? Same things we usually cover. I am not kidding. We share actions. We form teams to pursue ideas. We ask their ideas on priorities. The CAB is a catalyst for you to change your company and move it forward! They are not just helpful to you as the CEO. They can help everyone in your company. The CAB is an advisory group who, in the long run, should touch your whole company.

Whenever one of the CAB members would be in town, I would call a staff meeting and invite the customer to join us at the table. I would invite them to our all-company meetings. Jeff Bezos, CEO at Amazon, does something similar. He periodically leaves one seat open at a conference table and informs all attendees that they should consider that seat occupied by their customer, 'the most important person in the room.' I love this concept, but I would rather have the customer in the room!

4. Build a Customer-Responsive Organization

If the customers are putting pressure on you, then something is most likely broken in your organization. You have to get in there and fix it. Lead the change yourself. But you cannot do it all on your own; your whole team has to respond to customers. You are going to have to change the culture within your team. It's everything we have talked about, especially in Chapter 2, which will enable you to lead this and make it happen! It starts with Chapter 2, but it may not be just that. Maybe it is your new product development that is broken (see Chapter 4).

If you remember one tip from this book, remember this:

The most important thing you can do as a leader is to focus first on the customer. Find a way the customer can succeed by utilizing your products and services. Learn their challenges. Help them overcome them! Trust them to give you expert advice.

Why? Because you will be successful as a company, and have a lot of happy associates making their dreams come true, if you provide your customer with truly valuable products and services that they love! Make them raving fans of your company and your people!

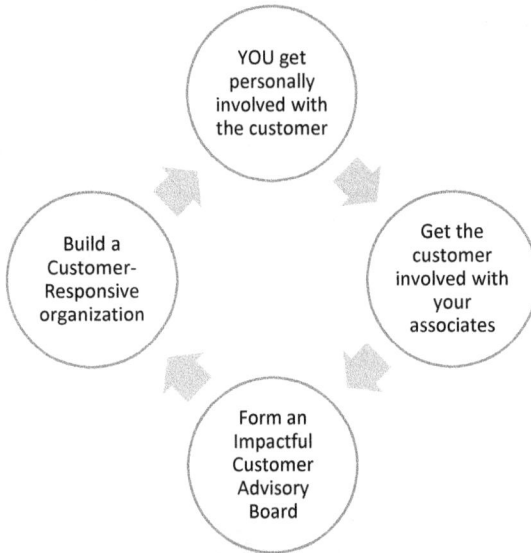

MANAGING THE EPICENTER – LEADING YOUR TEAM

"Your role as the CEO is to set the direction, increase the speed with which we operate, and in general, function as the organization spark plug."

We talked with you in Chapter 1 about building a growth culture, and that you can build a team of raving associates by implementing the **CHEER** principals in your company:

Communicate
Hold
Enable
Energize
Recognize

Focus on each principal, – and take the time to handle each of them awesomely well. This will reduce the epicenter pressure you get from associates.

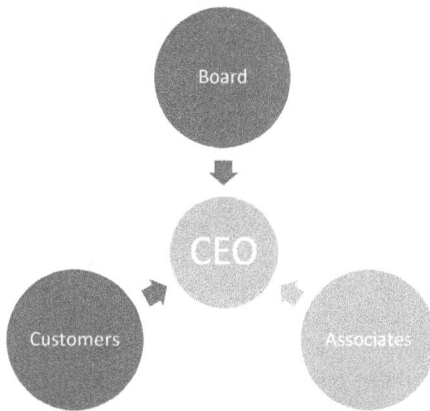

Your Relationship with Your Management Team

I believe it is my role as CEO to lead all the managers in the company. I do not delegate this. And I do not delegate to my direct reports and spend the rest of my time in my office. I believe this creates separation and kills teamwork. Get involved with them. On the ground is where the work is getting done. Let them hear directly from you – your passion and the importance of the customer.

I energize this with quarterly management meetings where we bring everyone with a manager title (regardless if they had direct reports) and get them into one room. We talk together about the company and where we are going and what issues we are having. This is also about building teamwork and camaraderie! We pick a topic at each meeting, such as "Execution." Alternatively, we might have an outside consultant come in and train our team on leadership. We talk about the business, strategy, key programs, and strive to educate our leaders. I learned the importance of this focus on the managers from 14 years of leading in a Fortune 500 company, a management training ground, but since then I have refined my ideas in smaller, faster, and more nimble companies, including startups.

Your Relationship with Your Staff

For those of you who have played sports and been on teams, you will understand what I am about to say. One of the biggest reasons you are hired as a leader is to put a great team together. When you aim to do that, and you go through the ups and downs with that team, and you accomplish unbelievable things for your people and your customers, everyone becomes very close. The sad thing is... at some point every team breaks up. Just like a college basketball team might break up as seniors graduate and move on. Putting together your management teams ends up

233

being the same thing! It is so fun... and so difficult to have this happen. But I do love the whole ride.

I sit humbly here looking back at the teams I have built, and the honorable, hard-working, talented people and diverse teams of all cultures and countries that stood behind me and fought with me in the pursuit of success. I am so grateful for them. So grateful.

BUILDING A TEAM CULTURE – In the Middle of Epicenter Pressure
When your company or leadership team is not performing, it is usually not because the team is not skilled or talented. It is almost always other conditions. I believe you can address those conditions and reduce epicenter pressure by effectively executing the *4 Success Factors for Staff Teambuilding*:

1. Build Trust
First, in your quest to lead your team to the promised land, you must build trust. Do you look at your staff and feel trust and love towards them? Why not? I recently heard the Navy football coach talk about his team and he said, "We have a simple culture and everyone understands it. 'We love each other.' That's it!"

Do you know that your team has toiled and labored and laughed with you to help **you** achieve greatness? They want to win. They are fighting side by side with you, even those teams in the past that may have "failed." Focus on helping them, and you will succeed!

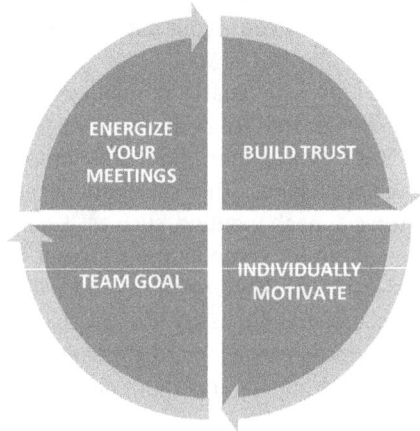

Let me give you an example of something I would do to energize trust. At least once a year, I have an exercise in my staff meetings where we go around the room and each person writes down two qualities about the person to the left of them that makes them great at what they do personally and professionally! We then pass the note to the person they wrote about. This becomes a special team moment. You can see walls come down and a mutual respect build. This is an example of an opportunity where, as their leader, you can show that being political is not acceptable.

2. Individually Motivate

I believe the second staff team building success factor is recognizing that you have some very talented people on your staff and to manage each of them individually. They are most likely all working hard. You have to stay with them in their own way; guide them, push them, CHEER them, and know what individually motivates them.

When I moved to Europe as President of a $50M operation that spanned across EMEA, we would have many meetings with my HQ staff and the country managers. My European staff always asked me to stand up after dinner to say a few words to everyone. They really looked forward to it! My approach in this kind of setting is to walk around the table, and as I get to each of my direct reports chairs, I say a word about them – first something funny, and then something special. Each person. Something different. Something about their accomplishments. Something heartfelt. Those moments were bonding.

To my dedicated European HQ and country teams: how I loved you all! Your talent, your resiliency, our bond together. I felt completely humbled when my French country manager approached me prior to my return to the States and said to me, "Gary, you are the best team builder I have ever seen." So humbling coming from European group that does not envision themselves ever being the United States of Europe!

How do we achieve this as leaders? What is the formula? I have thought a lot about this, and I want to help you achieve the same thing! Thinking about these things brought me to The Growth Cube concepts I am sharing with you in this book.

3. Get Everyone to Commit to the Team Goal

Look at any great team that accomplished the impossible or difficult, and they all shared one common characteristic: passionate and relentless commitment to achieve the team goal. There needs to be a team goal, an aggressive one, and the best way to get to the team goal is to sit down as a team and discuss and commit to the goal together. From this, you get commitment and reduce pressure by being collaborative, open to ideas, and discussing and involving your team. You cannot get this simply by dictating to them. In my experience, this has proven to be the best way. It will take extra time, but it will pay off for you in the long run!

You should own your goals together as a company. This applies to all of the associates. Make sure everyone on your team owns them, and that everyone in the

whole organization understands where you are going. Become synchronized be-hind your company goals. Although everyone has their own department goals, everyone must also be pushing for the mothership to succeed. It's like a football team. Each of the players on a football team has a goal to improve their skills and get more tackles or interceptions or improve their yards-per-carry percentage. Those goals are important, but more important than those goals is the team goal. The team goal is the most important goal of all.

> *"The strength of the team is each individual member.*
> *The strength of each member is the team."*
> —Phil Jackson

My son Tyler is the ultimate motivator; he is a future CEO. You want to follow him because... well just because. He just has that special motivating quality. Tyler was a very successful high school and college track and field athlete, so we spent many times over the years in camps. I went to a football camp out of state with him one year, and I watched the head coach move throughout the day. As his staff was running drills all over the field for their specific positions, the head coach would move around to each area, and he would jump in and help where needed. At the end of the practice, everyone would come together in the middle of the field, and the coach would talk to them. You have all seen something like this in teams you have watched. After that, they all stood up and came very close together in a tight circle with the coach in the middle. The coach would yell, "One Team!" and the players and other coaches would yell, "One Dream!"

"One Team!" ... "One Dream!"
"One Team!" ... "One Dream!"
And they went on.

It was motivating to me, and I wasn't even in the circle. But I wish I was, because I wanted that! That's what we have to try to build in our company teams – that same passion and closeness! It's not easy, but the rewards are incredible.

Recently, I met with one of my former VPs. We were talking about one of the teams we worked on together, and the VP said, "Gary, the team we had together was the best team I was ever part of. Everyone around the table actually trusted each other!"

Wow! That is very rewarding as a leader to hear someone on your team say this. This is especially true because of how many days you feel like you are not making progress, and yet it is a goal all of us leaders strive for. If you feel you are not quite there today with your team, it illustrates that it can be done. You can break through!

4. Energize Your Meetings

Most of the time during the week, you and your team are on the move: meeting customers, handling customer escalations, managing projects with deadlines, etc. Yet you are always together as one intimate team during your staff meeting. This is the opportunity that is often missed. If you believe in team goals, you cannot spend your whole staff meeting getting individual department updates. It has to be team-oriented and energizing!

As I evolved as a leader and ran many, many staff meetings, I realized that going around the table and having each department manager give their update created silos in our company. To combat this, I changed the format to focus instead on the customer, and as such, those who serve the customer. We would still cover the financial results and other key metrics, but this approach of focusing on customers and people did something very beautiful. It built teamwork around a common goal, and ultimately, it helped create an atmosphere of openness and working together.

I also like to bring in other key leaders from across our company and have them present their project update to our team. This is a leader we want to develop or to head up an important project, and the topic is always something focused around the customer or those who serve the customer. As an example, I would have the Manager of Customer Success come in and talk to us about our churn / retention rate programs and how those are working. It develops that leader, keeps focus on the customer, and it spices up your meeting.

Also, note that I mentioned looking at "financials and other key metrics." Are you creating raving associates in your company? How do you know that? What is your associate churn rate (turnover)? What is your employee morale score? You and your team should be looking at raving associate metrics. You should be looking at similar customer metrics at these meetings as well. This is what really matters, and this is what your top executive team should be focused on.

You can alleviate much of the epicenter pressure and take your team all the way to the top if you can execute on the teambuilding success factors I am recommending:

(1) make sure you are building trust and supporting each other and respecting each other; (2) build a relationship with each person and individually motivate them; (3) get the whole team pursuing the same aggressive and meaningful team goal; and (4) be creative in energizing the company around moving forward.

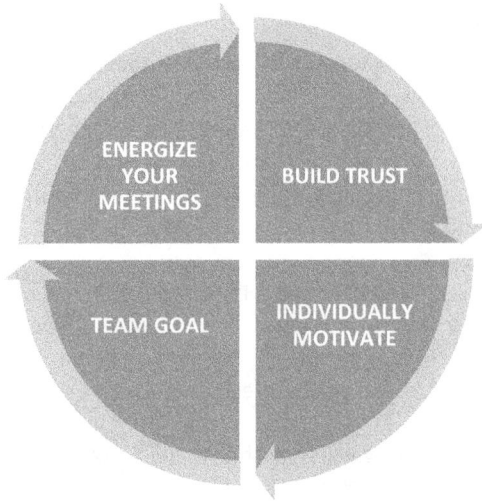

Managing the Epicenter – LEADING YOUR BOARD.

To lead your associates and manage that epicenter pressure through all your up quarters and some down quarters, and to experience success with them, is a challenging and rewarding opportunity. At the same time, there is another group of people who will be going through it all with you. For the most part, they will be challenging you and pushing you. Sometimes this is even to the point that it seems that they are against you! That group is the board.

I have had the opportunity to lead 5 companies as President and CEO. Some have been large, some small, some public, some private. I currently have a board for my startup company. I also coach CEOs today, and I see their challenges and understand their board situations intimately. The point is: every CEO has a board. It could be just the CEO and a family member. It could be the owner and a few of their friends that own stock. It could be a larger, more formalized version that we all envision when we say the word "board." Regardless, there is typically someone above the CEO. Someone you are ultimately accountable to who are in the approval level on the most critical and strategic decisions. Someone who can create pressure.

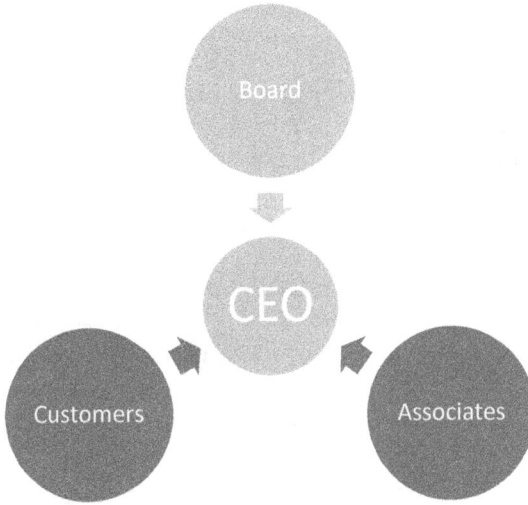

I have also been on the other side of the table – having served and currently serving on dozens of boards myself, so I understand and have experienced the dynamic of boards and CEOs from that perspective. It is certainly a different view being a board member. At a high-level, the board is responsible for improving performance and ensuring compliance. In a public company, the board has fiduciary responsibility to shareholders: it must deliver short-term results and assure the long-term health of the company. The board has the final responsibility for the success or failure of the company, and therefor the board will get involved in selecting the CEO and deciding how it should operate to best meet the objectives of the company. The biggest of companies with the smartest of people can mess this up. As an example, check out the board fiasco at Hewlett Packard (HP) over the past decade. How does this happen? Because the board members have egos and particular friendships and sometimes different agendas than the CEO, and as a result, it can get very political. It is the shark tank within.

MANAGING THE EPICENTER – LEADING THE BOARD

Differences Between Public and Private Company Boards

BUSINESS FRIENDS/NO FAMILY vs. PERSONAL FRIENDS AND FAMILY
In a small or private company, the owners want the same thing as the big public companies, but it is typically more tightly held by a few people at the top. The fact that the board of a family company are multi-millionaires on paper is offset by the fact that they also have to back their company personally and may be cash-strapped currently.

SHORT-TERM vs. LONG-TERM FINANCIAL
Public boards are oriented more toward short-term, and they are more heavily focused on monthly and quarterly performance and its effect on stock price. Private companies are more focused on annual profit improvement, cash flow, and maintaining company legacy.

ALL BUSINESS vs. EMPLOYEE LOYALTY
A small family company is focused on cash flow just as much as a large public company. However, they also contain a unique aspect – a personal connection to associates who may be the owner's own relatives or friends and a loyalty to people who have stayed with them. Changes made in family companies are often drawn out, highly scrutinized, and sometimes stopped if it is a friend or family, regardless of performance.

TEAM PLANNING PROCESS vs. INDIVIDUAL DECISION-MAKING
In a public company, there are regular interactions around monthly business, organizational, and financial updates. The discipline in reporting and management processes are impressive. Communication in a private family company is more informal and sporadic.

**DEGREES AND MULTIPLE COMPANY EXPERIENCE vs.
HANDS-ON EXPERIENCE FROM CHILDHOOD**
The board members in a large public company are going to be seasoned, financial, multi-degreed individuals. The board members in a family company are most likely going to be family members who grew up in the business and may not even have a degree. Both are very talented and should be respected.

The first challenge for the CEO is how do we possibly manage someone above us on the organization chart? It is difficult. That's why you have me coaching you! It starts by understanding what motivates and drives the board members.

I want to start by telling you one of my stories, and how I was initially trained. I was a Division President in a $20B global company, and went to HQ for quarterly board meetings in "the Pit" – the basement of the building. The CFO who reported to me went with me. No one else on my team came along. The CFO was not allowed to talk. The training in this company was that the CEO should know their business, which means understanding every number. As I presented the results of my business with 3 screens of spreadsheets on the wall behind me, I was expected (and learned how) to be able to explain every number in every cell of every chart. I presented to and was contentiously challenged by the top people in the company and their analysts – who studied all my schedules days before I arrived. Was I successful with that board? To be honest, at times it felt like I was, and other times it felt like I wasn't. However, I was promoted 4 times in 14 years and was President of the largest service business in the company (600 people) when I left, so I believe we did pretty well! It was a team effort, and it was excellent training. I It certainly trained me on the financial focus of a board and the dynamics of dealing with a powerful group outside of your operation.

I have also led small family companies where the owners and family members were the board. I have been part of some crazy and odd board meetings that I will not elaborate on here because what happened specifically is not the issue. The point is that you have to be ready for anything. Just as important, you have to be confident in yourself and your team because you will get challenged! In some of my smaller companies, I would bring my executive team at points into the board meetings and board level discussions. That is good training. They are able to feel the increased epicenter pressure from the board in these cases, which is certainly not for everyone. Most executives get to the top because of their talent, but those who fail lose it for other reasons, and it's mainly due to pressure and mistakes caused by that pressure.

From my experience, the epicenter pressure from the board to the CEO is always there. Sometimes has nothing to do with performance; you could have exceptional financial and customer results and the pressure still comes. It may be our ability to internalize and handle pressure that propels people like you and me to the top in the first place.

241

We often talk about boards like they are one unit; in actuality most do not operate like that. Boards could benefit from a Growth Cube™ teambuilding workshop! My point for you, though, is that the board is simply a group of people. These are people who have ownership in the stock or company, and therefor they have a personal interest in your results. In the end, try to develop your relationship with each board member individually. From this point on, to emphasize this, I am going to refer to the board as the board members. Those board members love leaders who listen and act on what's important to them (wouldn't you?).

One example of this for me was George Tamke. George was co-chairman of a Fortune 500 company while I was moving up the ranks, and George was a key decision maker in many of the technology and service growth successes we had. He had intensity, energy, and a market focus that always impressed me, and although he challenged and pushed me, I felt like he was on my side of the table fighting with me, and that we were making decisions together. Most of all – I felt that he believed in me!

Keep in mind that you are accountable to the board members, and you have to deal with them! They are the owners of the company, or at least a large share of the owners. They can hire and fire you. In 2016, the average tenure of Fortune 500 CEOs was 4.9 years. You have a runway, but the quicker you get things moving, and the more consistently you do it over time, the more highly you will be viewed. How would you grade your performance this past year if you were a board member? As long as you are getting results, you will most likely stay in that role. Getting results starts with competing hard. Something like this:

> *"Every morning in Africa, a gazelle wakes up. It knows it must run faster than the fastest lion or it will be killed.*
>
> *Every morning a lion wakes up. It knows it must outrun the slowest gazelle or it will starve to death.*
>
> *It doesn't matter whether you are a lion or a gazelle: when the sun comes up, you'd better be running."*

This is how your board members think, and this better be how you think if you are the CEO! In the business world, it is all about competing. You need to make tough decisions and you need to make them quickly. You cannot stand still, and you

<u>must</u> move boldly ahead. You cannot just hold the reins where you are today. You were hired or put into the top role because you had ideas and talent that could move the company *to the next level*. Your competitors – some of them you may not even recognize yet – are moving and aggressive. If your organization is not moving and aggressive as well, you will be left behind, and your board members will not be happy. If you were trained like me, you have been coached and trained to set high goals and hit them. You are a competitor. You have high aspirations and a high bar yourself! In the end, many times it is you and me – the CEO – who actually push the targets higher.

"I have been impressed with the urgency of doing. Knowing is not enough; we must apply. Being willing is not enough; we must do."
—*Leonardo da Vinci*

These inspirational words are from one of the greatest minds the world has ever known. I highlight them here because they capture the essence of what the board members want you to deliver as the company leader: results! Have an urgency about doing it. It's not about "moving in the right direction" or "understanding the issues and opportunities." The board members expect the CEO to execute the plans that were committed to the board members. They want you do what you told them you would do, strategically and financially. You should want that too! CEO pay is typically tied to hitting the same targets! For this reason alone, you should make sure your strategic and financial goals are defined (hopefully around all 6 dimensions of The Growth Cube!). It does not matter what you did last year or over the last 5 years. It is about now, about tomorrow, and about this quarter. As good as you are, you will have months and quarters where you miss goals. If you are an executive long enough, you will learn to deal with the board member pressure of making the month, making the quarter. Do not panic.

"When you have a great quarter, say little.
Push higher. Business as usual.

When you have a poor quarter, do the same.
But also have new ideas and be proactive
with a sense of urgency."

Someone may tell you, "Well, if you clarify and document the roles and responsibilities for the board and the CEO clearly, it should never be contentious in the board meeting, and everyone will work together." That is a good start, but it's not enough. It takes a team-oriented mind set by everyone to be productive and move the business forward. It starts with the attitude and approach of the CEO. Remember that you are responsible for the results, and the board members have experience and connections that can help you win in the market place! Be smart. Utilize them.

CEOs are partly to blame for some board members who are skeptical, challenging, and sometimes belligerent. All of these CEO mistakes are within your control as CEO:

1. Some CEOs who implode do so because they *are not upfront* with their board members. They do not tell them the whole story. This is the worst thing you can do. Tell the good and the bad. Tell both sides of the story. Give them the full picture, along with your recommendation.

2. Some CEOs *are not team players* and miss the big picture. If you are part of a larger company, make sure you are not only thinking about the value creation within your unit, but how you can help drive the value in your parent company, and how you can partner with colleagues running other business units.

3. Some CEOs think they can do what they want and just *avoid or ignore* the board members. CEOs in smaller companies and startups may underestimate the board members. You should reach out individually to each board member and develop a relationship. If you think it is insignificant or not important, you will do this at your own peril. In a small company, the "board" may be just one owner.

I made some of these mistakes. One thing is certain, though: I always try to be the expert in the room when it comes the 6 dimensions of The Growth Cube (The Growth Cube 6). You should too! Make sure that topics around customers and associates are on the board agenda. No matter what, you cannot let a board member who is further removed from the business than you push the company into a decision that will significantly hurt associates or customers; that will hurt the business. That is your responsibility. You also have to do what YOU think is right. On one occasion, I successfully moved one of my companies into a new business direction that we believed was vital for our future survival, and many of the board members did not support us. We did it anyway because it was the right thing to do for the business. Guess what? Today, it is a resounding financial success and the owners love that new business! I don't make it a practice of doing that kind of thing, though!

There is a reason why I communicate to my CEO friends that you need to lead YOUR board. In the end, you need to view this as YOUR board. As best you can, control the topics, lead the discussion, listen, and fight for what you believe in! At a high-level, my advice to you is that the CEO needs to be themselves, listen, be coachable, and make their own decisions to move the business forward. You will have up and down results. Hopefully most of them are up! Positive results in the market will almost always make everyone happy. Try to make your board meetings (and they are YOUR meetings) stimulating and productive. If you are hitting your targets, the board will probably even have some fun!

To this point in my career, I have participated in over 600 board meetings as a President/CEO or as a member of a board myself. Leading your board is an art and a dance. It is high-pressure and challenging, and your ability to bring balance and perspective to the discussion will be a constant fight. If you are reading this book, you are motivated to improve and do more for your company. Whether you are a CEO currently, a board member currently, or on the way up to either, I am hopeful my view and recommendations will help you be more effective in your endeavors!

And amidst what may sometimes seem insurmountable, scary, and lonely moments, we as CEOs need to have resiliency, a never-give-up-attitude, and skills to develop relationships and build teamwork. In the end, our ability to be courageous and take the whole team forward – including the board members – and get results, will inspire our team and inspire our board members!

15 TIPS FOR LEADING YOUR BOARD

DEVELOP RELATIONSHIPS

1. Get to know the board members individually outside the meeting.
2. Listen to the board members and learn from them.
3. Do not confuse light talk and laughter with the board members being pleased with your performance. But it does help.

AGREE ON EXPECTATIONS

4. Agree on strategic and financial goals for the year. Set your strategy in all 6 Growth Cube dimensions!
5. Deliver results on everything you commit to.

BUILD CREDIBILITY – YOU ARE THE CUSTOMER EXPERT

6. Make sure to get associate and customer topics on the agenda and fight for them!
7. Strive to be the most knowledgeable person in the room on your markets and your customers.
8. Take control. It's YOUR board meeting. It's YOUR board.

OOZ PERSONAL VALUE

9. Communicate good and bad.
10. Be a team player. See things from the board member and parent company perspective.
11. Be humble but have a sense of urgency.
12. If you ask for help, you will get it!
13. Do not take challenges personally. Always be professional.
14. Stand up for your people. If you are faced with a belligerent board, shield your people.
15. Stand up for your values as a person.

Aly Raisman, our USA 3-time gold-medal Olympian and captain of the women's gymnastics team in 2012 and 2016, recently talked about the biggest difference in her life now that she is not competing versus when she was competing at the top level in her field. She says, "Now I can finally rest." That is the number one thing that comes to her mind?! Out of everything she could have said? It just goes to show you how hard she worked to get and stay on top. The whole time she was training and competing over all those years, which most days was 8 hours of pure training, she was tired. Yet she pushed through it because she wanted to be a champion. Great leaders exhaust themselves in the preparation to be great.

"I have never met a great coach or a great player who was not obsessed with their performance."
—Urban Meyer
Ohio State Football Coach and Multiple National Champion

MANAGING THE EPICENTER – FINAL THOUGHTS

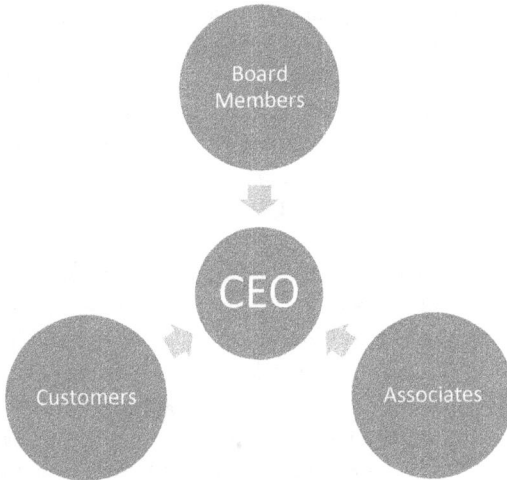

There is no job in the world like the role of CEO. You have the honor to lead a group of people to an inspiring goal that everyone should benefit from. To get there is so fun and rewarding. Even with that, the epicenter pressure is intense. Managing the epicenter is about developing all of your skills so that you can deal effectively with your customers, your associates, and your board. It is about the

pressure that impacts you professionally and personally and how you handle that and manage it. You have to set that example and walk the talk every day. You also have to deliver the numbers to stay in the seat. In the end, managing the epicenter of a company is what makes a CEO's job special and challenging, ultimately, valuable to the company. The greatest CEOs are able to deliver financial results while also building associate talent and customer commitment.

The epicenter involves an enormous gut-wrenching battle; it is there every day. There is an undeniable tension, a conflict, at the epicenter. It takes courage to succeed and survive. This feeling is what I want you to remember, and recognize that the challenge of the CEO is that he/she sits at the epicenter of sometimes conflicting priorities. It is the triangular conflict between a board's relentless pursuit of increased financial performance in the short run, a set of associates who want to trust and respect their leaders, and a customer base who wants their vendor partner to listen, respond, innovate, and do it today! At the center of this high-pressure, high-stakes conflict is the leader – you.

That is the challenge of managing the epicenter.

You must face this challenge if you want to be a well-rounded and successful CEO. The excitement, the fear, the frustration of this role, and the positive impact you can have on people's lives when you succeed, make it one of the most special leadership opportunities in the world. So special and such a thorough training ground, that a CEO has now become President of the United States.

MANAGING THE METRICS THAT MATTER

We have talked a lot in the book about strategy, motivation, and teambuilding, and we have given you many ideas, tools, and techniques that can help you to better manage the pressure at the epicenter. But what specifically do you do when you walk into the office every day? You can't just react to all the pressure. No matter what your Growth Cube™ priorities become, it is vitally important for you to put together a financially viable and growing company. No matter what condition you took over the business, you and your team must deliver continuously improving financial results and become industry leading! To do this, you need focus and you need a game plan.

"The ultimate goal of the CEO is to increase the value of the business."

So what do you look at on your CEO dashboard when you start in the morning? How do you know if you are winning the battle? Cash flow is important. Profit growth is a key element. Revenue growth is too. Yet, if you grow one of those and not the other, you have a major issue. What about the type of revenue or profit? Even if total revenue is growing, there could be mixed issues. For example, if recurring revenue is declining but project revenue was up this year, this could be a major issue as we look out over the next couple quarters. As CEO, we have to understand the financial details of the business we are running. We need an overarching goal that we are shooting for financially, but I believe the overall financial goal that the CEO is aiming toward is increased company value.

It is very simple. If you look at the impact of what you did during your tenure as the leader, did the value of the business you are leading increase? Notice I said, "During your tenure as the leader." This is the ultimate barometer of your accomplishment. To increase value, we need high-performance year after year. As an example, tell me who the most valued franchises are in sports? They are the ones who consistently make the playoffs year after year: The Yankees, The Patriots, The Red Wings. They deliver consistently at a high level over many years.

What about another example: Michael Phelps. The most decorated Olympian in history. He won at least 4 gold medals in 4 straight Olympics from 2004 to 2016. Think about that level of performance! It is his consistent, high-level of performance over a long period of time that makes him so unique and special. As a CEO, we want to do the same thing – continued high-level success over multiple years where we are outperforming competitors and investors are winning!

There are critical building blocks across all 6 dimensions that enable this to happen, but the roads all lead to one overarching goal: increased business value. I am proud to look back at every President / CEO role that I have had in my career, and they all have resulted in increased value over my tenure (and beyond). Some significantly more! This is how a CEO is ultimately judged. If we get strong results for our company over a multi-year timeframe, we will establish a valuable brand in our markets and unlock higher valuations for our company.

So how do you do it? How do you get increased value? What are the metrics that help you drive higher valuation? The answer is not black and white, and it depends on the industry and the business, but this can be figured out for your company and your business. A similar and related question I ask my clients is this: What is the value of your business today if you were to sell it? How did you arrive at that number? Valuation of your company is much more complex that 5x

EBITDA. I know because I led the sale of a $20M SaaS business to a P/E firm, and I have been intimately involved in 15 acquisition transactions myself. I also coach companies on valuation improvement today, so I have seen a cross-section of many different types of technology and service companies of varying sizes. Company value is also not just about the numbers, but it also includes the people, the processes, and the technology of that company. It's also about the value you are creating for your customer! So there are building blocks or milestones that you want to get right to increase company value.

Focus on the Milestones – the Building Blocks.

Let's look at a high-performing winner, Clemson. Clemson's football team has now been in the National Championship game two years in a row and won it the second time. Behind Alabama, they are now out performing everyone in college football. What do you think their goal is at the beginning of each season? To win the national championship? Actually, it's not.

Dabo Sweeney, Clemson head coach, sets 5 milestone goals with his team – the same milestone goals every year – that they track performance against. They believe that if they accomplish these 5 milestone goals, they will be in contention to win the National Championship. If we applied this concept to our business, what if we set goals like this? Our 5 business goals could look something like you see in the chart!

CLEMSON FOOTBALL	YOUR BUSINESS
• 1. Win the Opener	• 1. Hit first quarter targets
• 2. Win the State	• 2. Be the best in the state
• 3. Win the Division	• 3. Win in the core business
• 4. Win the ACC	• 4. Win in target verticals
• 5. Win the Closer	• 5. Hit 4th quarter targets

As another example, let's look again at Michael Phelps. If success is winning, he has won! In fact, a total now of 23 gold medals. The next best Olympian ever has won 9. You and I would probably be ecstatic to win just 1! Think about this! It is amazing performance. How do we get to this level of success where we are the best in the world, year after year after year? What has Phelps focused on that we can learn from? ESPN interviewed Phelps, and I found this very revealing as a leader. Although we as fans are impressed with his number of gold medals, Phelps said he and his coach never focus on winning gold medals. They focus on Michael's times; how to continue to get better and better times. Can we learn something here?

The first thing I see is this: we should never be satisfied as a leader, whether it is in our professional or personal life. Keep pushing higher. We should be working on continuous improvement with our management teams. Whatever your starting point, keep pushing to be at the top of your industry.

> *"Don't just talk about being the industry leader, become it!*
> *Your customers will love you for it!"*

Secondly, what are we trying to accomplish as a business, and what are the building blocks that will help us get there? I believe the point for us is that, although increasing our business value is the overarching goal, it is the milestone goals and building blocks that we focus on and execute on that actually get us to the goal we want. I have found through my success and my learnings that those building blocks are the 6 dimensions of The Growth Cube. I call these "The Growth Cube 6." It's those 6 dimensions that we must execute on and be successful with. Drive those, and you drive higher value. Let's break them down now into more detail to give you an even clearer roadmap.

251

THE GROWTH CUBE™
Unlocking the Growth Potential of Your Company

THE CEO DASHBOARD

Do you have a CEO dashboard? I build one for my customers that is constructed around the 6 dimensions of The Growth Cube. It includes the analytics and Key Performance Indicators (KPI's) that are most important, packaged around The Growth Cube 6. How often should you look at it? Every morning. Focus yourself on what really matters. I am hopeful this dashboard will enable you to move from ideas into concrete targets that, if achieved, can result in increased value for your business!

CEO DASHBOARD DIMENSION 1 – RAVING ASSOCIATES

Do you have an awesome culture? Are your people excited to work for your company? Yes? How do you know, and what percentage of them?

To get growth and increased value, we need to be able to measure our success at building what I call a "growth culture." And as we have learned, a growth culture is a company asset, and it creates company value that investors will value. I build a growth culture by implementing the inverted pyramid and the CHEER process

Are people staying, are they happy, and are they engaged?

- Associate Retention Rate / Churn Rate
- How many people hired in the past 3 years are still with the company?
- How many internal associates have been promoted in the past 2 years
- Associate Survey Morale Score
- How many of your leaders are doing quarterly performance reviews with their associates
- Number of new ideas from Associates
- Number of associate teams formed and active in the past year
- How successfully have you implemented the inverted pyramid process
- How successfuly have you implemented a training and certification process
- How successfully have you implemented the CHEER process

that provides the glue to keep your team inspired. The inverted pyramid philosophy is designed to focus the organization on the customer at the top of the inverted pyramid (raving customers) and those who support the customer (raving associates).

Your people are going to be engaged if you involve them through the CHEER process (remember CHEER stands for: **C**ommunicate, **H**old, **E**nable, **E**nergize, **R**ecognize) and invest in their development. We do this through the Level 3 Certification Program that not only trains the sales team but everyone in your company, and positions you as a thought leader in your space.

To put all these programs in place requires your personal involvement and commitment. They take time, focus, and teams to implement. Teams that are engaged and want to make things happen! We talked about the 4 steps to building a great team culture. These programs can take multiple years to rollout successfully. You have to be determined and focused on the end goal. Stay with it. Culture building is a marathon, not a sprint, but let's get started! Take it a step at a time, but move forward and start today!

"The most important marketing question a CEO should ask is: when my customer experiences my product or service, do they love it?"

CEO DASHBOARD DIMENSION 2 – RAVING FANS
To get growth and increased value, our current customers have to love what we are doing for them to the point that they are telling others about us! To measure this, we should know our CSAT and NPS scores. Do you know those numbers for your company? How about your customer retention rate? If you want a key metric, think about this: a 5% increase in your customer retention rate increases profits from 25%-95%!

A lot of these metrics are simply tracking the level of happiness of current customers, which is important, but in order to grow at high rates, we need the customer base to grow. This is why we track recurring revenue growth – a combination of current customer retention, current customer add-ons, and new customer adds.

Remember you customer base is an asset. You should measure your customer progress like you measure your financials. More importantly, what are the specific

Are customers staying, are they happy, and are they buying more of our products and services?

- Customer Retention Rate ($ and #) and Churn Rate
- Customer Sat Rating and NPS Rating
- Customer Traction Rating
- Recurring Revenue Growth ($)
- How many quarterly performance reviews are you doing with customers each month?
- Number of new launched ideas that came from customers
- How active and impactful is the Customer Advisory Board?
- Growth in Revenue / Customers
- How successfully have you implemented the Raving Fan Triangle[TM]?
- How successfully have you implemented the 5-Step Customer TouchPoint Plan?

programs and actions that we are implementing to improve our customer analytics over the next year? No matter what your starting point is – no matter how bad it gets – your goal is to continue to improve, continue to move forward, and to focus on becoming the industry leader. Anything short of that is not going to excite anyone, including tour board, your associates, and your customers.

We have learned about the 5-Step Customer Touchpoint Plan and how that can help you optimize the experience when your customer touches your company. You now know that the Raving Fan Triangle will guide you in building closer, long-term customer relationships. We identified the 6 windows to growth within your current customer base, that if done well, will put you on the way to doubling the size of your company! The beauty of all of this is that when the customer loves your current product, they will look forward to your next product. This will pave the way for upsells and add-ons, but these are earned because of the resource you have become for your customer, which is why we want to track growth in revenue per customer.

The key to current customer analytics success is to build the growth of your business on a strong foundation of loyal customers who believe in your company. If you can get these metrics moving in a positive direction for your company – a growing customer base, established annual contracts, strong relationships, and related annuity streams – this will significantly increase the value of your company.

> *"A 5% increase in customer retention yields a*
> *30 percent increase in the value of the company."*
> —Bain & Company

CEO DASHBOARD DIMENSION 3 – WINNING NEW CUSTOMERS

How many SQOs did you generate last month, and where did they come from? What did it cost your company to get those leads? Is your sales pipeline growing or declining? How many new customers did you win this year versus last year? What is your CAC ratio?

In many ways, it's a numbers game. The more opportunities you can move from lead to qualified opportunity to sale, the more successful you will become. So you have to watch traffic and activity at your website and social sites, and you have to understand your pipeline activity and make sure your pipeline has integrity. We learned about how you can build a marketing model framework to build a program in your company to generate SQOs. We showed you how to build your own Marketing and Sales Strategy Roadmap!

Winning new customers is so vital to your business. It's not just that it generates new revenue, but it is also a vindication that what you are offering is special enough for a customer to leave what they are currently doing to come with you. Those potential new customers are probably in your database today, and you have to be able to develop a relationship with as many of them as you can. We have learned that the customer / prospect database is one of the Big 4 assets of marketing.

The analytics around winning new customers is about better management of your marketing and sales resources. Marketing activities are very difficult to measure in terms of ROI, and that frustrates many CEOs. Leading sales is an art and a science – and the "art" part is not easy. How do we best motivate a sales rep? To get the growth we want from the business, we have to figure out the formula that works for our company. We know that if we can free up 23% of our sales reps'

time, we can double our company sales! I think that is enough to make it worth our focus. This result alone will significantly increase the value of our company.

Are we generating leads, growing our sales pipeline and winning new customers?

- Number of SQOs generated
- Lead Source of SQOs that were won
- Cost Per SQO (separate marketing and partner channels)
- How well do we undersand our website analytics?
- Sales pipeline by stage and velocity
- Customer Acquisition Cost (CAC ratio)
- New customers won vs prior periods ($ and #)
- How successfully have you defined your sales and marketing plan?
- How successfully are you managing the Big 4 assets of marketing?

"Don't just track the numbers – make them move!"

CEO DASHBOARD DIMENSION 4 – LAUNCHING NEW PRODUCTS AND STARTUPS
Show me the number of active development projects you are working and what system you are using to manage the progress. How do you decide which projects get developed? Do you have a process for screening and evaluating new ideas? Do you have a product roadmap? What percentage of revenues do you spend on R&D? Of the products launched in the past 3 years, how much of your company revenue does this represent? This will tell me the effectiveness of your new product launch efforts!

We introduced you to the Cars on the Road™ development process as a way for you to manage and ignite your development efforts. What cars are on your road? The Cars on the Road program reinforces something that is vital to the most innovative companies – speed. Are your cars on the road moving with speed, or are they stuck in the mud?

A startup business is simply a major new product development effort. When I say major, I do mean major. However, because startups have many of the same components as a new product development effort, many of the same questions and metrics apply. A technology startup needs to focus on doing 3 things successfully: make an awesome product, find a customer who will buy it, and raise enough funding until it can stand on its own. You also need a great financial and strategic plan that can guide your efforts and spend your funds in the smartest way. Many startups make strategic mistakes that eat up all their money.

In the end, your goal is to build awesome products, keeping in mind that awesome products are made by awesome people.

Are you generating ideas, and launching successful new products or startup businesses?

- Do you have a defined product strategy and road map by product line?
- Do you have a defined process for new product development?
- How would you rate your technical leaders in understanding the customers business?
- Number of ideas generated this year versus last year
- Lead Source of products that launched successfully
- ROI/Profitability by product
- Products launched vs prior periods ($ and #)
- Cars on the Road™ Status Report. What stage are the products currently in.
- What % of revenues were invested this year in new product development?
- What % of total company revenues are coming from new products launched in the past 5 years?
- For each of your new products, how many are "awesome:" 1. cool, unique design; 2. it simply works, and 3. it has extreme customer service?

The analytics around launching new products and startups is about building something awesome! This is possible by better managing our development efforts with much more energy, involvement and a focus on speed. Like other aspects of The Growth Cube 6, the CEO has to get involved and cannot sit back and delegate to your technical people. It involves the whole company.

257

Customers and prospects are looking for you to innovate and see out ahead of them, to guide them into new solutions they have not even thought of yet – solutions that help them win new customers! Being able to consistently launch new products and startup businesses out of your operation is a special skill that will significantly increase the value of our company!

"Think Speed."

CEO DASHBOARD DIMENSION 5 – EXPANDING TO NEW MARKETS
What is your revenue by vertical today, and what new verticals make the most sense for you to expand into? How about your geographic expansion potential? What is your revenue by geography today? Do you have international expansion potential? You learned about the 6 keys to international business success that will help you if you do take this step, and if you decide you need a partner to make it happen, we showed you a formal process utilizing our Partner Scorecard to help you pick the right partners to support your new market entry.

Are you generating market expansion ideas, establishing partnerships and getting into new markets?

- Annual customer analysis competed (non-traditional depts., geographies, verticals
- Do you have a defined market expansion plan for your business?
- Do you have a defined process for evaluating potential partners (e.g. Partner Scorecard) partners against established critical success factors?
- Number of market expansion ideas generated this year vs. last year
- ROI/Profitability by product by geography and by vertical
- New markets penetrated this year vs prior periods ($ and #)
- What % of total company revenues are coming from new markets penetrated in the past 5 years?
- What % of total company revenues are coming from acquisitions completed in the past 5 years?

What acquisitions have you successfully completed in the past 2 years? Have you hit the synergy plan for them? What acquisitions are you targeting in the next 2 years? What is the strategy behind them? How do you evaluate one candidate versus another? You learned you can succeed with acquisitions by making sure the target company is adding real value, and that this done by putting together a strong plan and assigning a leader who has the passion to drive it to completion.

Many companies are not looking seriously at the potential they have in expanding to new markets. If you take time to do a customer base analysis and identify the non-traditional departments, geographies, and verticals, and you ask yourself, "Can we do this for other customers?" – you will find great opportunities! The market expansion strategy we are sharing with you in The Growth Cube is unique. It reduces your risk over other types of market expansion strategies because it leverages current customer relationships and offerings you already have in place today. It focuses on extending to target markets that are adjacent to what we already do today. If you can show success in this arena, you will establish credibility and confidence that will translate into higher value and more potential to expand with more funding!

CEO DASHBOARD DIMENSION 6 – LEADERSHIP AND FINANCIAL ANALYTICS

What percentage of your business is recurring revenue? What is the growth rate of the recurring stream? Have you developed multi-level service offerings, and are there an active sales / marketing effort to move customers to higher levels? If you are a subscription-based or SaaS businesses, Bessemer's "6 Cs of SaaS" are fundamental – a must have for your dashboard. Do you know what those 6 metrics are? How are you doing?

I have spent a lot of time helping my companies, and the CEOs that I coach, to develop subscription offerings and recurring revenue streams. Why is this important? Because it builds a long-lasting relationship with your customers and establishes annual (or longer) contract commitments that have value. This recurring stream and repeat contract customer base is very valuable to the board and outside investors. It will increase your company's value. Remember that there is also a direct relationship between retention and company value.

- One study by Bain & Company indicates that a 10% rise in customer retention yields a 30% increase in the value of the company.

- Another study by the investment firm SaaS Capital found that a 1% improvement in customer retention increases company value by 12%!

In most of the small to medium businesses I coach, there is a keen organizational focus on profitability, cash flow, and costs. This is great, but what is sometimes missing is a focus just as intense on the revenue potential (the dimensions we talk about in this book), and on technology investment in operations. Do you have any active internal technology projects? What percent of revenues do you reinvest in the technology of your operations? For example, what technology can you implement in your customer service area that will enable you to be more productive with more volume? There is an opportunity to launch profit improvement programs with new technology that improves efficiency and will put the company in position to scale with increased growth.

Are you building up the value of the business?

- For subscription or SaaS businesses, Bessemers' "6 C's of SaaS:"
  - 1) Committed Monthly Recurring Revenue (CMRR)
  - 2) Cash Flow
  - 3) CMRR Pipeline (CPipe)
  - 4) Churn
  - 5) Customer Acquisition Cost (CAC ratio)
  - 6) Customer Life Time Value (CLTV)
- What % of total company revenues are recurring? How is it trending?
- What % of your time are you spending with current customers?
- What is your customer retention rate and do you have defined programs to improve it?
- What % of revenues do you reinvest in the technology of your operations?
- What are your revenue and profit growth rates by product line?
- During your tenure as leader, how much has the value of the company increased?
- What is your performance grade on the 6 Assets that build value:
  - 1) The Team you have built; and a Growth Culture
  - 2) Your Customer Base and Related Contracts
  - 3) Your partnerships and related contracts
  - 4) Website and Content
  - 5) Database and Followers
  - 6) Sales Activity Tracking

Leading smaller businesses made me much smarter in learning the balance sheet and cash flow statements. There is so much opportunity in the balance sheet, especially for smaller organizations. How to drive more positive cash flow, improve the current ratio (ratio of current assets to current liabilities), and reduce debt are key drivers for a stronger balance sheet. Removing and reducing company risk areas is important as well. Some companies, especially small and medium, have not considered all the risks and are exposed. I saved one of my small businesses from a $3M risk exposure from a benefit plan they had initiated a decade ago. Liability built up, and they had completely forgot about it. To make the balance sheet improvements, surround yourself with talented legal and financial advisors and executives to help you manage this. I like to conduct an annual partner briefing to bring all our partners into the company, show them our plans and strategies, and get their financial and legal advice.

Tell me how you value your company today. Do you know the values and sale price of other companies acquired in your space? Are you driving the metrics that matter to increase your company value? What are those? Do you have an exit strategy? Who is most likely to buy your company in the future? Have you tried to get investment in the past, and what was the feedback? At one of my companies, I managed and led a one-year process with an investment banker that resulted in a significant investment. This was a vote of confidence for the results we were achieving and how well we were positioned for the future. I have also raised significant dollars for startup companies. I understand your challenge! The answer to the questions above will tell me how ready we are to stand in front of an investor and talk with them about our company!

In summary, the growth of your company and success of your performance is more than just about achieving nice operating margins, although that is a great start! What we are really trying to do is significantly increase the value of your company by focusing more of our time and investment on The Growth Cube 6!

- Team you have built, and Growth Culture
- Customer base you have built, and related Contracts
- Partnerships you have established, and related Contracts
- Sales Process, CRM, and Pipeline Activity
- New Products and Innovation Process
- Website and Content; Database and Followers

THE 6 ASSETS THAT BUILD VALUE

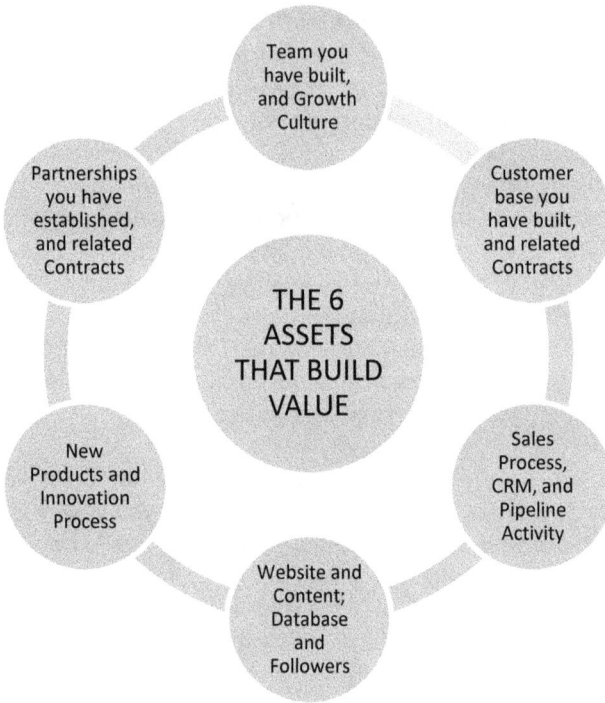

DIMENSION 6 WRAP UP – LEADERSHIP AND FINANCIAL

At one of my companies, we acquired a company, grew recurring revenue nearly 40%, significantly grew the number of new customer wins, and sold the company to private equity at a solid *multiple of recurring revenues...* in less than just three years! That's a pretty good set of results, and they demonstrate our ability to increase value as a leadership team in a short amount of time.

This is what makes the CEO and the executive leaders so important to the company. Leadership and the financial metrics and analytics we drive are the foundation of the company, and they are the foundation of The Growth Cube. It makes everything else possible, and your leadership and your financial focus needs to be in synch. You cannot lead by saying, 'Innovation is important," and not invest significant dollars in new product development! You cannot lead the company saying, "The customer is most important," and not put any investment in customer support, creating raving fans, or increasing customer retention rates! Remember – a

5% increase in your customer retention rate increases profits from 25%-95% – so customer metric performance has a synch with driving financial performance.

I have shared with you the biggest mistakes I have made as a leader, and they are all people related. I also gave you 4 tips to help you not make the same mistakes. Many CEO mistakes are caused by pressure – most of that coming from the epicenter where you are managing three sometimes competing forces between customers, associates, and the board. You learned a lot of ideas on how to handle and manage these pressures.

We now know that the ultimate goal of the CEO is to increase the value of the business. No matter what your Growth Cube priorities become, it is vitally important for you to put together a financially viable and growing company. It is equally important that no matter what condition you took over the business, you and your team deliver continuously improving financial results and become industry leading!

Grading your financial and leadership performance as the leader is very simple: if you look at the impact of what you did during your tenure as the leader, did the value of the business you are leading increase? I have shared with you the 6 specific assets you need to build and grow value. I have found through my success and my learnings that you can best build value by strategizing your business around The Growth Cube 6. Focus there, and you will take your business all the way to the top!

THE GROWTH CUBE –
SUMMARY AND WRAP UP

"In regard to selecting CEOs, it's always easier to trim and optimize and cut costs than to figure out something new. What firms need now from their CEOs is growth."
—*Boston Consulting Group, March 2017*

I know you want to be a stronger leader and deliver better results. You would not have read this book if you did not care. What you might have been missing is a clear roadmap that works for your company and your situation. It all starts with you as the leader.

Once again, the skills required for effective company leaders are changing. In the past, being strong financially is what counted. Being able to sit at the top of an organization and manage financial concerns and perform acquisitions to grow the top line and achieve synergies to improve profitability were the leadership's most important tasks. Boards were looking for leaders who were strategic, financial, and good with cost efficiency.

Then, leadership shifted to analytics. Leaders needed to be able to take big data and get quicker visibility to issues and trends and opportunities – through the analytics of data – to understand more quickly what was happening in the markets and competitors, and to be able to adapt and move to compete.

However, for many companies, there is still something missing: organic growth.

The top-line revenue growth that companies were getting in the past were sometimes achieved through acquisitions, and when you take those away, the core organic revenue and profitability are not growing. We know that the ultimate goal of the CEO is to increase the value of the business. Many CEOs simply are not delivering on this.

This gap in performance is resulting in the search for a new breed of CEO, a CEO who is able to manage across a wider dimension and put together teams and motivate them to higher levels of performance. Businesses now need CEOs who

are gifted at setting and executing on ambitious goals. CEOs anchored on the core business that can also effectively motivate people and teams to go after them.

I am confident that The Growth Cube's unique approaches, tools, and techniques can make the "business of doing business" fun, rewarding, and challenging for your associates. They will help push your business to new heights. The Growth Cube ideas, tips, and techniques are all original content that has been vetted and has worked for me in my companies! It is my greatest wish that you will be inspired to apply my lessons to your career and life in order to enjoy even greater success than you enjoy today.

> *"The Growth Cube process provides a*
> *road map to bring everything together*
> *and make your path forward clear."*

The challenge that we face as leaders is seeing the whole business, prioritizing our focus, and executing. We see a lot of issues, and we see a lot of opportunities. We cannot get to them all, so what do we focus on? The tool that can guide you to success is The Growth Cube. This is the path to unlock the growth potential of your company, and to achieve the dreams you have been chasing as a leader!

If you hold a cube in your hand, you will notice there are 6 equal sides and that you will never see all 6 sides at once. This is the same challenge that many company leaders and small business CEOs encounter when trying to grow their business. Many only focus on 2 or 3 dimensions of their business at one time – some because that's all they have time to do. Are those the best 2 or 3 opportunities in front of them? My learnings from working on this in real companies is that, if you implement The Growth Cube process in your business, you will be able to more effectively analyze and prioritize across all these dimensions. This makes it possible for you to grow and increase value more quickly.

The 6 dimensions of The Growth Cube are all important, and they are related to and integrated with each other. For example:

1. Your success at creating Raving Fans is directly related to your success at creating Raving Associates.

2. Your products need to be awesome if you want to win new customers, and keep the ones you have.

3. To succeed as a business in the long-term, the pre-requisite for winning new customers, launching new products, and expanding to new markets, is to have current customers who are raving fans.

I hope you have picked up something very important about the cube-business metaphor. If any of the sides of a cube fall, the whole cube falls apart. This can also be true in any small business or startup. Major issues can occur that sometimes make you feel like you are not going to make it. But you can. If you focus on what's most important. Additionally, your chances improve even more if you have a process to pick the right spots for your business. I have tested you to consider letting go of perspectives and assumptions that are limiting your growth, and to trust The Growth Cube process to excite your team, your customers, AND your board!

The Raving Fan Customer Is the Secret Sauce
As a leader, the most important thing you can do is to focus on the customer and find ways to help them succeed by utilizing your products and services. You have learned that if you adopt the Raving Fan Triangle and the Inverted Pyramid models, you can get there. These are leadership models that set the tone for what's important. The focus is on the customer and those who serve the customer. When you serve your customer, they will stay with you. When they stay with you, Bain & Company research proves that your profits and company value will both increase!

- **A 5% increase in your customer retention rate increases profits from 25%-95%**
- **A 10% increase in customer retention yields a 30 percent increase in the value of the company**

Because of this, you should lead from what I call "the fault line." These are the critical Touchpoints where your people touch your customer. Find out for yourself:

- Does the customer love the experience?
- Does your associate love the experience?
- Do your associates have the tools and training to succeed?

267

Remember that the most important marketing question a CEO should ask is: "When my customer experiences my product or service, do they love it?" And if the answer to that is not a resounding, "Yes!" then you have work to do.

You have to move forward; you cannot stay the same. Many companies fail because, even though they have identified the right idea and goal, they simply cannot execute successfully. I know you are very busy, but you will find many execution tips, tools, and techniques throughout this book to help you focus and be more productive in your growth endeavors. The Growth Cube process can get you there.

You know now that the most important quality of a great leader is courage. The courage to adapt to changing events, changing technology, and changing dynamics. You must evolve and continue the pursuit of a goal that inspires people. I want you to know that as a CEO myself, I have felt the discomfort and challenge that you feel in trying to achieve greatness. Also like you, I have felt the customer excitement and the associate enthusiasm that propel us forward as leaders and as a team of associates. By applying The Growth Cube process in your company, you can be inspired again, and inspire your team again like when you first started your business or first took on a new leadership role.

To become that great leader, you will have to overcome fear and gain courage. The stories I am telling you in this book, and the roadmap I am giving you, will put you on the path to developing the tools and techniques to do this, and I am here to support you. Your people on your team, and your family and friends, want the "true you" to emerge. They want you to inspire them!

So go ahead and do it. Create your opportunities and your success. You have faced victory and failure throughout your career already. Your ability to see yourself through it all has brought you to this point. Now The Growth Cube can take you beyond that and push you closer to the top. If you can succeed in your business while also keeping your values and faith intact, your family together, and your team proud of you as their leader, you will positively change your life!

THE GROWTH CUBE – NEXT STEPS

Where do you go from here?

IDEA #1 – Revamp your strategic planning process

Incorporate The Growth Cube process into your next strategic planning cycle. Get the book for you and your staff and work on the details together as a team!

The 10-Step Plan –
a new approach to your annual strategy planning

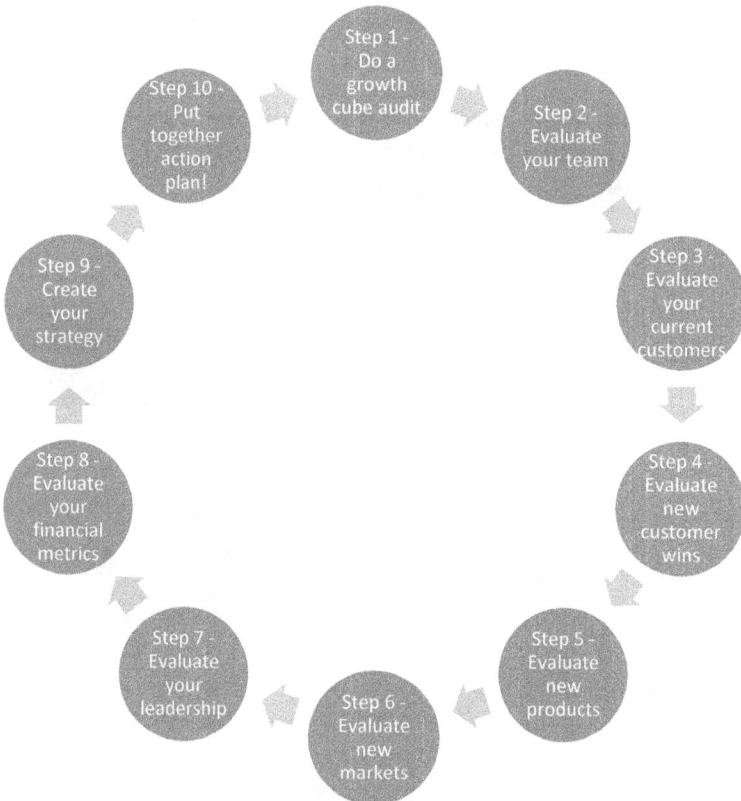

IDEA #2 – Engage with Gary directly.

There are **3** basic ways to engage with Gary:

1. Have Gary and his team do a Growth Cube **Audit** for your company:

3. EXECUTE

Prioritize and develop execution plan with you - and then help get them done!

2. STRATEGY

Deliver document outlining strategy for all 6 dimensions

1. AUDIT

1-2 month review and report

2. Have Gary and his team do a **Workshop** for your team around one or all of The Growth Cube 6

    1. **PEOPLE, TEAMWORK AND CULTURE**
    2. **CURRENT CUSTOMER OPPORTUNITY**
    3. **WINNING NEW CUSTOMERS**
    4. **LAUNCHING NEW PRODUCTS**
    5. **ENTERING NEW MARKETS**
    6. **LEADERSHIP AND FINANCIAL FOUNDATION**

3. Have Gary and his team provide you with one-on-one **Coaching**

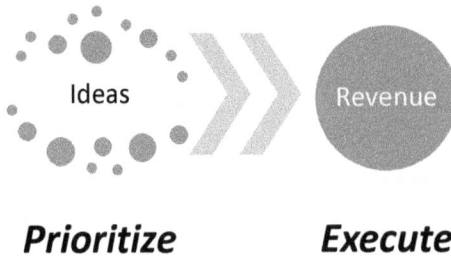

Ideas >> Revenue

Prioritize   *Execute*

For more information:
- Check out www.thegrowthcube.com
- Order the book for your team and colleagues
- Sign up for Gary's Growth Cube Newsletter
- For CEO's wanting to startup a new company, check out: www.HelpMeStartup.co
- E-mail Gary: gary@inspireyourselftoday.net

www.ingramcontent.com/pod-product-compliance
Lightning Source LLC
Chambersburg PA
CBHW060543200326
41521CB00007B/470